The Soulmate Strategy

My Imperfect Plan to Conquer Heartbreak and Find True Love

Corey Seemiller

SHE WRITES PRESS

Published in 2026 by

She Writes Press, an imprint of The Stable Book Group

32 Court Street, Suite 2109
Brooklyn, NY 11201
https://shewritespress.com

Library of Congress Control Number: 2025918198
ISBN: 979-8-89636-068-1
eISBN: 979-8-89636-069-8

Interior designer: Katherine Lloyd, The DESK

Printed in the United States

Names and identifying characteristics have been changed to protect the privacy of certain individuals. The events, places, and conversations in this book are the recollections of the author that have been recreated from memory and/or supplemented and/or condensed.

Praise for *The Soulmate Strategy*

"Through humor, honesty, and hard-won wisdom, Corey Seemiller invites readers into her year-long journey from devastation to self-discovery, showing that healing isn't about finding 'the one,' but about finding yourself again. This isn't a fairy tale about love, it's a real story about courage, clarity, and the messy, beautiful work of starting over. *The Soulmate Strategy* reminds us that every ending holds the possibility of an empowering new beginning."

—Sarah Prout, author of *Dear Universe*

"I love love love this book. It's raw, hilarious, and so freaking relatable. If you've ever ugly-cried in your car or questioned your entire worth over a breakup, this will make you feel seen in the best way while providing the hope you need to make it through the day. *The Soulmate Strategy* is the book you can read instead of obsessively googling how to get over your ex."

—Dorothy AB Johnson, breakup coach and host of *The How to Get Over Your Ex* podcast

"In this real, raw, and laugh-out-loud honest memoir, Corey takes us along as she navigates heartbreak, the search for her soulmate, and her classically Virgo Soulmate Strategy. From psychic readings to speed dating, she tries it all, and with every awkward encounter, hopeful misstep, and hilarious experiment, we feel like we're right there beside her—cringing, cheering, and laughing through it all. It's messy, unpredictable, and completely relatable: a truly wild ride through love, life, and the sometimes outrageous quest for 'the one.'"

—Bethany Nicole, astrologer, author, and relationship expert

"The quest for love is universal, and readers of this book will find themselves enthralled with Corey's journey while reflecting and maybe even healing their own. It is heartwarming, engaging, and an honest look at what it takes to move through heartache and be ready for your soulmate."

—Cassie Parks, money manifesting coach and cohost of the *Manifest It Now* podcast

"If you've done the therapy, read all the books, journaled your heart out, and still found yourself wondering, 'Am I going to die alone?'—this one's for you. In *The Soulmate Strategy*, you get insights to tools to build a healthy relationship that starts with you. It's beautifully written and a must-read."

—Dagmar Kusiak, relationship coach and founder of InsidesMatch

This book is dedicated to my mom, who always inspired me to embrace life's challenges, live boldly, and be humble and compassionate in all I do.

Contents

Part 2: Getting Out

Part 3: Getting Through

Part 4: Getting On

Prologue

This book is about my journey . . . but it could be about yours, too. Sadly, heartbreak is universal because we, as humans, regardless of identity or life experience, have the capacity and yearning to love and be loved.

What is also universal is the desire to heal and move on, as evidenced by the countless books, articles, podcasts, and seminars designed to get us "over" one person and onto the next. And because heartbreak hurts, we will often try just about anything to feel better so we, too, can find love again.

This is the story of my year-long messy path from heartbreak to healing following a devastating breakup. From feeling terrified and lonely to invigorated and hopeful, I could never have expected what would come next . . . except that it had been there all along.

Introduction: Naked and Afraid

"I'm gonna die alone." The words looped in my head as I scanned the crowd of drunk ladies, some sporting only bikini bottoms. Maybe spending the Fourth of July at a lesbian pool party I found online *wasn't* the best idea.

With my heaping plate of potluck food in hand, I nestled into the lone vacant patio chair next to a group of women engaged in a lively conversation. They continued chatting while I nodded along as if I knew who they were talking about. Not one of them acknowledged my presence. But being ignored in the gossip circle sure seemed better than being balled up on the floor at home, soaked in tears, dreading my imminent breakup.

After a few minutes, I turned my attention to the dozen or so ladies bobbing up and down in the pool. *It would be so much easier if you were here*, I thought. *We would mingle, chat with folks, and leave with ten new friends like we always do at these events.* I could feel the tears weighing on my eyelids, ready to pour out. *Suck it up, Corey. You are here to have fun.*

I took a deep breath, gobbled up the last bit of food on my plate, and then shot a text to my friend TikTok—so nicknamed for her obsession with the social media platform.

At this party. All old lesbians like in their fifties and sixties. No prospects. Several going around topless. There is an old lady wearing a bulletproof vest over her swimsuit.

You know I love a silver fox. It's probably a life preserver.

That's what I thought until I looked closer. A bulletproof vest for sure. There were ammo pockets. This is so weird. I don't know if I should stay or go. People-watching is fun, but . . .

Wait . . . I need a pic, please. At least stay an hour.

Ha ha. I'm waiting to see if anyone new walks in. I'll stay thirty more minutes.

Okay. Odds . . . there has to be at least one potential there. You just have to talk to people.

TikTok was my wingwoman from afar, after having met six years earlier at a lesbian Meetup event in Ohio. We made an unlikely duo—she, a curvy woman with spiky hair who often wore hot-red lipstick and leopard-print pants, and me, a Sporty Spice with a ponytail who could only be found in workout clothes. But, for whatever reason, at every event in Ohio we were both at, she would whisk me around to meet the regulars. I wished she were here in Tucson at *this* pool party, whisking me around. Instead, I was alone.

As I sat there feeling sorry for myself, a skinny woman in her sixties ran over to the oversized speaker beside me, a can of Natty Light in hand. Within seconds, she had synced her phone and "Single Ladies" started blasting.

Suddenly, hordes of inebriated, sun-scorched women sprinted toward the speaker. They surrounded my chair, grinding and pumping to the music, bumping into me with every beat of the bass and spilling warm beer all over the patio and some onto me. I finally figured out why this lone chair had been empty when I arrived.

I texted TikTok, hoping to get some more attagirls from her.

I'm next to the dance floor, and these old ladies are going to town.

Oh hell.

Ten minutes, and I'm going back to the buffet to hang out.

As soon as I sent the text, I knew I couldn't make it for ten more minutes.

Was it BYOB?

Yes. I brought lemonade.

Damn girl. You got some game.

When there was finally a lull in the dancing, I bolted inside to get another serving of pasta salad. I was going to need some comfort food as I attempted to come to terms with my total lack of game.

Before I had a chance to grab seconds, a short, fit woman with spiky gray hair came barreling up to me, cornering me behind the table. Only the cheese platter was within reach.

"Do you like hiking?" she blurted out, as she pushed up her black-rimmed glasses.

That's an odd question to open with, I thought, until I remembered I was wearing a hiking T-shirt and baseball cap with a little figure of a hiker embroidered on it.

"Yeah . . . you?" I stared at the pasta salad on the table just beyond her.

"Oh yeah, I love hiking!" Her eyes flashed with excitement. "I go all the time. Do you like survival shows?"

"Yep. I like *Survivor*," I said.

"Never seen it. But I like that show *Naked and Afraid.* You know, the one where they are naked and have to survive for twenty-one days in some random part of the world?"

Who hasn't watched Survivor*?* I thought. *It's been on for decades.* But I did like *Naked and Afraid.* I decided to stay positive. "I love that show. I would go on it if I could just wear shoes. That's it. Shoes, and I'd be good."

"I would cover myself with mud so I wouldn't get bug bites," she said. "That's what most of the women do. The men laugh at them, and then they end up with bites all over their bodies the next day."

I perked up a little. At least someone was talking to me, and it was somewhat interesting.

"Totally agree. I would also bring mosquito netting as my one item," I said.

"I would bring duct tape."

As she launched into a three-minute monologue about the many possible uses of duct tape, I nodded and popped cheese squares into my mouth.

". . . And why don't they ever take those shoulder bags off?" she continued. "I mean, they try to squeeze through crevices in caves, climb trees, and do other stuff where it doesn't make sense to bring the bag! But they have the bag strapped over their shoulders. The network must make them carry it. That's the only thing that makes sense."

"Maybe they put the microphone pack in there," I said.

When what felt like a thirty-minute discussion about tape

and bags seemed to have run its course, I saw an opening and changed the subject. "So, have you ever hiked Tumamoc Hill? It's one of my favorite places in Tucson."

"Yes. I love Tu-MAAM-ick," she said, correcting my pronunciation. "I talked to a Native person who told me us white people are saying it all wrong."

"Really? I had no idea." I held back a laugh. Perhaps I was saying it wrong, but in twenty years I had never heard anyone call it Tu-MAAM-ick.

"So, what do you do when you're not hiking?" I asked.

"I'm a lawyer. You?"

"Professor. I live here but teach online for a school in Ohio."

By this time, a pack of women had relocated to the potluck area, cramming up next to us to grab seconds. I shuffled backward a few steps. Although we were more than a year out from the onset of COVID, I was still squeamish about crowds.

She pulled her phone from her pocket. "You on Facebook?"

"Nope," I said as someone bumped into me while beelining for the restroom.

"I love Facebook. We should be Facebook friends," she said.

That's where my soon-to-be ex was. I wasn't about to tell her that, though. So, I just shrugged and said, "I'm on LinkedIn. You can link with me."

We both laughed—and the conversation came to a dead halt.

"Well," she said, "I gotta run."

"See ya," I said as she walked away. We didn't link.

Once she'd disappeared, I messaged TikTok.

> Talked to someone for a while. She might be a nice hiking friend (not really my type for dating).

> Well, it's a start.

I forced myself to linger just long enough to eat another helping of pasta salad while hovering around the edges of the party. No one noticed me leaving, just as no one had seemed to notice my arrival.

The second I climbed into my car, I burst into tears, sobbing so hard my chest ached. Despite my conversation with *Naked and Afraid* lady, I didn't feel empowered or excited about my impending journey into singlehood. Instead, I felt more alone than when I had gotten there. My heart hurt for the love life I was about to bid farewell to and my destiny—figuring out which half-naked, drunk lesbian would be my future life partner.

"I'm gonna die alone!" I yelled through the tears. "I'm for sure gonna die alone."

Part 1

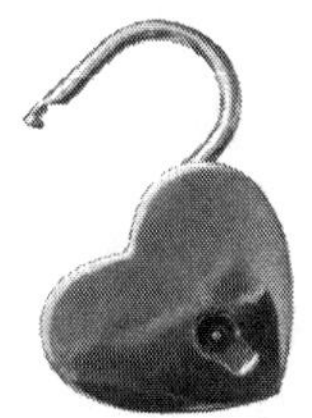

Getting Up

Tangled

"Why can't you just get divorced?" I pleaded with my dad. "All you do is yell at each other."

We were out walking our dog, Soxy, like we did every night. My dad pulled on the leash, and we all came to a stop. "It's not that simple," he said brusquely.

I stared at him, waiting for more of a response. But he just stared back—words unspoken but message clear. Even at eight years old, I understood what his look meant. Divorce would be too much. He wasn't willing to upend all our lives, including his own. So, he would put up with the arguments and the absent love because the certainty of mediocrity if he stayed was far more comforting than only a possibility of happiness if he left.

My shoulders dropped. I knew there was no point in pressing further. We continued around the block, and not another word was said about it—that day or any day.

Six years passed, and the constant fights and cheating on my dad's part finally pushed my mom to the brink and my dad out of the house. Their divorce was messy—years of lawyers and custody struggles. After that, I swore my future marriage would be different.

"I'm gonna marry her," I told my mom.

In my entire twenty-eight years of life, I had never said that about anyone. After having crossed paths at the university some time back, serendipity, or rather, a mutual friend, reconnected us five years later. Before we knew it, we had made plans to travel from our respective sides of the country to meet up at Zion National Park. I nicknamed her "Zion" because of that trip.

"Don't get ahead of yourself. You've only been back for a day," Mom cautioned me.

But I did get ahead of myself.

Two months after the trip, Zion's stuff arrived at my tiny apartment in Tucson—and before long, we had a mortgage, joint bank accounts, a commitment ceremony, and later on, a daughter Zion gave birth to with the help of an anonymous sperm donor.

Once our little girl was in the picture, it was easier to divert our attention to raising her rather than acknowledge that our relationship had been on a slow downward spiral over the nearly twelve years we had been together. While there wasn't cheating or incessant arguing like with my parents, the love between us had simply faded. Autopilot, it turns out, is no way to make a relationship thrive.

One night, when our daughter was four-and-a-half, Zion called me into the kitchen. When I found her sitting at the table with a serious look on her face, a terrible heaviness landed in my stomach.

"Our relationship isn't good," she said. "And you know it."

My eyes filled with tears.

"We're gonna move out," she said in a definitive, rehearsed kind of way.

"What?" The heaviness grew even heavier.

"I'm taking the kiddo," she said matter-of-factly. "We'll work out a schedule so you can see her."

She got up from the table and headed to the bedroom, where

she began pulling clothes out of the dresser and stacking them on the bed.

Within minutes, Zion and Kiddo were packed up and gone. Tears streamed down my cheeks as I stood alone in our quiet house. No bedtime story to read to my daughter and no hand to hold when falling asleep—a ritual Zion and I had kept alive until the very last night we slept next to each other . . . more out of habit than affection.

Over the next few days, I kept pleading with the universe for Zion to burst through the front door, bags in hand, and say she wanted to come home. She was supposed to be my person, and we were supposed to figure this out. But she never did, and we never did.

And that ended up being a good thing.

Our unlove for each other was from detachment—simply growing apart. While our situation felt different from my parents' unlove, which was born from continuous conflict, I eventually came to learn that unlove is unlove, no matter how it comes about.

My dad was right, though, in saying "It's not that simple." Zion and I trying to untangle our lives made it easy to see the allure of staying no matter how bad things get. After we finalized the last detail of our separation, I vowed to never tangle lives with anyone again.

But the universe didn't listen to my request. Five months after the breakup, I met someone—Runner, an easy nickname given her hobby of running. I was attracted to her from the get-go—boundless enthusiasm combined with a feminine appeal that wasn't overly girlie. She was the epitome of my type.

"She'll be coming over after her half-marathon today," I told my mom on our daily call. I could feel myself grinning ear to ear. "I just cut up orange slices for her."

"Well, that's sweet," Mom said cheerfully. "I want all the details."

I put the phone on speaker and started rinsing the knife and cutting board. "You'll be the first to know!"

Runner and I spent nearly every minute together those first few months. She would take me to fancy restaurants, surprise me with my favorite coffee, shower me with gifts, and bring toys for my daughter. She paid the kind of attention to me that I had been craving for more than a decade. I fell for her quickly, and so did Kiddo.

With both of us enamored, right around the six-month mark, I asked her to move in. I was giddy with excitement the day she unpacked her clothes, placing each item neatly into *her* dresser in what was now *our* bedroom.

Our day-to-day continued to be magical. We talked, laughed, and shared affection—such an unfamiliar state of affairs coming out of my relationship with Zion. I loved being in love. I loved living together. But I wasn't interested in marriage.

"I just can't end up like my parents," I told her early on, "legally trapped in a relationship that's run its course—"

"But I'm not your parents," she said.

"—and then my failed relationship with Zion when I did try to do things differently."

"I'm not Zion either."

I knew how insulting it sounded to assume we would eventually grow to loathe each other and that I basically wanted an escape hatch for when it happened.

"I know. But I just can't see myself getting all tangled up again, at least legally. That doesn't mean I don't love you or want to be with you."

"If that's true, then I don't understand why you wouldn't want to marry me."

"It's not that simple," I said. "Let's just enjoy what we have."

And for the next six years, we did.

"I love this," I said to Runner as we unpacked boxes. "I can't wait to hang it up."

I pulled out a framed print of the US with three hearts inside, one situated in each of the states we had lived in—Arizona where we met, Ohio where we lived until I got tenure, and then California where we had followed Kiddo after Zion relocated. Now, we had decided to hunker down back in Arizona to weather out COVID.

I looked at the print again. "Home is where the heart is," I read from the caption.

She smiled.

And I thought we both believed it . . . until the package arrived.

Fun Home

Just a few months after returning to Arizona and nearly one year before the lesbian pool party, Runner and I were sprawled out on the couch, doing what everyone else was during the pandemic: binge-watching TV.

In the middle of some house-flipping show, she suddenly jumped up, grabbed her phone, and beelined for the kitchen. "Gotta get some water," she called as she disappeared from view.

I paused the episode.

A few minutes passed, and she hadn't returned.

"What are you doing in there?" I finally yelled.

"Filling my water!" she yelled back.

"How long does it take to get water?" My stomach did a flip. "Hurry up! I want to see if the owners are going to stay or sell the house."

"Just a minute!"

After a bit longer, she bounded back into the room, flopped down on the end of the couch, and slid her phone face down under the pillow.

She didn't have a water glass.

Pandemic days continued—work from home, go on walks, and watch TV. This slow, quiet life stood in stark contrast to the fast track we had been on together for years—traveling, socializing, and attending events, always doing something different. Now, every day was exactly the same as the one before, with one exception: Runner's grip on her phone tightened, and excursions to get water seemed more frequent and longer.

A few weeks after my initial stomach flip, a package came for Runner. She tore it open as soon as it arrived.

"What is it?" I asked.

She pulled a paperback from the shipping box. "A book."

"What book?"

"*Fun Home*," she said.

I noticed her name was handwritten on the box label. "Who sent it to you?" I asked.

She glanced away as her voice trailed off. "A friend."

"Oh, cool. Who?" I didn't need a name to know this was no buddy.

"Just a friend." She started skimming through the book, barely looking up at me.

"Do I know this friend?" I asked casually.

She walked across the kitchen, carrying the box to the recycling bin. After sharing only her first name, she then said, "She's in my Peloton group."

Runner had invested in a Peloton bike at the outset of the pandemic and had practically become an evangelist for the company. Not long after getting the bike, she'd found a virtual LGBTQ+ Peloton group and offered to host a video happy hour every week. At first, I didn't understand why people would want to get together online to talk about their bikes. But after overhearing bits and pieces of their conversations for several weeks, I realized their gatherings were about more than riding a stationary bicycle. And now some woman from the group had sent her a book. *Who was she?*

When we crawled into bed that night, Runner flipped over, back to me, and buried her head in the pages of her new book.

"I didn't know you liked graphic novels," I said.

"I've never read one," she mumbled. "But this one is supposed to be really good."

"Actually," I said, "I didn't know you even liked reading." I snickered, knowing it was a jerk thing to say. But I just wanted to get some sort of reaction out of her—something besides indifference.

She didn't respond or even turn around, and instead, she read on, turning each page with what seemed like unabashed anticipation. A familiar uneasiness surged through me.

"Is there something going on with you and the Peloton lady?" I asked as we lay in bed one night later that week.

She had just put *Fun Home* back on the nightstand and rolled over to face me.

"No." Her eyes shifted to the side. "Not really . . ."

"What do you mean, 'not really'?" I demanded. "Is there something going on between you or not?"

"I texted her and told her I was interested in her, but she said she didn't want to be with me because of the pandemic and because I was already in a relationship."

"What?!"

Silence.

The vomit came halfway up my throat, and tears—not the

sad kind, but the angry kind—welled up in my eyes. I looked right at her. "What, exactly, did you say to her?"

"I don't remember the exact words." She glanced away. "Can we be done with this conversation?"

My voice increased in decibels as my heart raced faster and faster. "How do you not remember? Look at the text!"

I waited a moment, but she didn't reach for her phone. Instead, she just lay there silently.

"For the record, just because she didn't take you up on your offer doesn't mean we are done with this conversation!" I said.

She looked back over at me.

My heart ached. "Why did you do it?"

"I've felt really disconnected from you," she said.

"Did you think about talking to me about it rather than, oh, I don't know . . . *cheating* on me?"

Even being on our respective sides of the bed felt too close.

"It wasn't cheating," she protested. "Nothing happened!"

I sat straight up. "Yes, it was!" I was not up for debating semantics.

For another ten minutes, I kept probing, and she kept attempting to respond. But after all of it, I still didn't have any answers. And she didn't seem to want to read me the text. Deep down, some part of me understood that not hearing those words was probably for the best.

"Do you want me to sleep on the couch tonight?" she finally asked.

My breath escaped my chest, and the weight of my tears made it hard to blink. All I could do was nod.

Without another word, she got up, grabbed *Fun Home* and her phone, and left the room.

For hours I tossed and turned, shifting my pillow, as I pictured her crafting her "Do you want to be with me?" message. I imagined her writing something and then deleting it and then writing something again, reworking each line until the wording was perfect.

"Cheating is a deal-breaker for me," I'd told her when we first started dating. "No forgiveness; no second chances."

What I should have said was, "Cheating is *not* a deal-breaker for me. I will stay even if I'm cheated on." Because that's exactly what I did.

⟷

"Is there anything you want to do to make things right?" I hadn't planned to say this, but the words just fell out of my mouth.

After days of hardly speaking, we had decided to take a walk around the neighborhood together. Nothing like chirping birds, sunshine, and a light breeze to calm the storm between us. But we didn't make it more than a few steps before I had blurted out my question.

"I just want to move past this whole thing," Runner said.

We were just crossing the street. I stopped, with zero care for any car that might run me over. She stopped too.

"We aren't going to just move past this like it never happened!" I said, my voice escalating. "You cheated!"

"I didn't cheat!" she snapped back. "I never even met her in person!"

I was sure the neighbors could hear us, but that didn't matter to me.

"You don't have to physically cheat to cheat," I said, incredulous I had to explain this fact to her. "You developed an emotional connection with someone who wasn't me and then pursued it. You literally asked her to be in a relationship with you!"

The storm in my stomach roiled through my body as our stroll plummeted into a heated debate over the definition of cheating. Once it became clear to me that we weren't getting anywhere, I stopped talking.

We walked home in silence, the sun still shining bright in the sky above us. It didn't matter. I could feel the heaviness of my own dark clouds approaching as defeat took over.

Over the next few weeks, this scene continued to repeat itself with the same lack of resolution. I felt I was never going to get what I wanted, which was for her to love me so much that she would move mountains to save our relationship. Instead, it felt like a never-ending argument.

At my urging, we started couples therapy, which ended up consisting of numerous unsuccessful sessions where the focus was on reconciling our opposing views of what constituted cheating rather than attempting to rebuild trust.

The only thing I could think to do was write her a heartfelt letter begging her to see my perspective. After several edits, I printed it out and hand delivered it to her in the living room where she had been lying on the couch, scrolling through her phone.

She immediately sat up. "What's this?

"Just read it." I went back to my office, plopped down in my chair, and waited nervously to see what might happen next.

Within minutes, she ran across the house and into my office. She said she got it; she understood; she was sorry. The words sounded so good . . . so believable. I wanted them to be true.

We managed to make it through the next few months riding on her supposed enlightenment, but our life had become a tinderbox waiting for the strike of just one match. Periodically, that would happen. First, something would trigger one of us, leading to a full-blown argument about cheating, trust, disconnection, and all the other fun words we had explored in therapy. Then she would throw a bunch of clothes in a bag and walk out.

While I was usually enraged and devastated, it was the uncertainty that got to me the most. *Will she ever come home? What if she ends up dead in some ditch?*

But after a day or two, she would return. The moment I could hear the key in the door, my anger would subside, devastation disappear, and worry vanish. More so, the gaping hole in my heart would fill with hope—hope we could work it out, hope that she loved me, hope that she would fight for us . . . this time.

"I'm done!" Runner shouted.

She grabbed several trash bags and stuffed them with her T-shirts, underwear, and nearly every other piece of clothing in her dresser. I just stood in the hallway and watched as she stormed out, yet again, hauling the bags one by one to her car.

I texted Mom. My hands were shaking so much my thumbs could barely find the right letters to press.

She is leaving for real this time.

Okay, let her go. She's not in it.

I wiped my tears with the back of my hand. I needed Mom's tough love.

I know. I'm sad.

The door slammed.

Of course you are. Call me.

I rushed to my kitchen cabinet and grabbed a bag of jelly beans—my biggest vice. I shoved a few into my mouth before texting her back.

I'm eating jelly beans.

You can eat jelly beans and talk at the same time.

Mom answered on the first ring.

"Okay. I'm done being sad. Now I'm just pissed," I said while chomping. "Even if she comes back and dumps all her stuff into her drawers and says she's sorry, it's too much." A fat tear rolled down my cheek, and I popped another jelly bean into my already-full mouth.

"She will, with all sorts of apologies," Mom said. "But how much more can you take?"

"Not much," I mumbled, and I knew it was true. I had reached the end of my rope.

"You heated the chips?" I asked, settling onto the stiff couch.

It had been a week since we had decided to officially separate, right after Runner returned from her latest walkout. We were taking things very slow—starting with her inviting me over for dinner at her "new place," which was essentially a furnished short-term rental.

"I know how much you love warm tortilla chips," Runner responded as she put salsa *and* guacamole on the table.

"You never heat the chips. And we never have guacamole."

"Well, things are going to be a lot different."

Another week passed, and I couldn't shake the regret I had for separating in the first place. Runner seemed to be trying to make things right. She had heated the chips, after all. So, I asked her to come back, and she agreed.

"I printed us both all the workbook pages," she said, sitting down at the kitchen table. We were just a few days into our reconciliation.

"That's a thick stack." I flipped through mine with my thumb.

"Well, we have a lot to work on," she said. "And I'm ready."

"Okay. First exercise. Describe your relationship vision," I read out loud. We both scribbled on our respective pages.

This might just work, I thought.

Our foray into the self-guided six-week relationship boot camp program, though, came to a screeching halt before we even made it halfway through the exercises. We had another heated debate—about marriage, about moving to another state, about our very different desires for our lives, and, yes, the definition of cheating. Finally, it was clear: Runner and I were at the end of the line. No more couples therapy, "please listen to me" letters, warm tortilla chips, or relationship boot camps. No more trying and no more hoping.

I was done.

Stuck on You

It was the day before Runner's official move-out date, and Hiker—a friend I had met years earlier on a Meetup hike—had texted me about a stray mama cat with babies living in her carport. I'm sure she reached out to me since Runner and I had previously fostered several kittens and would likely know what to do in this situation.

As soon as the message came in, we jumped in the car, ready for an epic cat rescue. It felt ironic that this would be Runner's and my last hurrah: saving something together, despite not being able to save our own relationship.

When we arrived, we corralled the cats into the carrier—including the mama, whom I dubbed Cujo after the Stephen King novel for her demonic eyes and excessive hissing. We then sped off to the shelter.

While my plan was to drop the kitties off and wish them the best, in the chaos of everything, I had somehow agreed to foster the whole litter, along with Cujo. And I would do it without Runner.

"You have to keep the babies warm, and the mama cat needs these eye drops twice a day," the shelter vet said. "Bring her back in five weeks, and we can try to adopt her out. You'll keep the kittens for another few weeks after that."

The vet handed me the meds. *You can do this*, I told myself. But I wasn't so sure.

The next morning, after Runner moved out, I had my first solo visit with the kitties. I creaked open the door and tiptoed into the storage room in the garage we had outfitted for them.

The three dark gray tabby babies were nestled up next to Cujo, who was busy licking their foreheads. They looked so sweet . . . so loving. I sat the food plate on the floor and crouched down to fill the water dish.

As I stood up, I sensed the piercing gaze of Cujo's eyes upon me. She sprang from her pile of kittens, burrowing straight to my chest, clinging onto me with her sharp claws. She hissed, her warm breath on my face.

"Aaargh!" I grabbed her around the midsection and yanked. "Get off!"

But her claws had punctured my shirt. With each pull, both the fabric and my skin ripped, and still she wasn't letting go.

She hissed one last time before finally releasing her grip and dropping to the ground. Shaken and bleeding, I ran out of the room, slamming the door behind me.

Oh crap, I thought, as soon as I was safe on the other side. *I didn't give her the eye drops.*

Day one of singlehood officially sucked.

Aside from Cujo and her kittens, the house was absent of any signs of life. Runner was gone, and Kiddo was in California with Zion.

The quiet wasn't as noticeable during the day, as I was typically occupied with work and my daily walks. But when dusk rolled in, the air would become still and quiet as the thunderous sounds of fighter jets from the nearby military base subsided for the night.

Birds stopped tweeting as they nestled in for sleep, and neighbors settled in at home with their families. These were what I called the witching hours, where the darkness and silence would summon all the emotions I had kept at bay during the day, reminding me there was no one to love and no one to love me back.

The clock would slowly tick for hours until it was time to go to bed. So, I tried to fill every moment with some distraction. I pulled out my old Lego bins and made architectural art pieces, played songs I had written decades before on my guitar, sang karaoke in my living room, attended virtual writing group meetings, and tried to keep Cujo and the kittens alive. If time really did heal all wounds, I was sure I would die of loneliness—or at least from sheer boredom—before then.

After five weeks of singlehood, Runner reached out to reconnect. She said all the right things, and my heart fluttered. During the course of our conversation, she had also offered to help me return Cujo to the shelter, which came as a welcome relief, even if only for my safety.

A few days later, Runner pulled into the driveway and parked, like a houseguest would, and together, we were able to get Cujo into the carrier with little fanfare. I tucked the unused bottle of eye drops into the side pocket. And off we went to the shelter.

Once we got back to the house, I invited Runner to join me for my walk. This time, the birds really were chirping, and the sun really was shining. And there were no dark clouds. As we walked and talked, I felt myself getting pulled back in again. And I was okay with it. I was addicted to her—the energy, the attention, the undeniable chemistry. It felt so good.

But there was no stopping fate. Over the next few weeks, we went through the same old push-pull. We had another epic argument, this time while she was out of town during a month-long work trip. Days followed with texts, calls, and voicemails from her pleading for my forgiveness. She even scheduled a flight home in the middle of the trip, promising to try couples therapy again. But her arrival time came and went, and she never showed up. She never called. She never even texted.

I called Mom.

"What if something bad happened to her? Look at me . . . totally ghosted by my partner of seven years, and I'm still worried about her."

"I'm sure she's fine." Mom sighed. "Walk away."

I hung up and texted TikTok to ask her to check Runner's Facebook.

Active twenty-one minutes ago. No posts, though.

Guess she's still alive. She just didn't get on the plane.

Tears welled up. I finally had to accept what I knew all along—she wasn't going to fight for me, and she wasn't going to move mountains for me . . . no matter how much I wanted her to.

A week later, an apology text rolled in, with her again pleading for forgiveness. We'd been here before, but this time, I couldn't do it. I wrote a response but wanted to wait a day before sending it. In the meantime, I went to the lesbian pool party.

The next morning, after revising my breakup text ten more times, I took a deep breath and hit send. It was finally over.

But really, the journey had just begun.

Finding Grace

"How are you?" my therapist asked. She was a familiar face, having helped me through the breakup with Zion and more recently, the chaos with Runner.

I fixed my gaze on the canvas painting filled with dozens of colorful squares hanging on the wall behind her. Even on video, I could see the detail. "We split up. This time, it's for real. Like, I'm not even communicating with her."

She sat silent for a moment, then asked, "How are you feeling?"

I sighed. "I miss her. I miss our life. I mean the good times . . . not the last year or so."

"I'm sure you do."

"But I've also been beating myself up. Why did I stay so long, especially when it got so bad?" I paused. "And the times we did break up, I would just run back to her when I had the chance." I exhaled and then focused on another one of the little colorful boxes on the canvas.

She nodded. "You didn't this last time."

"I know. But I should have left for good a whole lot earlier. My dad stayed too long in a loveless relationship, and I hated that for him. Then I did the same thing with Zion . . . and now, with Runner. It's like I'm programmed to think it's okay to stay in unhealthy situations."

"Why do you think that is?"

I rattled off everything that came to mind. "Maybe fear—of the unknown . . . or maybe I don't want to have to deal with the difficult emotions that change would bring. Or . . . the status quo feels safer, or maybe I'd regret my decision, or maybe I don't want to be alone."

Therapist nodded and scribbled in her notebook. "Perhaps. But you've handled tough emotional situations before. Are any of those things what you think you're really scared of?"

Silence.

"Not really, I guess."

"Then what is it?"

I took a deep breath. "Maybe my fear of failure—like I don't want to admit to myself that something is bad, and I'm incapable of fixing it."

"Sit with that. I think you might be onto something."

Therapist wasn't the only one getting an earful about the breakup. I was reaching out to everyone I knew, even my very first love from my college years.

Hey, you wanna chat tomorrow?

Maybe this weekend. Bad news, though . . . I was diagnosed with breast cancer last week. Trying not to get too overwhelmed. It's a lot.

Cancer? My dad had lung cancer a few years back and witnessing him experience immense suffering and then eventually die was horrid. I didn't want to say that to her.

I'm so sorry. Is there anything I can do to help? Even if I just listen.

Just being friends again is enough for now.

I felt a huge lump in my throat, the kind that shows up right when you try to hold back tears.

I'm here . . .

But it had been more than two decades since I had been "here" for her.

First Love and I met just before my senior year in college. We were counselors at a summer camp, where we spent our days leading games and our evenings in tiny cabins talking tween girls through their woes.

First Love had long, bushy, brown hair that she usually tied back in a ponytail. She wore the same outfit every day—shorts, camp T-shirts from past years, and athletic sandals. Several fabric bracelets were wrapped around both wrists, each handcrafted by a camper. Her laugh filled the room, and she always seemed to sing the loudest and cheer the hardest, spreading camp spirit everywhere she went. The kids would follow her around, waiting patiently to get one of her bear hugs.

Our friendship developed quickly, and we both kept saying how it felt like we had known each other all our lives. We would stay up late at night sharing our innermost thoughts by the flickering campfire, long after the kids were asleep. And just before leaving with the girls on my weekly backpacking overnights, she would tuck a handwritten note into my bag. I would wait until everyone dozed off and then slide the note out of my pack ever so quietly and read each word over and over.

As the summer went on, my connection with her grew to

affection and then ultimately attraction. I wasn't sure what was happening and wondered if it was normal to feel this way about another girl. I couldn't risk telling her. So, I kept my confusion to myself and continued along our "best friendship" path.

During our last night at camp, after all the kids had gone home, First Love and I lay down next to each other on one of the bunks in my empty cabin. I rested my head on her chest, and she stroked my hair.

"I can hear your heartbeat," I said.

"It's beating just for you," she whispered back in my ear.

No more confusion on my part, and apparently none on hers. And while we both "didn't want to be gay," there we were, wrapped in each other's arms during our one last night together.

After camp ended, we went back to our respective colleges. However, our connection continued to grow. She would make the two-hour bus ride every Friday from her university to mine to spend the weekend with me. When money started running low, we both began selling CDs from our music collections to piecemeal together enough cash for the tickets. Thankfully, she was able to transfer to my university at the semester break, which meant no more hawking our belongings just to see each other—and, more importantly, no more tears on Sunday nights, thinking of spending the next five days apart.

Our love felt like a fairy tale, but the social climate in the early 1990s wasn't supportive of people like us. So, we kept this big secret—from everyone.

After tiptoeing around for more than a year, a mutual male friend expressed interest in her.

"I really want to see where things go with him," she said. "You and I can still be best friends, though."

Tears came flooding out. I cried so hard I could barely gasp for air. "I can't just be friends," I sobbed. "And I can't watch you with someone else."

My chest tightened, and my heart ached. The hurt and suffering had only just begun, and because we had been so very good at keeping our love a secret, I was going to have to weather this storm alone.

Every Christmas, for decades after, First Love would reach out to reconnect as friends, and I would politely respond that I wasn't ready. It was during my first "break" with Runner that I finally reached back, twenty-five years after my heart had been shattered by her. Maybe it was because my life was in turmoil, and it felt nice to have someone connect with me. Maybe it was because I was feeling lonely. Or maybe it was because I thought I needed to find forgiveness with people from my past in order to move on. Regardless, it just felt like time.

Our reconnection began with a few text exchanges and ultimately a video call. We chatted for a few hours, meandering from discussing kids to hobbies to work to "Whatever happened to . . .?" I brought her up to speed on my imploding love life, and she filled me in on her divorce.

During our conversation, no feelings of unrequited love nor unresolved emotion bubbled up. All of it had dissipated—even the supposed hurt I had been grasping onto. The anticipation of reconnecting after all these years had been far scarier than the reality.

Over the next several months, we stayed in touch through text. When I learned about her cancer diagnosis, our messaging amped up, and I checked in on her every day. It wasn't long before I told her about my final breakup with Runner. She had nothing but reassuring words for me.

> It's okay to not be okay right now. This part is awful. It feels like forever, but it will pass. And cry. It's okay to cry . . . just don't live there.

I want the yucky sadness, hurt, and anger to pass.

It will, but it might take a while. Give yourself some grace in the healing process.

Time and grace might be great in theory, but it had taken me decades to heal from my relationship with her. I was never going to let myself go through that again.

"And now you can see why I'm never going to sit in my hurt again." I had just finished telling Therapist about First Love. "This time, I'm gonna take control of my life and not wait decades for the feelings of hurt to go away on their own."

"When you say, 'take control,' what do you mean?" she asked.

"Like do anything and everything I can to not feel like crap forever."

"What do you envision doing?"

"I'm not sure. I've been told I have to *feel* the feelings." I leaned back in my chair and let out a sigh.

"Yes, if you go around them or ignore them, they'll just reappear later," she said.

"Probably cry a lot then. Maybe hang out with friends, walk more . . . I don't know yet. But I'm not sitting around. I'm going to take control of my life."

She jotted down some notes and then said, "Let's talk more about the fear-of-failure stuff we started to explore during our last appointment."

I stared at her canvas painting and then said, "Yeah. I definitely think that's why I stay in relationships too long. Leaving would say to the world, 'I can't make this work' and 'I'm not strong enough or smart enough or persistent enough.'"

"Well, it might be more of a failure to compromise your happiness and well-being than to leave an unhealthy situation." She paused. "Not everything can be fixed . . . or even should be. You *can* walk away. And doing so doesn't mean you're a failure."

"It sure feels that way now."

Paper Airplanes

"I need to get the eff out of town so I can shake this horrid breakup slump," I wanted to say. But that wouldn't win me any parenting awards. Instead, I said to Kiddo as we packed up the car, "It'll be so nice to be up in the mountains with the whole family and get out of this heat."

We finished loading, drove to Phoenix to pick up my sister-in-law and nine-year-old niece, and made the two-hour drive to the rental house we would call home for the weekend.

After arriving in town, we turned off on a road that took us to a quaint neighborhood filled with rustic homes and towering trees alongside a trickling creek.

"There it is!" Kiddo shouted as she pointed out the window to the top of a hill.

I took a deep breath and then carefully inched the car up the steep dirt driveway. We had hardly come to a stop before Kiddo threw open the door. A cool, pine-scented breeze blew in. *This should get me out of my funk*, I thought.

The four of us made our way inside, immediately scoping out all the amenities—a wraparound patio, hot tub, pool table, and enough games and movies to last a year. Kiddo and her cousin did an even deeper dive as they sped around the house, exploring every closet and opening each drawer.

My brother and mom arrived a bit later. As soon as they unloaded, Mom went to the patio to read, and my brother challenged me to what was sure to be a rousing game of eight-ball. But I couldn't muster up the energy and opted instead to curl up on a twin bed in the basement to surf my iPad . . . alone.

Runner was supposed to be on this trip, so her absence was noticeable, at least to me. Several times that evening, I found myself looking around, expecting to see her in some corner of the room, checking her messages every thirty seconds. Even though the thought of that made me nauseous, I would rather she was there on her phone than not at all. *So much for breaking out of my funk.*

"Look, Mama!" Kiddo yelled from the living room loft the next day. She scurried down the ladder and then opened her hand to show me her bloody tooth. "Now the tooth fairy gets to come here!"

Shit, I thought. The tooth fairy was definitely not prepared to arrive that night; I didn't have any cash with me. *And why does my twelve-year-old still believe in the tooth fairy, anyway?* But there was no way I was going to ruin the magic for her.

When Kiddo lost her first tooth at Zion's house many years earlier, she couldn't wait to tell me all about it.

"Twinkle, my tooth fairy, wrote in tiny writing on a miniature Post-it note all about who she is," she said. "She left me a two-dollar bill folded like an origami cat."

Who has two-dollar bills and an origami instruction guide on hand? I grimaced, anticipating a lost tooth under my watch. *Thanks, Zion.*

It wasn't long before Kiddo did lose a tooth at my house. Thankfully, Runner kept two-dollar bills in her nightstand drawer.

I stayed up late folding the bill every which way, trying to make a cat, but it only looked like a wadded-up ball of paper. After abandoning the "Origami for Beginners" video I found online, I ended up making a paper airplane and left that and my fairy-font, handwritten Post-it note by her bed.

Early the next morning, Kiddo came darting into my room. "Mama, who do you think Sparkle is?"

"Who?" I asked.

"The tooth fairy signed her name as Sparkle. My tooth fairy's name is Twinkle." She gave me a perplexed look.

Uh-oh. I could have sworn it was Sparkle. Thinking fast, I said, "Tooth fairies have jurisdictions and the road between your two houses splits our region. Each has a different fairy assigned to them."

She brightened. "That's cool. I have two tooth fairies!"

Another parenting bullet dodged. I sighed with relief.

In the years following, Sparkle made many visits to Kiddo, always with a paper airplane crafted from one of Runner's two-dollar bills.

"What am I supposed to do without a two-dollar bill?" I whispered to my brother and sister-in-law while sitting on the couch at our rental house. "It's not like I can run to some bank in this tiny town on a weekend."

My brother pulled a bill out of his wallet. "Here, leave her a twenty. It was a molar, you know."

"Are you serious?" I said in a loud whisper. "If she gets twenty bucks for this tooth, she'll expect some big wad of cash for each of the rest of her teeth. I can't afford that!"

"What are you gonna do then?" he asked.

I sat, contemplating. *Runner would have a solution.*

Finally, I jumped up from the couch and started rifling through the drawers of a desk in the corner of the living room. I found a tattered pad of paper and pen and started writing in my fairy font.

Everyone watched, waiting for me to share my grand idea. "You'll see," I said.

The next morning as the adults were having coffee, Kiddo came running into the living room, beaming. "I got a note from the intern!"

Everyone looked puzzled, except me.

"What intern?" my brother asked.

"Sparkle's intern," Kiddo explained. "My tooth fairy couldn't get here. So, the intern came instead. She also forgot the two-dollar bill. It's okay, though. Sparkle will come when I get home. She'll leave me a paper airplane like she always does."

My brother shot me a "This was your solution?" look.

I smiled, for what felt like the first time in a while. *I don't need Runner to save the day. And I don't need her stack of currency. I'm over that stupid funk, and I'm going to be just fine without her.*

We All Need Love

"Nothing much happening on her Facebook," Mom told me during one of our daily calls a few days after the trip. "Just some pictures from an event in California."

While I had decided to go no-contact with Runner, which meant I wouldn't communicate with her at all, many people in my life—my mother included—had offered to stay "friends" with her on social media to keep me up to date. Whenever Runner posted anything interesting or questionable, I got a call or text from at least one person in my inner circle.

"Are there any comments?" I asked Mom, my body tensing.

"Yeah, one from someone who said she enjoyed finally meeting her and the lady she was with."

"What lady?"

I took a deep breath.

"I don't know. It just says, 'I enjoyed meeting both of you.'"

Shit. Is it Peloton Lady?

Saturday rolled around, and Kiddo and I were knee-deep in cleaning the house. All was fine until I got Hiker's text.

Has your mom told you about Runner's post? I can send a pic. I don't want to upset you, though.

She just blocked my mom the other day. Definitely send it!

In came a screenshot of Runner wrapped in the arms of some woman I'd never seen before. They wore matching red dresses and were all smiles. I read the caption: "In a relationship."

The blood drained from my face, and queasiness hit me like a ton of bricks. I stood in the bathroom, sponge in one hand and phone in the other, staring at the image. My stomach turned again, and I dropped the sponge. I hadn't seen the photo my mom had told me about from the Facebook post earlier in the week. So, I wasn't sure who exactly this was. But what if it was Peloton Lady?

I wanted to yell, "It's been three weeks since we split up! During that time, you started a relationship with some lady and then was sure enough about it to announce it on Facebook?"

Since Kiddo was within earshot, I decided to forgo the shouting.

I staggered over to my bed and shoved the phone in my pocket. As much as I tried to hide my reaction, Kiddo knew something was up.

We both sat down, and she put her arm around me. In a faint whisper, she said, "I miss her, too."

With those words, I burst into tears—more from devastation and shame than sadness. I didn't want my twelve-year-old daughter to have to console me, especially when I knew she was holding in her own feelings of sorrow and loss.

I laid my head on her little shoulder and just let it all out, my whole body shaking.

"I love you." Kiddo squeezed me tighter. "It'll be okay."

I wasn't sure it would. But it did feel nice to be loved.

First thing the next morning, I drove across town to Hiker's. She had offered to let me look through her phone to see Runner's posts. I hated the feeling of wanting to know the details but hated not knowing at the same time. As soon as I walked in the door, Hiker handed me her phone, and I began furiously scrolling through posts and comments, photos and emojis.

"At least sit down," she said.

I didn't take my eyes off the screen as I dropped down onto her weightlifting bench.

"Look at all the likes," I muttered, holding up the phone to show her.

"Well, I didn't like it," she said. "And I don't recognize those names."

I started sobbing.

"Good." I sniffled. "It's not like everyone knows then. I can just be horribly humiliated in front of strangers."

As soon as I woke up the next day, I grabbed my phone from the nightstand and started scrolling through my Meetup app. *I'm going to find an event that will distract me from all this horridness.* The first thing that came up was my lesbian group's weekly "sit under the tree" gathering at a nearby park. I had never participated before because it entailed sitting still and making small talk, both of which I wasn't a fan of. But I figured, under this tree, I could hide from my woes. I wouldn't be Runner's ex. I wouldn't be someone whose heart was crushed. I would just be Corey.

Once I arrived at the park, I saw one familiar face among the dozen or so women and set up my lawn chair next to hers.

As soon as I sat down, she leaned over and whispered, "So, what's up with Runner and her new lady?"

Oh my God. It's not just Hiker and me and a bunch of strangers who know. Everyone knows! The revelation hit me upside the head, and my eyes started filling with tears I hadn't planned for.

Suddenly, a lady's voice bellowed from across the circle, "Aren't you the woman who posts those hikes at like seven in the morning?"

The group quieted and looked my way. *Oh no. She's talking to me.*

"Yep," I said, preoccupied by images in my mind of everyone I had *ever* met reading Runner's post—colleagues, professionals in my field, my students, friends, and apparently random Meetup group members.

I didn't even have a moment to wrap my head around that humiliating realization before the lady shouted back across the circle. "That's too early."

Like a tennis match, everyone's gaze returned to me.

This was the last thing I needed, defending the choice of my hiking time. I wanted to say, "Eff off lady. Stop criticizing other people's events. My ex humiliated me, and I have to sit here and listen to you complain about my hikes being too early. If you don't want to go, don't go." Instead, I said politely, "If you want to go on a later hike, then you can organize one."

She didn't respond and went back to talking to the woman sitting next to her. I waited five more minutes, managing to avoid the earlier question about Runner, then folded up my chair and marched back to the car with tears streaming down my cheeks.

I spent the next few days trying to smile through it all so I could enjoy time with Kiddo for the little we had left of summer. She was set to head back to California soon to start seventh grade. But I just couldn't gather the strength to do that, or at least do it well. The cycle was feel terrible, feel terrible for feeling terrible, and then feel more terrible. All Kiddo wanted to do was spend time together, and all I wanted to do was cry. So, when my emotions would bubble up, I would squeeze my eyes, take a deep breath, and hold in the sobs begging to come out. I didn't want to ruin summer vacation for her.

One afternoon, I got yet another text from someone in *my* social circle that Runner had friended on Facebook.

Who's the new lady?

This was similar to the other ones I had received like, "Saw Runner's post . . ." or "You two broke up?" A few others like, "Are you okay?" were sprinkled in the mix. I was embarrassed for me, embarrassed for her, and I had to live it over and over with every text that came in.

Three days before Kiddo's return to California, I got a call from the cat shelter asking if I would take another litter of kittens. After having returned Cujo and her babies, my plan was to be litter-free for a while, at least until I could get myself together. But Tucson's growing cat population didn't care about my intolerable heartache.

While I was chatting with the adoption coordinator, Kiddo sat by patiently, waiting for the verdict.

"I'll have to think about it," I said to the staffer before hanging up.

"There is nothing to think about. We have to go now," Kiddo said. "Like now!" She jumped up from the kitchen table and ran her lunch dish to the sink.

"I don't know." I frowned. "You're leaving. I would have to take care of these kittens on my own."

"I'll get everything set for you—food, litter . . . everything. I promise." She darted into my bedroom to get my keys and wallet and came rushing back to the kitchen. "Now, can we go?"

I was no match for her enthusiasm. "You are quite convincing," I said. "Yes, we can go."

We got in the car, and I called the shelter on the way. When we arrived, two calico kittens with Egyptian names were curled up in the back of their carrier, beady eyes shimmering from behind a bunched-up blanket. They looked at me with skepticism. Frankly, I looked at myself in the mirror like that every day.

We brought them home and, given the treacherous summer heat, decided to put them in the hall bathroom instead of the garage. When I opened the carrier, the two scampered out and hunkered down behind the toilet.

I texted Mom to tell her the news, attaching a photo. She wrote back right away.

They are really cute!

I'll do anything at this point to distract myself from feeling so crappy. No matter how hard I try, everything still sucks.

They sound exactly like what you need right now.

The next few days flew by, with Kiddo on kitten duty while I wallowed in sadness. But then she left, and I had two kittens looking to me to care for and love them.

The first morning I did my solo feeding, I had flashbacks of Cujo puncturing my chest with her sharp claws. But when I saw these tiny kittens sleeping, one on top of the other, behind the toilet, the traumatic memory passed. I put the food down, filled their water, and went on my way.

An hour later, I returned to check on them. They were in the same kitten pile as before, snoozing—but their food dish was licked clean, and the floor in front of the litterbox was an absolute mess.

"Who did this?" I asked. "It's only been an hour! Plus, I thought we had a plan: I love and care for you, and you keep the place tidy."

Three more times that day, I found myself on my hands and knees scrubbing the floor.

"Kitties, we're in a pandemic, and Clorox wipes are hard to come by," I scolded them gently. "And what about our plan?"

All I got in return from the sleeping kittens were soft purrs.

The next morning, Mom checked in.

How's it going with the kittens?

They make quite the mess. But they are adorable and have really been a great distraction for me. I have a lot of love to give these days. I might as well channel it into these little babies.

They are very lucky to have you.

I think I'm the lucky one.

"Dear Soulmate"

Within a few days, the kittens and I had gotten into our routine. I clean, and they keep me company. That seemed like a good plan, except that two drowsy cats hunkered down behind a toilet were never going to be able to take the place of the human interaction, connection, and love I so badly craved.

One night during the witching hours, I was overcome with this deep sense of loneliness. I didn't want to go one more day without those things, especially knowing *I* was suffering while Runner was presumably off enjoying life with her new lady. So, I hurried to my desk, pulled out a pen and paper, and scribbled across the top, "What do you want in a partner?" Then I wrote down everything I could think of until the whole page was filled.

I massaged the resulting cramp in my palm while I read my list out loud. Although I liked the sentiments expressed, I couldn't get past the grammatical inconsistencies on the page. Some things I'd written were feelings, some traits, some nouns, and some adjectives. My list was a mess.

I started to try to clean it up, but it was late, and I was so exhausted. The changes I made only led to even more confusing language. Frustrated, I pushed the paper away and peeked in on the sleeping kittens before heading to bed.

I'll try again tomorrow.

The next morning, I returned to my scribbles with a fresh eye. After fixing the grammar issues, I read everything over a few times.

"Perfect," I said aloud.

I stared at the first item on the list—soulmate love. *This would be like no love I'd had in the past. Instead, it would be true love, never fading away or leaving me heartbroken and alone. And, once I found this person . . . my soulmate . . . the one I'm supposed to be with, the universe would make sure I never got hurt again.*

I jumped on my computer and started researching "soulmates."

After reading several blogs, posts, and articles, I came across two books that seemed intriguing: *The Soulmate Secret* by Arielle Ford and *Calling in "The One"* by Katherine Woodward Thomas. I ordered both.

Two days later, they arrived. I began with *The Soulmate Secret*, immersing myself in the first few chapters and noting interesting passages. Then, I came upon it . . . the key to soulmate love—make a list of what you want in a partner.

I grabbed my handwritten notes sitting on my nightstand and waved them in the air. "I'm so ahead of the curve!" I shouted to my cat. "My soulmate will be here in no time."

The following morning, I put on my old hiker-embroidered baseball cap, grabbed a bottle of water, and set out for my daily walk. As I made my way through the yard to the sidewalk, I pressed the timer on my watch and then hit play on my phone. One of the many breakup podcasts in my queue came blaring through my earbuds.

I started speeding along as usual, past saguaro cacti, mountain buttes, and neighbors out walking their dogs. After thirty minutes or so of "you'll find love again" affirmations, the podcast host said, "Remember that while you're looking for your soulmate, your soulmate is also looking for you."

As soon as I heard the words, I stopped short, almost tripping over my own feet.

"Write a letter to your soulmate inviting them to connect with you and reassuring them that you are out there looking, too," he advised.

This is brilliant! I immediately turned around and hurried home to write my letter. The moment I made it through the door, I sped straight to my desk, grabbed a pen and paper, and—referring to the list I had already made—started writing.

Before long, my hand was aching again. But I couldn't slow down. *The longer it takes me to write this letter*, I thought, *the longer it will be before we are together.*

> *Dear Soulmate, I know you are here in Tucson. That is why I have such a strong pull to live here. I see you as fit; athletic; in your forties; smart; funny; witty; liberal; goal-oriented; tidy and organized; a cat lover; loving to travel; preferably vegetarian; sporty-looking; honest; loyal; with good grit and follow-through; career-minded; financially secure; light or nondrinker; loving to snuggle, kiss, and be intimate; well-educated; independent; close with family; extroverted; and ready to give me love, support, fidelity, commitment, trust, loyalty, equity, and interdependence. You laugh at my jokes, want to be close to my family, will love my kid, want stability, seek adventure, and want to live in Tucson.*
>
> *Game on.*

It had been two days since I had crafted my "Dear Soulmate" letter and two days of repeatedly reading it out loud. Yet nothing had happened. *How long does it take to summon a soulmate? Maybe Arielle knows.*

I reached over Phoenix, my kitty, who was nestled up next to me in bed, to pull *The Soulmate Secret* from my nightstand. I leafed through the entire book but couldn't find a definitive timeline. Feeling impatient, I tossed it aside and rummaged through the drawer to find *Calling in "The One,"* which I had tucked away for later reading. I smiled when I saw the answer was right on the cover: "Seven Weeks to Attract the Love of Your Life."

Just six weeks and five days to go. I could definitely make it . . . now that I had a timeline.

Gone Grill

A week after writing my "Dear Soulmate" letter, I was preparing my daily cafeteria-tray lunch—the usual banana, nuts, and an assortment of other picnic foods, when I was suddenly overcome with nostalgia for the days when Runner was a part of this routine. We always ate together, with her scooping up far too much hummus and me complaining that she wasn't going to leave me any. We would then both laugh. Back then, lunchtime was full of banter—a part of the day to look forward to. Without her around, lunches were quiet, and I had more hummus than I needed.

As the ache in my chest intensified, my yearning for the "good ol' days" quickly devolved into hysteria.

"Why? Why? Why?" I yelled, tears welling up in my eyes. I looked up as if gazing at the heavens, seeking some answer to my question. But there was no response and no sign from above. Just the sound of Phoenix purring from a nearby rug.

I slumped down onto the cold, hard kitchen floor and mumbled one last "Why?" before allowing my face to fall into my hands. As tears seeped through my fingers, I shouted, "Because you're an awful human!"

I looked over at Phoenix, who had perked up and was staring at me.

"I don't mean that," I reassured her. "I'm just hurt and angry . . . and sad. I want to move on and not feel this way. And I *don't* want to be alone." Resolve flowed through me, and I picked myself up off the floor. "I'm *not* gonna be alone," I told Phoenix.

I dashed to the other room, grabbed my "Dear Soulmate" letter, and returned to my spot on the kitchen floor. Legs sprawled out, leaning against a cabinet, I began reading it out loud while tears streamed down my face. "Dear Soulmate, I know you are here in Tucson . . ."

After reciting it a second time, I didn't move. I gripped the letter in one hand and lifted the other to wipe away the wetness on my puffy, red face. I exhaled and then let my eyes wander from the new white cabinets I had gotten installed in the kitchen during our first relationship hiatus to the huge patchwork rug where Phoenix was curled up. Then, I noticed a reflection from the backyard shining through the sliding glass doors. It was from the big metal grill Runner had bought years earlier.

"Your stupid grill!" I yelled.

I thought I had already gotten rid of everything that reminded me of her. I'd replaced our cat throw-pillow covers with ones with mid-century modern geometric shapes. I'd donated all our old picture frames, convinced that any new photos I put in them would only be renting space from our memories. I'd even sold the expensive set of pots and pans she'd bought me to the first person who'd offered a few bucks for them.

But I had missed the grill.

I threw the letter down on the floor, got up, and stormed out to the patio. I tilted the grill onto its two back wheels and dragged it across the gravel, all the way from the backyard to the front of the house. When I finally made it to the sidewalk, I let go of the handle, and the whole thing landed with a loud thump, narrowly missing my foot. But I didn't have time to thank my lucky stars that I'd just avoided breaking my toes. I was on a mission. I stomped back inside, grabbed a piece of paper and a marker, and wrote "Free Grill." I then rushed back out, taped the paper on the side facing the road, and left it for anyone who wanted to take the metal behemoth off my property.

Emboldened by the grill disposal, I marched into the house with purpose.

"What else did I forget?" I asked Phoenix.

She gave me a bemused look as I started scouring every kitchen cabinet for anything I might have missed. And as soon as I flung open the door of the corner cupboard, there it was—her favorite coffee.

"How did I miss this?" I shook the bag at Phoenix and tossed it into the trash bin.

Unperturbed, she began to groom herself.

I then found Runner's gluten-free flour. I grabbed the bag and threw it into the trash, too. It landed with a huge *thud*, which gave me an adrenaline rush. When it hit the bottom of the garbage can, though, the bag split and flour shot upward, covering the floor with a snowy topcoat.

"What the hell?" My shoulders drooped as the excitement of the moment slipped away. I spent the next ten minutes scrubbing the floor on my hands and knees.

After cleaning, I went outside to check on the grill. "No shit," I said, standing in my driveway. There was no grill in sight.

I then walked back inside and immediately ordered a five-star-rated sage cleansing spray. It arrived the next day, and I wasted no time spritzing the house while chanting about replacing negative energy with love and positivity.

With the house cleared out, I was sure I would feel empowered and free. Instead, as the silence of the space we'd once shared enveloped me, a deep sense of loneliness set in—one I had never before experienced.

I had to find my soulmate. And I needed to do it soon.

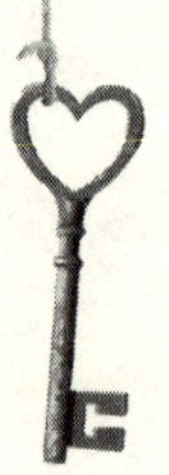

Gotta Love Tucson

You called it, pal! Do you want me to send you her post?

I was on my way to the shelter with the kittens for a checkup a few days after the big cleanse when Hiker's text popped up on my screen. It could only mean one thing.

I pulled onto a side street, parked the car, and took a deep breath before furiously typing my response.

Married?

Three little dots flashed on the screen. Finally, a message appeared.

House

She then sent a screenshot of a Facebook post saying, "Cheers to new adventures!" with a picture of a two-story home.

"What the fuck?" I said out loud. I didn't swear often, so my language even caught me off guard. I took another deep breath, exhaled slowly, and replied, asking her to send the comments.

Screenshot after screenshot loaded onto my phone. I couldn't read fast enough to see all the likes and celebratory words from dozens and dozens of people whose names I didn't recognize.

"Congratulations, gals!"

"❤ So excited for y'all!"

My face felt like it was on fire as more flooded in. I texted Hiker back.

I bet she got married too. That way they could buy the house together.

She responded right away.

I would put my dog on my mortgage over a woman.

Ha ha

Although I typed the words, I sure didn't feel like laughing.

I turned around to look in the backseat. "Kittens," I said, trailing off in a near whisper. "She just moved on . . . like I didn't even exist."

I managed to hold it together for the shelter visit and the rest of the day. But that night, I laid my head on my pillow and fell asleep, yet again, in a puddle of tears.

Want to see a screenshot? I'm waiting for you to tell me to stop . . .

I hated Hiker's texts, especially the ones with photos. And it had only been a couple days since the last bout before this one rolled in.

Married?

I asked again.

Three little dots popped up.

I stopped eating my lunch. I didn't want to risk choking to death on a carrot while getting this horrifying news.

No, but I think they are here in town. I'll send it.

In came a picture of Runner and her lady taken at our favorite resort, with the caption, "Gorgeous morning hike! ❤🌵☀."

A faint feeling rushed over me. At least she wasn't getting married. But she was *here*, in town, and at *our* special place—a place full of memories we'd made together.

I stared at the picture. They were both smiling from ear to ear, skin glowing in the sun. Witnessing her elation and knowing she posted this photo despite how hurtful it could be to me was like a gut punch.

More posts popped up over the next few days, and I wanted every update I could get. With my continuous encouragement, Hiker fed them to me by the spoonful. And before I knew it, I was back down the rabbit hole, bypassing the messenger and looking directly at Runner's social media account on Hiker's phone.

The pictures made me feel awful inside, especially the one in front of the cat shelter we had fostered so many kittens from. But part of me felt as though knowledge was power. If I knew what she was up to, I could have some sense of control—although over what, I didn't know.

After having spent an inordinate amount of time analyzing the barrage of posts about *her* "new adventures," I felt more compelled than ever to find my soulmate and have *my own* new adventures. So, I registered for a lesbian online speed-dating event. I figured if my soulmate was also searching for me, I had to make it easy for us to find each other.

I'd attended two of these events back in the spring when Runner and I were on our hiatus, so I knew how it worked. You got paired with a random woman in a breakout room for four minutes, then after the timer went off, you were rotated into a different one to chat with someone else. After each conversation, you had to click a button to indicate your interest—date, friend, business contact, or none.

I hadn't had much luck at the first two events. The one designated for any lesbian in America brought me the longest four minutes of my life, having to chat with a Linda Ronstadt–obsessed truck driver.

"Were you at her concert in 2017? I was there. I had a stop-over on my route in Tucson," she said. "Maybe we were there at the same time?"

"I've never been to one of her concerts." I stared at the embroidered patch of her name stitched on her shirt and the countdown clock as she droned on and on about Ronstadt's greatest hits.

After deciding to narrow the field a bit, I attended one for vegetarians, which ended up being the most interactive recipe swap I had ever experienced with zero viable prospects for dating.

But the one I had just signed up for was supposed to focus on professionals. I thought I might meet some women who loved their work, just like me. After suffering through four minutes with a retired lunch lady who didn't even like her job when she *was* employed, I rotated into a room with a twenty-something eccentric with a nose piercing and half-shaved head. While she was not my physical type, our conversation flowed, and the time flew by. She was the only person I marked as "date." The feeling must have been mutual, as we were matched by the speed-dating algorithm the next day. Although I still had a lot to learn about her, she was the closest I had to a soulmate contender so far.

Llamas

"Welcome," she said with a warm smile. "It's so nice to meet you."

"You too," I said, before taking a deep breath of the lavender aroma wafting in the air. I gazed around the room and was immediately drawn to the wall with floor-to-ceiling shelves filled with energy healing books. *Only experts have that many books. She must know what she's doing.*

We sat at a small table adorned with a lace tablecloth. On it was a pad of paper and a pen.

She then asked in a soft voice, "What do you hope to achieve today?" Her grayish-brown bob haircut swished as she leaned forward to take notes.

"I just had a breakup and need to clear any negative energy I'm holding onto," I said. "I thought I'd try Reiki. I had acupuncture done, but having all those needles sticking out of my skin made me feel out of control and anxious, not relaxed and spiritually free."

She smiled. "Well, I'd love to help. I might suggest we start with something called Access Bars, though. It's a technique designed to unblock energy fields. I think it would be good to do before Reiki, which we can do next time."

I nodded. "Whatever you think is best."

She led me into a small room with a dim night-light and then asked me to lie down on what looked like a massage table. She placed a sheet on top of me and turned up the heat from below. The warmth flooded through my body, helping to offset the chill from the air conditioning blowing from a nearby vent. The soothing sounds of a trickling creek played from a speaker across the room. I closed my eyes and tried to relax, despite having to breathe through my heavy cloth face mask, which was COVID protocol at the time.

"I'm going to move around you, holding my hands above each of your chakras to unblock your energy," she said. Her voice was quiet and comforting, although barely loud enough to hear over the sounds of the water.

"What am I supposed to do? Think about something, or clear my mind and meditate?" In truth, I actually had no idea how to clear my mind.

"Just relax," she said. "Maybe say a mantra in your head."

"I am grateful for my healing process" immediately popped into my brain. *That seems like a good one*, I thought.

She moved around me ever so slowly, the warmth of her hands floating over my body. My silent mantra was on loop like a broken record.

Suddenly, tears started rolling down my cheeks, flowing almost involuntarily. I kept on with the mantra, though, until a voice inside my head shouted, "There's no way you can genuinely be grateful for feeling like crap." I immediately put a stop to the mantra, and the tears dried up.

I then filled my absence of thought by running through my to-do list for the day—errands, work tasks, and grocery items I wanted to pick up on my way home. By the time I finished fixating on my afternoon agenda, my mind drifted, and nonsensical visions appeared. *At least my mantra didn't come back.*

Suddenly, I heard, *gong!* The sound ricocheted through the room, jarring me out of my wandering thoughts. She walked around me, swinging her mallet. *Gong!* It ricocheted again.

I slowly opened my eyes.

"You can join me back at the table when you are ready," she whispered.

"How do you feel?" she asked once I sat down.

"Sleepy, but good," I said, keeping tight-lipped about my mantra experience. "Do the visions mean anything?"

"Did you have one?" She raised her eyebrow.

"Yes. There was a llama wearing a red bandana standing in some far-off mountain range . . . nowhere I've ever been to. What does it mean?"

"What do *you* think it means?"

"I'm not sure." I took a swig from my water bottle.

"Usually, people feel the effects of energy healing within about twenty-four hours," she said and then smiled. "Maybe the vision will make more sense later."

The next morning, I woke up, not feeling any different from the day before. I headed out to lead a group of lesbians from my Meetup group on a walk along a river path that loops around Tucson.

Several people showed up, including Naked and Afraid, whom I hadn't seen since the pool party nearly two months earlier. She brought two women she'd recently met at a happy hour. One was a tall, athletic hippie-type who looked to be in her mid-fifties. Her shoulder-length blond hair fell just shy of the neckline of her T-shirt. The other seemed to be a little younger, around the same age and height as me, but with short brown hair and glasses. I could see her defined shoulders under her tight T-shirt. *I want muscles like that.*

Once we got started, groups broke off by pace, and I found myself at the front of the pack with the lady with the muscles. She was speedy, but I kept up. Naked and Afraid and Hippie were hauling along, too, right on our heels.

After the walk, the four of us headed to a nearby café and sat on the patio, chatting for several hours.

"So, what's your bucket list hike?" I asked everyone.

Naked and Afraid jumped in. "You know I worked on Everest."

"Wow! What did you do? Did you hike the whole thing?" Hippie asked, before taking a bite of her bagel sandwich.

"I just stayed around base camp. Some of the shit I've seen is terrifying. No way I'd do that whole hike," she said. "I've always wanted to do Machu Picchu, though."

"Me too!" I said.

The others agreed.

"Maybe we could go together," Naked and Afraid said. "We could have sherpas with llamas carry our stuff."

Suddenly, the image of the llama from my vision flashed through my mind. I glanced at my watch—twenty-four hours since the energy healing appointment. I let out a small gasp, but thankfully, no one seemed to notice. No need to share this story with my new friends yet.

"We should start with the Grand Canyon to prep," Naked and Afraid said.

Everyone seemed to be on board.

Naked and Afraid looked right at me. "Just text us the details."

We all laughed.

"I'll get on it," I said, still grinning, less about her comment and more about my llama. I was definitely on the right path.

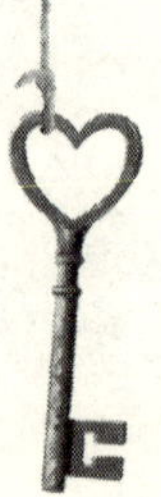

Whips

"What do you like to do for fun?" I asked the twenty-something eccentric from speed dating.

She leaned into her webcam. "I just bought a whip and am trying to learn how to crack it."

Over the next five minutes, she continued to explain the merits of whip-cracking. "You know they have competitions at the rodeo?"

"I didn't. We have a big rodeo here in Tucson. I wonder if that's one of the events."

"I'm going to master it. I'll keep you posted."

"Uh, cool."

And that was my first date with Whips.

"So, the text I sent you about not hiking because of botched LASIK surgery . . . I wanted to explain," Whips said on our second video date.

"Okay . . ." My response sounded more like, "Uh-oh. Something weird is about to happen" rather than a chill, "Sure, what's up?"

"Well, the surgery screwed up the nerves in my eyes, and I can't go out in the sunlight."

I breathed a sigh of relief when I realized we were probably just going to talk about good sunglasses.

"That's awful! Is there anything you can do?"

"Well, I used to drive two hours every month to a doctor who would make eye drops out of my blood. It was supposed to regenerate my nerves or something."

"Um . . . Did it work?" I leaned forward toward the screen, waiting for the story to unfold.

"Nope. I did it for nine months. Each month's little vial of eye drops was, like, a thousand dollars, too."

"Is that covered by insurance?"

"No. I had to pay out of pocket, and I was just a grad student at the time." She paused. "I had to *find* the money."

Something suddenly felt off. *Was she a drug dealer or an art museum thief? Or maybe a bank robber or someone who commits insurance fraud?* My mind raced from one illicit occupation to the next. I was sure she could sense my wheels turning with my prolonged pause.

"I was a dominatrix," she finally said.

Silence again fell over me as my thoughts shifted. I did not know any dominatrices, nor did I live in a world where I understood what one even did.

"Oh . . . What was that like?" I asked in my "I'm so cool with you being a dominatrix" tone.

She filled me in on the details, and by the end of the conversation, I marginally understood the dominatrix world.

"Sounds like a difficult situation," was all I could say. "How long did you do it for?"

"Two years."

"Didn't you only use the eye drops for nine months, though?" I asked.

"Yep. But I made good money, and I kind of enjoyed it."

What I wanted to ask was, "What did you like about it?

Why did you stop? Do you miss it? How were you able to use a whip back then, since you are just now learning how to crack one?" Instead, I said, "That's cool."

The next day, in came a video on text of her trying to crack the whip. Although she was in her backyard, just wearing jeans and a T-shirt, I couldn't rid myself of the image of her in some hotel room with a whip wearing black leather. I texted back.

Looks like you are making progress.

I wasn't sure what else to say or if I could even judge whether she was indeed making progress.

No response.

Later, I sent her a picture of me standing on a huge rock with the caption:

The weather was great, and the hike was absolutely wonderful.

Then, her reply came in, telling me I had nice muscles.

My chest grew heavy, and an overwhelming sense of unease came over me—the wave of lightheadedness that hits right before you faint. I had been working out and wanted other people to notice. And I liked Speedy's muscles. But flirtatious comments had been reserved for Runner—and I wasn't quite ready to hear someone else say them.

I waited until the physical sensation of overwhelm passed and then wrote back.

Thanks. It was a fun hike.

I later got a text from her, this time with no whip video, asking if her comment made me uncomfortable and if I would rather just pursue a friendship.

> I'd love to just be friends for now. You still want to chat this week?

Ghosted.

Back to square one.

Abundance Everywhere

I hadn't quite completed the seven-week soulmate search as described in *Calling in "The One."* But, after my visceral reaction to Whips's "nice muscles" comment, I knew I needed to heal from the breakup a bit more before continuing the quest for my soulmate.

So, I put the books in my nightstand drawer, along with my "Dear Soulmate" letter, and pulled out *How to Not Die Alone* by Logan Ury. Over the next few nights, I curled up in bed to read Logan's sagely advice on how to get through the healing process, none of which involved dating a person who cracked a whip. My new book made the witching hours fly by, and I felt less lonely, which was especially helpful since everything was quieter after having returned the kittens to the shelter.

Once I finished reading the last sentence, I closed the book and placed it in my drawer. I then pulled out my "Dear Soulmate" letter and read it aloud to the universe. I was back on track.

"Do you want great abundance in your life? Maybe financial wealth? Love? Good health?" said the overweight, middle-aged man broadcasting from his living room. Stacks of books and papers towered behind him.

"Yes!" I said. "I want all of those things, especially love!" The words came out of my mouth to no one, as, thankfully, my microphone was on mute.

"You *can* have everything you desire, simply by manifesting," he said.

All the little boxes on the video screen were filled with faces of eager people, like me, who stumbled upon this free virtual Meetup event, looking for a life of abundance.

"All you have to do is ask the universe for what you want," he said.

He talked about how he manifested his own personal elephant, which was a bit obscure, along with stories of others calling in their dream houses and jobs. "Write down what you want as if you already have it. Be clear about your intentions. Be descriptive. Express gratitude. And then let the universe do the work," he said. "The universe, though, will deliver when you are ready to receive. You must be ready, though."

During those ninety minutes, he taught us everything we needed in order to have great wealth, a successful career, and profound love.

While I knew this expert might be pulling a fast one—especially since I wasn't even sure someone could own an elephant—I still held out hope. If I learned how to manifest, my life would certainly change.

Right before wrapping up, an older gentleman in attendance asked if anyone wanted to form an online group to share the manifests we would be writing. I gave him my contact information.

As soon as we logged off, I began typing out an actual love manifest using my newfound knowledge and a lot of the language from my "Dear Soulmate" letter. I included a thank-you to the universe for giving me someone with those qualities and described how I would feel when we were together. After several iterations, I got it to sound exactly how I wanted.

⟷

"I feel good. I am in great health. My body feels good. My mind feels good. I just feel good." The older gentleman read for another couple minutes about all the ways he could possibly feel good. After finishing, he asked for feedback. The six of us in attendance at the virtual manifesting group offered suggestions on the wording. It seemed like a cool process.

"Does anyone have a manifest they would like to read?" he asked.

I stayed quiet, waiting for others to volunteer. No one stepped up. I wanted to share the beginnings of my love manifest, but I wasn't ready to divulge I was a lesbian and had just gone through a terrible breakup. I'd save those for our second time together.

Burning Tower

"Would you like a psychic or card reading?" the lady asked. She was sitting at a folding table in the New Age church's tiny kitchen.

"Um, a card reading, I guess."

She scribbled my name in the first available slot and took my twenty dollars.

"It'll be about ten minutes. Just move to the side here and you can wait." She pointed to an area in front of the stove that had a spot for one.

"Thanks." I took a few steps back and tried to avoid the crowd of people hovering over the table with the sign-up sheet. *Ten minutes . . . that's it. Then I will know what the universe has in store for my love life.*

My name was finally called, and I was ushered down a long hallway into a room with five folding tables, each with an intuitive awaiting their next guest. They all had pendulums, candles, and stacks of tarot cards. A lady in her sixties with short gray hair waved me over.

After I sat down, I couldn't help but fixate on her dangly earrings, which swayed back and forth with even the slightest turn of her head. She handed me a deck of cards to shuffle, which I did thoroughly. She then laid out five of them and started talking about someone who had been an important presence in my recent past but who was no longer in my life. While she was going on and on about this mystery person, who was obviously Runner, I couldn't help but notice the upside-down Tower card later in my spread. I knew little about tarot, but I figured a tower on fire with people leaping from the windows to their deaths was not good. I also knew getting a card in reverse was an even more ominous sign.

When she got to the Tower card, she said, "It seems like you are transitioning out of something really challenging right now . . . maybe having to do with a person who has brought negative energy into your life. This will likely continue for a while since the card is in your future spot."

"Why are people jumping out of the windows? Am I one of them?" I asked.

"The Tower is more about needing to escape from some type of chaos. Looks like you'll be dealing with this turmoil for a little while longer. Hang in there," she said. Her voice was calm and soothing.

"That sounds awful."

"It'll eventually pass. By the way . . ." She picked up the last card in my spread. "It looks like a very influential person has recently come into your life . . . maybe a lawyer?"

"I have a new friend who is a lawyer."

"Hmm. Well, she is going to make a profound impact on you."

As soon as I got to the parking lot, I called Naked and Afraid. She and I had been chatting nonstop since the Meetup walk, commiserating about our devastating love lives.

"I'm the lawyer!" she said.

"Of course you are! I don't know any other lawyers. It also looks like my tower is on fire, and people are jumping from the windows."

"What tower?"

"The burning tower of my entire life."

The Plan

During the days following the tarot card reading, I couldn't get the image of the burning tower out of my head. This was my life, and I was stuck, flames burning around me in a state of chaos, uncertainty, and angst.

Late one evening while lying in bed, an idea came to me. If I didn't want to sit in this burning tower or wait thirty years for the raging flames to die down, like I did with First Love, I had to take action. So, I did what any good Virgo, Type A personality would in this circumstance. I started to draft a plan, a checklist of sorts, of everything I could do to heal from the breakup and ultimately find my soulmate.

I began by typing the following: "Distract myself," "Talk with anyone who will listen," "Get therapy," and "Feel the feelings." I then added several more, ending with "Get energy healing," "Make new friends," and "Write a manifest."

I looked at my list, and all I saw was a haphazard summary of things I *had* tried and not a plan for moving forward. *Where was the strategy in that? You have to rethink this, Corey. This is your official move-on and find-your-soulmate strategic plan.*

I leaned back in my chair and took a deep breath. *Alright, then what else can I add?* I hovered over my keyboard about to type. *"Cut hair"? Nope. I like my ponytail. "Start a new job"? No way. I love being a professor. "Hook up with someone"? Not a chance. I'm way too traditional.*

I finally got up and wandered back into my bedroom. *My plan sucks.* I climbed into bed and started scrolling through the Meetup app. Then I saw it—a virtual session on attachment styles scheduled for the next day. I RSVP'd and then rushed back to my office to add it to what I now called The Plan. A tiny wave of excitement came over me. *Let's do this, Corey.*

Over the next two weeks, I attended well over a dozen self-help seminars about healing from heartbreak offered through Meetup. They covered topics such as building trust and breaking unhealthy relationship patterns.

I would text Naked and Afraid periodically to give her my thoughts.

I just finished one about how to pick better partners.

What did you learn?

I have a dominant personality but am often drawn to more laid-back people. But over time, I end up wishing those people were more driven and motivated.

Well, that's interesting. What ever happened with that women's circle you signed up for?

Most of the ladies had been divorced from their husbands for nearly a decade, and they all just cried a lot.

I checked that one off the plan. I want to at least get credit for trying it!

Once I made it through my short self-help stint, I was overwhelmed and exhausted with all the self-reflection and processing. I decided the key to my plan truly was balance—recover from heartbreak *and* search for my soulmate at the same time. I then remembered in *How to Not Die Alone*, the author suggested going to places you enjoy to meet people with the same interests. So, I added this idea to The Plan and then brainstormed possible places I could go—women's basketball game, local festival, karaoke bar, and used bookstore. Basketball season was months away, and I hadn't yet met anyone at a festival or while singing karaoke (admittedly in my living room). I figured I'd try the bookstore. And I'd go tomorrow. Someone who was well-read, enjoyed learning, and was a bit thrifty, like me, could be a perfect match, and I didn't want to keep her waiting.

As soon as the front door slid open, I was welcomed by the musty aroma of vintage books. The place was bustling with people sifting through the racks and skimming pages. Small kids gathered in the aisles of the children's area, an old guy shuffled through a stack of paperbacks on the employee suggestion rack, and a handful of avid readers were trading in their used books.

I headed to the LGBTQ+ section, as it made sense that my soulmate would look for me there. As I perused the covers of the romance novels, I noticed most of the books were not geared toward lesbians, unless seeing a sketch of a man with long locks of hair blowing in the wind was their thing. I then came across one that had a muted photo of two women in each other's arms. As soon as I cracked it open, the crusty binding started to come apart. I immediately closed it, slid it between two other vintage books, and made my way to the nonfiction area, where I leafed through a "So you just came out?" book. Once it occurred to me that I didn't want to send *that* message to a prospective soulmate, I shoved the book back on the rack.

None of it really mattered, though. After fifteen minutes, my mystery date hadn't shown up. So, I made my way to the exit. Despite feeling a bit defeated in that moment, I thought the bookstore strategy was genius. I just had to keep trying.

Pow, Boom, Bang

"I know you don't want to get married because of all the 'Been there, done that, I don't trust myself to leave if it's bad, and I can't be trapped' thing," Naked and Afraid said. "But what if you do find your soulmate? You really wouldn't marry her?"

We were trekking along the Linda Vista Trail, one of the places we had been training for our Grand Canyon adventure. Hiking with Naked and Afraid was always a combination of exercise, sunshine therapy, and soul searching as we pondered life's biggest questions in the beauty of the Arizona desert. And today was no different.

"I want the spiritual connection, not some stupid piece of paper that says someone gets half my stuff if we split up."

"Well, there are prenups, you know?" She laughed.

We finally made it to the high point of the loop and stopped.

As she chugged from her water bottle, I asked, "You ever hear of the saying, 'When you know, you know?' Or like love at first sight . . . chemistry . . . fireworks that light up the sky? That's *pow, boom, bang*. When I have it, I'll know I've met my soulmate and won't need to marry her because our connection will be much deeper than some contract. And if for some reason she doesn't end up being my person, I don't have to give her my house."

"*Pow*, *boom*, *bang*—is that some weird saying you made up?"

Right then, an elderly couple approached us on the trail. We both waited in silence as they carefully stepped past us.

Once they were out of earshot, I said, "I don't know if I heard it somewhere or what. But it's Hallmark movie love . . . 1950s photos of long-lost lovers' kind of love. *That*, I didn't make up."

"Have you ever had it?" she asked.

A few hikers were coming up behind us, so we started up again hoping to outpace them.

"Not yet. But I'm not settling for anything less this time."

She suddenly stopped and spun around to look at me. I too came to a screeching halt. She then said, "You know the lady I had the date with the other night?"

"Yeah?"

"I didn't tell you this because I figured you would think I was completely out there. But when we met in person, I felt lightning shoot through me. I just knew."

I looked her right in the eyes. "That's *pow*, *boom*, *bang*! And I'm gonna find it too."

"We can help you with breakup recovery. Just reach out and set up a free consultation with one of our coaches," the voice said at the end of the episode.

I sped around the corner back toward my street, practically tripping over myself to get home from my walk.

"You *can* move on from heartbreak," the voice continued.

"Yes, I can. And I'm gonna extinguish my burning tower!" I said out loud to no one.

I burst through the door, ran to my computer, and signed

up for my free consultation. I then added "Meet with a breakup coach" to The Plan.

Breakup Coach was a perky blonde who looked to be in her early thirties. She wore a classy blouse, appearing more professional than I was expecting for a video meeting.

"You noted in your intake form that your parents got divorced when you were younger. Tell me more about their relationship and eventual separation."

I shared all about the brewing misery that had developed between my parents over time. "They fought a lot, and they weren't happy. It was like they were trapped, and I couldn't figure out why one of them just wouldn't leave. The only reason they got divorced years later was because my mom caught my dad cheating. Then he left and married the other lady."

She scribbled in her notebook. I was sure she wrote, "So messed up" and "No hope for love again."

I went on to explain more details of the divorce.

"A lot of the ways we act come from our past trauma with parents, friends, exes, coworkers . . . really anyone," she said. "It's important to recognize and resolve our trauma in order to break unhealthy patterns of behavior. If not, you just repeat those as a way to cope with the trauma. And then you have trauma again."

I nodded.

I then told her about how I sat in angst for decades about First Love and witnessed my relationship with Zion die right in front of me. The more I talked, the more I realized I had never deeply processed any of it. Now, here I was again . . . trying to deal with my most recent heartache.

I filled her in on the specifics of my relationship and eventual breakup with Runner.

"Well, it sounds like you might be experiencing some trauma from this, too—particularly your last year together, how everything ended, and even the aftermath on social media."

"Yeah." I sighed. "Apparently, I have a lot to work out—between my past stuff and this breakup."

"It might take a while and some serious intention to move through it," she said. "Just don't stuff it down or ignore it. Tackle it head on."

"That's what my therapist told me too." I let out a small laugh, more out of discomfort than finding any of this funny.

We logged off, and I finally had a name for what I had been feeling—the heaviness and unresolve of trauma. The idea of it landed like a medical diagnosis that comes after years of doctor visits. At least I knew what I was up against. But I also felt broken, and I didn't want to feel broken.

Cosmos

Ever since Naked and Afraid and I had reconnected at the Meetup walk, she had been flooding our text thread with random links she *had* to share with me—political stories with her own captions, our shared Virgo horoscope, Gen X memes, and quotes about surviving heartbreak.

One day, she sent me a link to a podcast on the Law of Attraction. The episode began with a lady saying in a soft, soothing voice, "Think positive thoughts, which will generate positive feelings, which will, in turn, create positive energy. With positive energy, we can manifest our dreams and desires." I liked this lady a lot. She was full of optimism and said to focus on joy, which she called high vibrations, rather than negativity, or low vibrations.

While walking my neighborhood loop one morning, I found myself ruminating about the breakup again. I cranked up some music to drown out the thoughts. But the nagging what-ifs replaying in my mind overtook the thumping bass and loud beats flooding into my earbuds. I finally stopped walking and turned off the music. *Breathe, Corey. What would the nice Law of Attraction lady say?* I closed my eyes and took a deep breath.

Her voice whispered in my ear, "Any time you feel stuck in a state of anger, hurt, or sadness, redirect your thoughts to something that brings you joy, and let the positive emotions fill your soul." *Hmm. I need to feel my feelings but not get stuck in them. Got it.*

I then shifted my attention to Kiddo's upcoming visit and began walking again, picturing all the fun things we were going to do, like hiking, watching our favorite shows, and playing cards. Within minutes, my mood began to transform. And by the time I got home, I felt light, free, and full of joy.

It was obvious that "Embrace the Law of Attraction" had to go in The Plan.

"Repeat a mantra silently to yourself while you stroll through the labyrinth," a thirty-something man with a bushy beard told us.

I gazed at the twinkle lights laid across the grass in a circular maze pattern and then over at a group of children, whose distant laughter barely echoed from the other end of the park. About twenty people stood along the outskirts of the maze. While I wondered what brought each person to the labyrinth, I had zero interest in doing introductions to hear their stories . . . or share mine. All I knew is that I was on a mission to embrace anything the cosmos could offer to help me heal and find my soulmate. And if walking through twinkle lights would do it, I was willing to try.

We all lined up and entered one at a time. Once inside, I decided to give my mantra from the energy healing session another chance.

"I am grateful for my healing process," I uttered in my head.

I hadn't said it three times before realizing I still didn't feel gratitude for this awful process and was now stuck behind a bunch of slow people pontificating as they meandered through. I wanted to yell, "Hurry up. My mantra sucks, and I need to get out of here." But I didn't. I just silently strolled along, counting the seconds until I could make a dash for my car.

"You will want this one for healing and definitely a rose quartz for love." The lady behind the counter dropped both crystals into a small paper bag and handed it to me.

I stood there wondering why, after the labyrinth bust, I felt the need to buy crystals.

As quickly as the doubt poured in, a voice inside me tried to squash it. "Do not give up on the spiritual realm. Energy healing, manifesting, and the Law of Attraction seem to be working. If the crystals do, too, you could be healed and with your soulmate in no time." The voice paused. "Plus, these rocks are only a few bucks. Don't be cheap, Corey."

I gave in to the sales tactics of my subconscious and paid the lady.

Right before going to bed that night, I gripped the crystals in my hand and said my mantra again. I felt nothing except a sweaty palm and not any bit more grateful for my healing process. *I guess that's three dollars I'll never get back.*

The following morning, I woke up still feeling a lack of gratitude for my healing process. Maybe it was because The Plan thus far only included random things I had already tried, the slew of self-help seminars I dove into, scattershot suggestions from experts concerned about my loneliness, and questionable recommendations from Naked and Afraid. I was sure that *this* wasn't what Breakup Coach or my therapist had in mind when they encouraged me to work "through" the healing. I knew I needed to really take action in a more intentional way.

So, I headed into my office, opened a blank document on my laptop, and added a heading at the top of the page, "My Healing Manifest." Immediately, ideas began flowing out of my fingers, nearly faster than I could type. "Peace," "calm," "positive," I wrote. So many feelings landed on the paper.

Within thirty minutes, I had crafted a detailed description of an emotional destination I planned to arrive at two months out, which was a format suggested by someone in my manifesting group. She said to write in present tense as if I had already arrived at my intended outcome but date it for a future time period so the universe had time to work.

I looked at my manifest and decided to read it to Phoenix, who was curled up on my colorful, polka-dotted chair right next to my desk.

> *It's November, and my healing process is on the right track. Every day, I notice myself experiencing greater healthy detachment from the relationship, the situation, and my ex. I am also continuing to process my emotions, enhance my mental and emotional well-being, and expand my self-awareness. I am thinking more positive thoughts, engaging in fun and fulfilling experiences that make me excited and happy, and feeling a greater sense of peace, calm, hope, and ease. I now see both the breakup and the healing journey as an opportunity and blessing, feeling a sense of freedom, appreciation, and relief to live my amazing life. I am moving forward with self-love and am ready to receive the positive possibilities and good that are coming my way now and will continue to come in the future.*

After finishing my read-aloud, I knew I wouldn't be able to just say I'm healed, and poof, I'm healed. I would need to put in the work between now and November to get there. And that's where The Plan would come in—albeit a much more strategic and less reactionary version of it.

The Setback

At 3:54 p.m. on Monday, September 20, a text popped up on the home screen of my phone, right when I was in the middle of class. I typically taught with my phone face down, but I must have forgotten, and the message flashed on the screen. It was from Hiker, and I knew it was going to ruin my day.

Just saw a post from Runner. Engaged . . .

I flipped my phone over as if doing so would transport me back in time before I saw it. The room had already started spinning, though, and I could feel vomit splashing up in the back of my throat. I grasped onto the sides of my chair and tried to keep lecturing as if nothing had happened. How I didn't pass out, burst into angry sobs, or throw up, I will never know. For the next twenty minutes, I taught class while my hands uncontrollably squeezed the armrests, bracing for what felt like was about to be a turbulent landing on a plane.

As soon as all of our cameras were off during the break, I replied to Hiker.

Seriously

Sorry!

They've only been together for two months.

I know, pal.

Well, it's good she's doing this now, so that there is no waiting for the other shoe to drop. I can heal and move on . . .

Yes, and I'm sure you realize . . . you're better off. She's not the person you thought she was . . .

Hiker then sent me a screenshot of Runner's post. The photo was her, down on one knee, proposing in front of attendees at a major event *I* had planned to go to with her. There were hundreds of likes and comments.

Literally never heard of these people.

Talk to your friends, go on walks, organize hikes . . . keep busy! Give it time, and you won't give a shit.

Look at her hashtag. #whenyouknowyouknow. How she met the love of her life in a matter of days after our breakup is beyond me.

The fifteen-minute break seemed like mere seconds as the students' videos turned back on. The remaining hour passed in slow motion. At least I had finally let go of the death grip on my chair.

Once we wrapped up, I texted Naked and Afraid.

Just finished class, but I found out she's engaged.

Of course she is.

We just broke up!!!

Yes, but this has nothing to do with you or the feelings she had.

She hashtagged #whenyouknowyouknow.

Let her go. Can you do a hike and a sage burning?

Yes. Let's hike!!! I don't have any sage, though. Do you?

No, but we can pick some weeds on our hike and burn them.

I grabbed my pack and rushed over to her place, bawling the entire way. I pulled into her carport and jumped out of my car. Before I had a chance to go inside, she came out the front door to meet me. I fell to my knees on her patio, wailing into my hands.

No questions. She simply said, "Let's go hiking."

I got up and wiped my tears. "She left, moved on, bought a house, and is engaged. It sucks. I'm glad it happened now, though. I can rip that Band-Aid off and don't have to dread when these things are gonna happen. They already did."

"Why do you want to know this stuff? Nothing good can come of seeing her ridiculous, over-the-top social media posts about her new love."

"I don't want to be blindsided."

"Well, it's too late for that."

"What's hurting you most about this situation?" Breakup Coach asked.

I hadn't thought about that specifically since I was too busy being generally pissed off.

Our third meeting fell on the day after the news of Runner's engagement. Although we had spent the first two sessions processing my childhood and past relationships, I didn't want to talk about that again. Instead, I wanted to vent about the proposal. And I did.

Before blurting out "Everything," I paused. "The cheating, the stupid reconciliation process, her coming and going during the last year, the horrid way things ended."

"Was it more the relationship, the breakup, or what happened after?" she asked.

"I never got answers, and I feel like I didn't deserve any of it."

She started jotting notes.

"Seeing pictures on Facebook that she's moved on—buying a house, the extravagant marriage proposal. It's salt in the wound."

"Is there a part of you that wishes it was you she was doing those things with?"

"God, no." I exhaled. "At first, I missed her and our life. But . . . I miss that less and less every day. I'm still livid, though, and that doesn't seem to be going away."

"It sounds like you're moving past the grief of losing her and the relationship. But not so much with the trauma."

Here is the trauma thing again.

"Healing from grief and healing from trauma aren't the same. Some things might help with both—time, staying busy, and making new friends. But you have to process them differently."

I leaned into the screen as if her message was going to be louder or clearer if I was closer.

"The grief stems from sadness and loss about the present *and* the future you imagined. But with trauma, there are unresolved feelings and questions, because what you experienced, in your mind, was unexpected, out of your control, and undeserved. And it ties back to your other patterns of past trauma we've been discussing."

"I'm just now processing the hurt from my breakups with First Love and with Zion. I don't want to wait that long again." I paused. "I'm going to tackle all this trauma head on, be done, and move forward."

"Well, then you need to keep exploring all of this with your therapist, especially since we only have one session left."

"Definitely." I exhaled.

She then leaned in, looked right into my eyes, and said in a gentle, yet firm, voice, "You also need to tell your friends to stop sharing updates about her, and don't look anything up online—no exceptions. If you do, you'll keep becoming retraumatized any time she posts something."

I nodded again, like a compliant teenager, as a tear rolled down my cheek.

"Why do you want to know all these details about Runner's life?" Therapist asked at our session a few days later. I had told her about the proposal, the Facebook post, and my conversation with Breakup Coach.

"I just can't make sense of what happened and how she moved on so fast. If I can get to the bottom of that, I know I'll feel better."

"What you've learned so far doesn't seem to be making you feel better. Why do you think more information will?"

I leaned forward in my chair. "Because then I can deal with whatever comes from the truth and move forward. But without knowing certain information, it's like I'm always wondering, which makes me feel out of control. Then I speculate and make assumptions."

I paused while fixating my gaze on one specific red box on her canvas painting.

She waited for me to continue.

"I never got answers with Zion either, and now all that crap is bubbling up too!"

"You may just need to let go of your need to know," she said. "About Runner . . . about Zion."

"Or get answers," I insisted. "I can tell you one thing. Moving forward, I'm never going to live in a state of ambiguity again."

I pondered the conversation with Therapist all day and knew she and Breakup Coach were right. Scouring Runner's social media and getting updates from others was unhealthy for me. At the same time, having unresolved questions filled me with angst. I needed to find a healthier way to get answers, and I had just the idea.

Later that night, I sat down at my desk and typed out every question I had for Runner.

- Why didn't you get on the plane?
- Why did you start dating so quickly?
- Why did you post your relationship status online when there was a chance it would get back to me?
- How are you already healed and in love with someone else?

The list went on and on.

Since I knew I couldn't ask her, I spent the next several hours trying to answer these questions from what I thought might be her point of view. Tears rolled down my cheeks as I pounded away at the keyboard. Brutal honesty hurt.

Then, for each question, I asked myself, "If this answer were true, so what?" and "How does acknowledging that this might be true help me move on?" With every keystroke I typed, I felt the trauma pouring out of me.

It didn't take long for me to see from my responses that while I felt like I had been wronged, I had to take some responsibility in our relationship. I realized I could be a control freak; I had a tendency to slip into the role of parent rather than partner; and I wasn't willing to sacrifice for her. *Ouch.*

After a short break to dry my eyes and stretch my legs, I began typing again: "What I have come to accept," "What I have learned from this relationship," and "What I can do better or differently in my next relationship." Another hour went by. I wrote about boundaries, expectations, and compatibility.

Midnight rolled around, and my body was overwhelmed. Between the adrenaline and sleep deprivation, I didn't know what I was feeling—except relief and a tad bit of closure. The ambiguity was at bay, and tomorrow was a new day.

"You've made great progress," Breakup Coach said, after I recapped my late-night journaling sob fest for her.

"I even feel a little better, too . . . more from catharsis than anything." I smiled.

"Good. You have a lot to unpack with your therapist. But you will move through this."

I will move through this.

She took a deep breath. "So." She paused. "This is our last session together, and I *have* to put it out there: Have you considered dating again?"

I leaned back in my chair. I was thinking we'd explore more about my childhood, or I would get to rant more about Runner.

"I'm just coming to terms with all my trauma. I have a lot of work to do, and I'm finally realizing I'm not ready. I did that speed dating thing and have been trying to summon my soulmate, but I think I was doing all that just because I was hurting so badly and wanted my happily ever after too." I paused. "So, no. Not really. I don't think I'm ready to get back out there for real."

"You aren't going to wake up one day and be ready," she said. "You can work on yourself while also exploring possibilities."

"What if I make the same mistakes? What if I pick the wrong person?" My voice sped up.

"You need to trust yourself to make decisions in your best interest. That's part of healing."

After we logged off, I couldn't stop thinking about her suggestion—*dating could help with my healing*. And it sure seemed like the most obvious way to find my soulmate. I didn't know if I felt terrified or liberated by the idea. But I gave in, opened The Plan, and added "Date."

Part 2

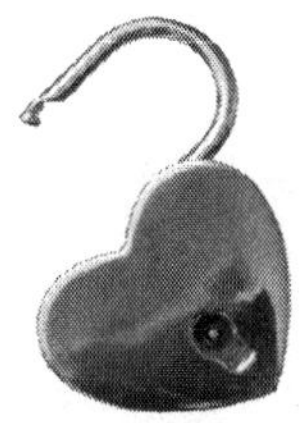

Getting Out

Practice Dating

Every day since the breakup, TikTok had been sending me several links to short videos. They usually involved some brokenhearted teen bearing wisdom about relationships, and a message with TikTok's own thoughts.

> This one hit home.

And another . . .

> I can't believe how spot-on this is. She's only a teenager, but she really has some great advice.

After telling TikTok about Breakup Coach's recommendation to get back out there, she stopped sending heartbreak videos and embraced her new gig as my matchmaker. One afternoon, while returning some emails for work, a text from her popped up on my phone.

> Here are some single ladies I found.

I immediately abandoned what I was doing to sift through the pictures.

How do you know these people?

I don't. They're in some lesbian Facebook group I belong to.

I looked over the photos again, this time with a keener eye.

Wow! It's like a buffet of women.
The one wearing the red shirt is more my type.

I went back to emailing. I hadn't finished drafting one message before she replied.

Okay, so I got some more info on that lady. This is her and her ex-wife. I DEF think she would be up to talk to you.

It's weird that she still has a picture with her ex up.

My bigger question was how TikTok would believe this random lady would "def" be interested in talking to me, let alone dating me.

It's probably an old photo.

All the other ladies are a bit more butch than I'm attracted to. If you find any sporty, hair-in-a-ponytail types, send them my way!

Another pause. Back to work. Within three minutes, a message arrived.

Okay. Here are some more.

Five pictures came in.

This one rescues kittens. I can find out more about whoever. Just let me know.

I skimmed through them.

I like the one with the kayak and the other with the dog.

Within seconds, more pictures arrived of the kayak lady.

Cool. How about the lady with the dog?

She got snagged. Lots of people hooking up with "soulmates."

Wow!!! Maybe there is someone more recent who hasn't re-partnered. It sure seems like the ones who joined the group in 2020 are COVID-bonded with others!

I knew shopping for a partner through TikTok's Facebook wasn't going to be the great *pow*, *boom*, *bang* love story I would tell my grandkids. Plus, I didn't want to look at screenshots of women from her nearly defunct Facebook group, and in the rare chance I did see someone I was interested in, have her awkwardly reach out to set me up. But the whole charade did get me in the headspace to tackle the "Date" item on The Plan. Not yet, but soon.

"You can't just write 'Date' in that plan of yours and peruse TikTok's random lesbian COVID pictures. You have to actually get out there and do it," Naked and Afraid said as we hiked along the Linda Vista Trail.

"I know. But I'm still not totally sure I'm ready, even though I wrote it down. Looking at those photos just seems like a safer way to wade into the dating pool."

"Well, nothing is going to come of that," she said. "How about instead of dating, you practice date? That isn't as scary, is it?"

"I don't even know what practice dating is."

"You create a profile, post some good pictures, and message people without sounding like an idiot!" she yelled back to me while speeding ahead. "You practice all the skills you need to actually date."

"That seems really shitty to do to someone if I'm not really interested!" As I shouted back, I realized all the other nearby hikers could likely hear our conversation. So, I raced to catch up with her to continue this nonsensical discussion at much lower decibels.

"You aren't *using* them for practice," she said. "If you click with someone, great. If not, you learn from the experience . . . like if your messages sucked or you came off as too eager, don't do that next time."

"So, if I do find someone cool, I'm not just 'practicing' my skills . . . I would be open to actually dating that person?"

"Yes!" She exhaled as she said it. I could tell the exasperation was from my line of questioning and not from the incline we were tackling. "And if you don't, who cares? You move on!"

"I'll have to research my options to find the best dating site."

"Seriously. Just get on one and post a profile! Do *not* overthink it."

"Overthinking is what I do. Haven't you figured that out yet?" I asked.

"Do *not* overthink this."

"What are you looking for in a relationship?"

I copied and pasted the question from the sample dating profile I found online into a Word document.

Hmm. Something short but poignant. I typed, "Passionate love."

I pasted another question. "What don't you like?"

I wasn't sure if I should write about my general dislikes or those in relationships. I opted to include both. "Olives, and when people check their phones all the time."

I spent the next hour sitting at my desk, organizing my responses to every possible question. When I was done, I sent my master Word document to TikTok.

Girl, you need to spice this up.

How?

Get a little flirty. What's up with olives? Don't put that.

I'll take that feedback under advisement.

I made a few tweaks, but my disdain for olives stayed.

After looking at several dating sites, reading reviews, and writing out the pros and cons of each, I landed on one designed for career professionals. The shortest membership option was six months, which either meant the site had no faith in my ability to find love or it was about the money. I hoped it was the latter.

I copied the responses from my master document into my profile and uploaded some hiking pictures. Within a minute, it was approved. *Hmm, that was a thorough vetting process.*

I went straight to my dashboard. Instead of being able to search, I found out the system matches you with possibilities based on the criteria you set. So, I already had three people in my queue—a professor, a woman with bleach-blond hair and beaming lights behind her reminiscent of a 1980s senior photo, and a lady whose profile picture was a selfie while sprawled out on top of a table. Those were my choices. I messaged Professor.

Hi! I just got matched with you and wanted to say hello.

That was it. One message, and the whole chase was over. The image I had of countless profiles of attractive, smart women waiting online for me to click and connect with was only a dream. When I got no response from Professor, I logged off and went to bed, a bit defeated.

As soon as I woke up the next morning, I grabbed my phone from the nightstand to check my inbox. There was a message from Professor.

Hi. Nice to connect with you.

I let out a sigh of relief. She was real, and she responded

After a few days of messaging on the app, I had finally gotten up the nerve to ask her out. She responded right away.

Want to grab coffee sometime and swap some stories of life in academia?

Sure. That would be nice.

To prepare, I bought a new pair of shorts, khaki ones with a zipper. I also pulled out a red-and-white plaid short-sleeved button-down from the back of my closet. Since zippers and buttons had been absent from my wardrobe for years, the whole thing seemed more like a costume than an outfit for a date. But I planned to wear it anyway.

The night before, I decided to map out directions to our meeting place. I knew it was a coffee house somewhere at the mall, but I couldn't remember the actual name of it. So, I opened the dating app to look back at our messages. As soon as I logged in, I saw that my matches had gone from three to two—only Beaming Light and Table Selfie. Professor had disappeared.

I gasped and then texted Naked and Afraid in a frenzy.

Just got on the site and Professor is no longer linked to me. But we have plans to meet tomorrow. Should I still go?

YES. Do you have her number?

No.

Go anyway. You can come to my place if she doesn't show. I am your designated wingwoman, you know.

Yes, you are. And I appreciate it so much!

On the day of our scheduled date, I put on my new shorts and fancy shirt and drove to the mall. I found a table at the only coffeehouse there, hoping that was our meeting place. I sat peering around for anyone who might look like a thumbnail picture of a lady with brown hair. Everyone looked like a lady with brown hair.

Right on time, I was approached by a woman possibly resembling Professor's profile picture. She was a few inches taller than me at around five-foot-eight and had a thin runner's body. Her bob haircut fell to just above the neckline of her stark white long-sleeved shirt. She was attractive, but I didn't feel an attraction to her. I was just relieved I wasn't ghosted.

She introduced herself and shook my hand. "You'll never believe what happened. My profile got hacked. After going ten rounds with the app people, I finally just had to close my account."

"That's awful. I actually noticed last night that our match disappeared. I wasn't sure you would even be here." An awkward laugh came tumbling out of my mouth.

"You still came, though," she said.

"I didn't want to stand you up . . . just in case."

She smiled.

Instead of coffee, she suggested smoothies . . . a way better choice for a scorching hot day. We got our to-go orders and sat on a nearby bench where she rattled off question after question. I could barely answer one before another was in the queue.

"Are you close to your family?" she asked.

"I am. My mom is practically my best friend, and I spend a lot of time with her and my brother. And his wife and daughter."

"What do you like to do for fun?"

"Ummm. Hiking, walking, softball, karaoke, basketball, going to festivals, traveling . . ."

"Do you have any pets?"

With each question, I felt myself scooching further away from her on the bench until I was straddling the end of it. Our conversation seemed more like an interview. All the while I was fielding questions, I was thinking about the hurt and pain of the breakup and how practice dating was weird and uncomfortable.

We exchanged numbers. I promised to send her information about the lesbian Meetup group I was in, and we said our platonic goodbyes with no plans for a future date. Once I got back to my car, I cranked up the AC to temper the blistering air that had been trapped inside all afternoon. Then came the tears . . . buckets of tears.

I laid my face in my hands and mumbled, "I'm gonna die alone! I'm for sure gonna die alone."

Cooking Fish in My Pan

Despite my post-smoothie emotional breakdown, I decided to stay on the dating site. But I only had the same two matches. So, to get more ladies in my queue, I made a late-night decision—I would change my settings from a hundred-mile radius to radius infinity!

Early the next morning, I awoke to dozens of matches from around the country and even an old smoker from Russia who had slipped through the extensive algorithm. While still lying in bed, I sent messages to a few of the more interesting ones. Two people responded right away.

The first was a woman from the East Coast who I had a lot in common with, despite her love for running and my desire to only do so if chased. We were both athletic, in similar career fields, and had kids the same age. I sent a "smile" and soon got one in return. Throughout the day, we chatted about our interests, music tastes, jobs, and favorite foods. But then, I got an odd message from her. I texted Naked and Afraid.

Someone from that dating site asked if she could cook fish in my pan. Is that some type of sexual innuendo?

She probably wants to know if you are okay with meat in the house since you are a vegetarian. If it's something sexual, I've never heard of it!

I responded to the East Coast woman.

I guess I wouldn't care as long as I wasn't cooking in that pan at the same time.

The second response I got was from a die-hard NFL fan from the Midwest. Her picture was her in a jersey at a football game. We exchanged several messages right away and then silence. I shot off another text to Naked and Afraid.

This one lady is from Minnesota and is so my type. But we were having a conversation and it just stopped.

Remember, if that lady ghosts you, it has nothing to do with you!

The next day, I gave Naked and Afraid the update.

Just heard from the Minnesota woman! She told me that her app logged her out yesterday and she couldn't get back into it. She reset her password today.

See!!! Always an explanation.

I feel better. I really like her. I'll wait to message back until later this afternoon. Or maybe she will reach out before I even send it.

Don't wait, fool. Just acknowledge her message.

I'll give it a couple hours. Don't want to seem too eager. But I won't wait until this afternoon then!

My banter with Minnesota came to an abrupt end a few days later. This time I didn't get an "I needed to reset my password" message. Just silence. I knew I was ghosted for real.

Once that happened, I realized I didn't want to leave anyone hanging out there. So, I replied with kind letdowns to every woman I wasn't interested in who had sent me a wink, smile, or message through the app and then removed them from my queue. No one, except for East Coast, remained.

Do I just delete this stupid dating app and head back to the bookstore? "No!" A voice boomed in my head. "You can't give up on this process. What are you gonna do—go back to TikTok's defunct Facebook ladies? You're just in the wrong place."

I contemplated my internal argument for a moment and then began feverishly typing into the Internet. A new dating site popped up. *I should have gotten on this one to begin with.* Once I got to the credit card portal, I ran to my bedroom to get my wallet. *No need to wait for destiny.*

Once my new account was up and running, I repurposed my profile and loaded my hiking pictures. This time, no fancy algorithm was going to find my perfect match. It was just me and some search filters. Like the other site, though, it became immediately apparent that there was no one in my local area. So, I widened my search to more than a thousand miles, and it was game on! There were so many women. I stayed up until the middle of the night surfing and sending out messages, smiles, and winks. I got two responses—one from a history teacher who ended up ghosting me a few days later and another who sent dozens of messages sharing gory details about her recent car accident before telling me I was "the one." *Okay, maybe this site isn't much better.*

"Hello?" she said, in a thick East Coast accent.

"Hello," I said while pacing back and forth on my patio. "How was your day?"

"I think this whole COVID thing has totally been blown out of proportion. I mean, c'mon. I'm so over it," East Coast said.

I've been waiting all week for this call, and this is your introductory conversation starter? "Have you had it?" I asked.

"Nope. You?"

"I had it in January. I wear a mask everywhere. I don't want to give it to my mom or my kid."

"I mean, I'm not some anti-vaxxer. I got my shots. It's just that a lot of this is over the top."

I noticed I had picked up my pace and was weaving in and out of the patio furniture. So, I made my way to the front of the house and then sped up and down the street to burn off the adrenaline that was building from our conversation. Suddenly, though, the awkwardness turned to silence, and then she changed the subject to something even worse—her ex. As she went on and on, I realized I would have rather spent the whole time talking about her cooking fish in my pan.

Later that night, I got a text from her telling me she enjoyed our call. It was the moment of truth. Our conversation was uncomfortable at best and off-putting at worst. But I liked that someone liked me. So, I replied.

Great chatting with you, too.

The next day, I got a "good morning" text. It seemed sweet, and just like that, the awkwardness of our phone call had become a distant memory. The texts flowed back and forth that day and over the next several. So, we set up another call.

"Hey. How are you?" I asked.

"Good!" she said.

"So, I've been thinking . . ."

I could hear a sigh from the other end of the phone. "What have you been thinking about?"

"I mean, I like you, and we have a lot in common. But you and I both know there's no realistic possibility here. We live thousands of miles apart, and neither of us is going to move."

"It *doesn't* make sense. But I also don't want to cut it off," she said.

Although we agreed that any potential relationship would be doomed, we kept chatting. Five hours flew by. This conversation was anything but awkward or off-putting; instead, it was interesting and comfortable.

"It's super late . . . especially for you," I said. "We still didn't resolve the distance thing, though."

"I like talking with you, and I don't want to stop . . . I agree, though. This is never gonna work."

"We probably shouldn't continue then." I felt a twinge of regret as soon as the words came out of my mouth. Going back to the starting line with this whole dating thing was not an option. "Let's not make any major decisions tonight, though. It's late," I said.

But then, we texted and talked on the phone the next day . . . and the next . . . and the next, and never about our conundrum. Instead, we would discuss mundane work meetings, explore deep issues about our pasts, and share silly stories. And when our text exchanges would get flirty, she would make sure to send an emoji that had images of ice cubes flying across my screen.

The connection was like an addiction for me. She asked questions, processed my life with me, and offered kind and supportive words, which affirmed that there were people out there who might actually move mountains for me after all. I knew this relationship would be impossible, but I couldn't help myself.

"You should come out this weekend," I said during one of our calls.

"Arizona is all the way across the country."

"Then let's meet in Nebraska for coffee. If that goes well, we hang out longer. If not, we both fly home."

Even though she laughed, I would have jumped on a flight to Omaha.

"I can't this weekend. Let's find a time for real, and I'll book a flight to come to Arizona."

A couple days later, she made a reservation.

I had to tell Naked and Afraid.

East Coast bought a plane ticket to come out in a few weeks.

Is she vaccinated?

Yep! And we can get rapid tests at the airport when I pick her up.

Wow . . . the new STD test. That will be sexy!

I know. Don't hug me . . . get a nasal swab first.

Ha ha. NO! You need to go with the passion.

Hug and then nasal swab.

Yes!

Maybe she will be the great love I have always wanted.

Or maybe she'll be some lunatic you just invited to your house.

Signs, Symbols, and Spirit Guides

October rolled around, and with East Coast's arrival still weeks out, I had decided to keep my attention focused on the most promising items on The Plan—energy healing, listening to podcasts, bookstore lurking, and manifesting. Despite my intense focus, I had a nagging feeling I was missing something that would be profoundly impactful to my healing process.

One night while lying in bed, it came to me. I hadn't noticed red flags in my past relationships because I didn't *want* to notice them. What I had wanted was perfect love—the opposite of what my parents had. I had shielded myself from seeing any warning signs. By the time the red flags had become obvious to me, I was too far down the road in the relationship to let it fail. So, I stayed, and I hoped.

I knew, though, moving forward, detecting red flags early on was an absolute must, or I would repeat this unhealthy pattern. Now, I just needed to learn how to *actually see* them. I decided to create a manifest summoning the universe to help me tap into my intuition so I would never miss or ignore any red flags again.

Because my epiphany was too much to hold onto until morning, I jumped out of bed, ran into my office, and furiously began to type. After some editing, I had the perfect manifest—dated for the future just like the other one.

> *It is November, and I have reinvigorated and reconnected with my deeper sense of intuition. I have created space for it to emerge and flourish within me and trust it to help me make decisions that feel right. I am in tune with messages from the universe, paying great attention to the signs that come my way. I am spending more time flowing downstream with ease, letting the current take me where I am supposed to go and changing course or waiting when I notice the need to do so.*

After writing this, I realized, November was going to be a busy month.

"Are you prepared for your intuition to go into overdrive?" a woman in my manifesting group asked. I had just finished reading my new manifest to them. "If it does, it might drown out your logic."

I hadn't thought about that since I was just excited about never missing a red flag again.

Others offered ideas for tinkering with the wording. But one woman actually suggested an intuition-building exercise to try. "Think of a decision you are considering and assign a symbol to one of the choices. Then, spend a couple of days just milling about as usual. If you see that symbol a lot, go with that choice. And if you don't, pick the other one."

After the meeting, I added "Look for signs and symbols" to The Plan. It was the perfect way to reconnect with my intuition.

How many cacti do I need to see? I wondered. As a researcher who likes to measure things, I struggled with the idea of a lot versus a little. Still, I was excited to try the exercise. And I had the perfect question to use: Should I seek out closure from Zion about *our* breakup?

My recent therapy had brought to light the heaviness I had been feeling around the ambiguity of our separation years earlier. If I just talked to her, I thought, I might get the answers I so craved and then finally be able to fully process and move on. Then again, I wondered if maybe talking to Zion about our long-ago split would be a terrible idea—opening old wounds and possibly being blindsided by her brutal honesty.

I thought then, *Give this decision to the universe!*

And I did. I selected the artistic rendering of a saguaro cactus, not the actual living succulent, as my symbol. I decided if I saw several in one day, more so than would be expected in Arizona, I would reach out to Zion to process our breakup.

On the day of the exercise, I saw several saguaro symbols, none of which I had noticed before—one on a neighbor's mailbox, one buried in a nearby mural, and one spray-painted on the glass of a storefront window. It seemed clear, even for my analytical brain. The universe was telling me to reach out to Zion.

But every time I thought about doing so, something in my gut stopped me. I already knew she wasn't happy by the time she left. *Do I really need all the details? No.* Even the mere thought of hearing them made my stomach turn.

So, I just kept my mouth shut.

"I'm here because I feel spirits in my house," a disheveled-looking guy said.

"I am so bad at making decisions," an elderly lady piped in.

It was my turn. "I need to pay better attention to my intuition."

"Well, we're here to help you." The voice came from the thumbnail video of a middle-aged man sitting in his cluttered kitchen. He then advanced his slides to one entitled, "What Is Intuition?"

I had high hopes for this Meetup session, wanting to know why the saguaro cactus exercise (talk to Zion) and my gut feeling (don't talk to Zion) pointed me in two different directions. But as the man clicked through the presentation, I could tell what he was sharing was not going to shed any light on my dilemma.

At the end of the session, an older woman who had been silent up to this point introduced herself as the co-host and invited us to put our email addresses in the chat if we were interested in private coaching. I, along with several others, did.

I then added "See an intuition coach" to The Plan.

A few days later, I logged into my virtual coaching session. The intuition lady was sitting at a table in what appeared to be her living room, with a stack of papers in front of her and a pen in hand. She was wearing a necklace with oversized beads and long earrings that hung below her short, wavy gray hair. The black-rimmed reading glasses perched on her nose made her appear as a wise elder ready to pass down sacred stories to her next of kin.

After a quick hello, she asked me to remain quiet while she closed her eyes and "felt my energy." For the next three minutes, I sat there as still and silent as I had ever been, waiting for something to happen. But this didn't feel like an elder ready to pass along wisdom about my intuitive capabilities; instead, it was like watching an old lady who had fallen asleep on the subway and feeling unsure whether or not to wake her to get off at the next stop.

Suddenly, her eyes popped open, jarring me from my subway scene, and she began scribbling on a piece of paper.

She then looked right into the webcam and said, "There are four types of perception. We have all of them. But we use some more than others."

I wrote the numbers one through four on my page.

"Your number one," she said, "is intuitive. You pick up energy and just simply know information . . . from your gut." She went on to give a full paragraph's-length explanation.

I started writing frantically, trying to capture her every word.

"Then, they are, in this order, visionary, feeling, and prophecy. Visionary is picking up on signs and symbols. Feeling is sensing energy through some type of physical sensation. And prophecy usually happens in the form of messages through dreams."

My hand couldn't keep up with the pace she was talking, leaving me with unfinished phrases and illegible words. But one thing I did know: I am a strong visionary and can trust signs from the universe, but only if my gut aligns. If the two go to battle, my gut wins. *I get it. The cactus symbol never stood a chance.*

"I will mail you the list of the descriptions of each of your perceptions. If you want more guidance, you can always set up another session," she said. "Before we go, though, I want to put you in touch with your spirit guides."

"What are spirit guides?"

"They are the angels who look out for you. We can ask the guides for their perspectives now. Stand up and close your eyes."

I got up from my desk chair, put my arms by my side, and stood in front of my webcam with my eyes shut.

"Lean left . . . lean right . . . lean forward . . . lean backward," she said.

There I was, swaying back and forth to summon my spirit guides.

"Embrace the love and support. Do you feel them around you, Corey?"

"Yes?" I felt nothing other than unbalanced.

"Let's talk to them. Ask them a question."

"Will I ever love again?"

"The spirit guides are telling me yes," she said. "You can open your eyes now. When I send you the paperwork about your perceptions, it will also include information about your spirit guides."

"Okay. Thanks so much for your help." I was still standing but a little woozy from rocking every which way.

"I'm here for you if you need anything," she said. "Goodbye."

Just like that, she logged off.

A few days later, an envelope arrived from the "academy." I tore it open at the mailbox and yanked out the papers, which looked like ditto machine copies from the 1980s. They were covered with several doodles and scribbles, along with a number indicating the supposed quantity of spirit guides I have: five. As soon as I finished skimming, I ran inside, plopped down on my office chair, and called Naked and Afraid.

"Remember the intuition coaching I had the other day? The handouts came."

"What do they say?"

I looked down at the papers I had spread across my desk. "It's just descriptions of what she told me in our coaching; you know, the types of perception. But the pages are covered with sketches of stick figure people and her notes. Weird."

"Well, for sure the swaying thing she had you do was odd. Not the fact that you have spirit guides, though. That's cool."

"I suppose. I guess I could really use one of them right now."

"I just passed a billboard for the home show this weekend," I said into the speakerphone. "I really want to go." I paused. "But I'll be in California. Maybe I can push my trip back."

"You can miss the home show to spend time with your daughter," Mom said.

The light turned green, and I started cruising along.

"I just haven't been able to find any place to stay or someone to watch the kitty for the three weeks I'm supposed to be gone, and I've been stressing about it for a while now." I paused. "I think the billboard was a sign from the universe that I should leave *after* the weekend, and was never really about going to the home show. I've felt it in my gut for days that I should change the dates. This only confirmed it."

We hung up, and I pondered my idea for the rest of the drive.

As soon as I got home, I reached out to Zion, who was on board with my proposal. She even suggested flying Kiddo to Arizona for the weekend and then have her drive with me to California on Monday, which we realized was a holiday. Within hours, everything fell into place—lodging, kitty sitter, plane ticket, and all. Not only was it far less expensive, Kiddo and I got to attend my niece's birthday party in Phoenix before we were set to head out to California.

I never made it to the home show. But that didn't matter. Everything unfolded exactly as it was supposed to. It wasn't even November, and my intuition was already starting to work again.

Garbage Trucks

Kiddo and I woke up early Monday morning to start our day-long drive to California. We played dozens of rounds of twenty questions and chatted about possibilities for her future career, including running an animal shelter or being a filmmaker. I listened to my favorite podcasts, she edited videos on her iPad, and we both ate a lot of snacks.

By the time we arrived, we were exhausted. We dragged our luggage inside the small apartment, and Kiddo promptly took off to investigate every nook and cranny in the place.

"Look, I have my own bed! We don't have to share!" she yelled from down the hall.

"I had to get a place with two beds. When I sleep next to you, you just dig your bony knees into me!" I shouted back as I was putting food from the cooler bag into the fridge.

She laughed. "And my own room. Now I can throw my clothes wherever I want."

"Oh, I don't think so."

We unpacked and then both headed to bed. I tried to doze off without streaming one of my fall-asleep-to shows, since we couldn't get the Internet to work. After lying there in the quiet, running through my to-do list for the next day, I finally nodded off well after midnight.

The next morning, I woke up at 5:30 a.m. to go for my walk before school drop-off. I looked out the window, and it was pitch black. The weather app on my phone might as well have said "freezing cold." I hadn't packed many warm clothes, since back home, the temperature still lingered in the nineties. My workout pants and windbreaker had to suffice.

Once I went outside, a chill ran through me—not just from the frigid air but also from the realization that this would be home for the next two-and-a-half weeks. When Zion and I had agreed on the "Corey can come to California a few times a year" parenting arrangement, it seemed like a great idea. But here I was now, on my first trip, unsure of how I would continue my healing process, train for the Grand Canyon, and take care of another human . . . all without the comfort of my routines and support network.

I put in my earbuds, opened my podcast app, and pressed play. A soothing voice came on, speaking kind words about how the universe loved me and wanted me to have joy and abundance. I liked my Law of Attraction lady. She made me feel good.

I walked around the hilly neighborhood of back-to-back apartment buildings near our place. The sunshine and beautiful mountain landscapes, cheery neighbors, and chirping birds of Arizona were a distant memory. And no warm breeze was going to fill my soul.

Instead, there was a garbage truck where two guys would jump off, yell at each other, bang the trash bins around, and head to the next stop. Everywhere I turned, the garbage truck was right behind me. It was so loud that I couldn't hear the lovely lady anymore. I turned up the volume. But something seemed a little off about her screaming that the universe loves me.

I rounded the corner and saw an old man smoking marijuana on the curb.

"What are you looking at?" he hollered.

I darted by and turned off Law of Attraction Lady. There was nothing she could share about joy that would make this situation better. I then cranked up Eminem, hoping he would drown everything out with his insightful rap. I sang each word as if we were performing a duet and occasionally yelled out my own commentary. "Yes, Eminem, I feel it too!"

When I returned to the apartment, I recognized that my peaceful, abundant, and supportive healing process would be drastically different in California unless I changed things up.

So, the next day, I headed to a new path thirty minutes down the road. I scurried along with runners, parents with strollers, and casual walkers also making their way through the rolling hills. The air felt warmer, and the sun shined brighter, and Law of Attraction Lady was finally pleasant to listen to. I was going to heal, no matter what it took. And no stoned guy or garbage truck was going to stop me.

Boots and Pants

Although East Coast and I had been chatting on the phone nearly every day, I was still messaging with a few others who had recently popped up on the apps, including two ladies who lived in California. Since I would be out their way, I scheduled in-person dates with each of them.

The first was with a woman who had a profile picture of her rappelling. She looked like someone I would hang out with—sporty and fit. But two days before we were planning to meet up for a hike, I got a text from her—she wasn't ready to date. My heart sank. After some back and forth, though, we still opted to go, but with friendship as the only foreseeable outcome.

I'm here. It's a small lot, and it says unauthorized vehicles will be towed.

I pulled off to the side of the road, bid farewell to Naked and Afraid, who I had been jabbering with on the way there, and replied to the "non-date" lady I was scheduled to hike with.

Is there anywhere else we could go?

My phone rang. I had never heard her voice before. It was high-pitched, and she talked fast. While I fixated on imagining how what was coming out of her mouth lined up with her rappelling picture, she rattled off options. We decided to park at a nearby grocery store so she could grab a candy bar. She asked if I needed to pick up a banana, which seemed strange until I recalled I had told her about my daily lunch routine. She remembered. I liked her already.

After the snack run, we finally met up at her car. She gave me a big hug—the kind reserved for reuniting with an old friend. I noticed we were about the same height and build. She had her long blondish hair pulled back in a ponytail and looked just like her picture, which I had learned is a rarity in the online dating world. More so, she was my type—a sporty lesbian with femme appeal. Her hiking attire appeared well-worn, and even her SUV seemed like it had been to remote places for amazing adventures. I felt an immediate attraction, which would surely complicate our friendship-only pact.

She opened the hatchback for me to load my gear. When I climbed into the passenger seat, an odd sense of familiarity washed over me—like we had done this before . . . many times. I couldn't figure out where that feeling came from. But it was warm and comfortable . . . and safe.

We chatted nonstop—on the drive and during the hike, sharing about our outdoor adventures, the woes of online dating, and the difficulty of finding nice dress pants. Everything with her felt easy, and the nerves I had on the drive over had nearly disappeared.

Naked and Afraid had been waiting for an update, which I sent as soon as I returned to my car.

Off the trail.

And in bed?

Going to lunch with her.

Are you smitten?

A bit—just friends, though, remember?

My non-date and I met back up at a nearby pizza place to grab lunch before our long drives back home.

"Hey, if you ever want to hike The Wave, and we could get a permit, I'd go," she said before taking a bite.

We had talked about The Wave, an epic sandstone hike in northern Arizona, during one of our first text exchanges. Seeing the stunning rock patterns had been on my bucket list for over a decade. But the lottery system makes getting a permit challenging. Only a handful of people are selected from thousands of applications each day.

"Sure. It would be quite the adventure," I said.

After finishing our pizza, we headed out to the parking lot. I wasn't sure what an appropriate goodbye looked like, so I just asked if she wanted to stay in touch.

"Like text and talk on the phone?"

"Yes." I tried to imagine what it would look like if we mailed letters or sent written notes with pigeon carriers. I hoped she didn't see my little smirk.

"Like, how-was-your-day kind of stuff?" she asked.

"Yeah, among other things. But yes, that could work." I spun my key ring around my finger several times.

"Okay."

Okay is what you say as a kind, yet empty, gesture. At least I tried. We hugged, and I was certain I'd never hear from her again.

Two hours later, I got a message.

Made it home. Thanks again for the fun hike. It was great meeting you.

Thanks for making that drive today. I had a lot of fun. Good scenery, fun trail, and great conversation . . . all finished out with some pretty good pizza.

Yes, it was a great day! Worth the drive!

Her text gave me butterflies. And that felt good—until I reminded myself; we were only going to be friends.

The next morning, I had another hiking date scheduled—this time, with a veterinarian who lived much further north of where I had been the day before.

When I woke up, the dark sky and constant drizzle seemed ominous, providing a stark contrast to the sunny, warm weather from my last hike. I drove for nearly an hour to meet at one of her "favorite" trails. Once I got there, I pulled into an empty dirt lot and waited in my car. A few minutes passed before she called to tell me the GPS had routed her to the other end of the park. I then offered her directions to her supposed favorite trail.

Fifteen minutes later, an SUV arrived. By this time, the rain was coming down harder, and the sun was still nowhere to be seen. I jumped out of my car into thick mud as a petite woman with shoulder-length brown hair walked toward me. I noticed her warm smile, which made me feel an immediate sense of comfort. While I didn't find myself attracted to her, she was pretty . . . in a femme, not sporty lesbian, kind of way. She was bundled up in a clean ski jacket, wearing boots out of the box and hiking pants with creases showing.

We introduced ourselves, and then she said in a soft voice, "I have the trail in my GPS, so I can navigate us."

While watching her struggle to bring up the route information,

I noticed the abundance of very obvious trail signage. But I didn't say anything. I just stood in the rain while she tapped and swiped on her phone.

We finally started up the trail. The rain droplets rolled down our faces, and our feet sunk into the deep mud with each step.

"What do you like to do for fun?" I asked.

"Spend time alone . . . or with my dogs. I'm kind of a recluse."

"I'm like the exact opposite—a true extrovert. I'm chatty and process everything. And I love being around people," I said.

"People just make me anxious."

Uh-oh. People who get anxious around people make me anxious.

Silence.

After routing us off-trail to an abandoned shack, she gave up on navigating and put her phone in her pocket. We turned around and made our way back to the main path where we saw the very well-marked trail sign. *Two miles to go.* I exhaled. *Thank goodness.*

But then she started slowing down, talking about how she felt a blister coming on. She limped along for another half hour, while we were both getting wetter and muddier and struggling to have even lackluster conversation. I wished I was with the woman from the day before. At least we'd laugh about it.

Once back at the car, I messaged Naked and Afraid.

Just got done. I forgot we're also supposed to go to lunch. Nice lady, but I want this to end.

Told you so.

I didn't remember her ever telling me so.

At lunch, I wolfed down my burrito, then dodged a potential goodbye kiss through pandemic masks. I never saw her again.

I'm going down to that outlet mall near where we hiked to get some dress pants later! What are your plans tonight?

The non-date woman and I had been texting incessantly since our hike two days earlier. She replied to my message right away.

No plans. Just gonna be home all day. Chores. Watching some TV, probably.

Well, if you get a wild hair, let me know!! Ha!

A few hours later, I got a response. She was in. Apparently, her need for dress pants was as pressing as mine. We planned to meet at the Columbia store at 6:00 p.m., not so much to get fancy clothes but because there seemed to be no place more fitting for two outdoor enthusiasts to convene.

I arrived right on time. But after a quick scan of the lot, I didn't see her SUV. She finally texted that the GPS had taken her to the other end of the outlet mall. To avoid any more navigational confusion, we opted for me to come her way.

When I pulled up, I could see her standing outside a women's clothing store, which, after all, was probably a better starting place than Columbia given our mission for the evening. She was wearing jeans, a T-shirt, flip-flops, and the obligatory pandemic mask. I parked in a nearby spot, released my tight grip on the steering wheel, and took a deep breath.

"Hey!" I said as I walked toward her.

"Hey."

As soon as we entered the store, both of us beelined for a table with a stack of black dress pants. She grabbed a pair and headed to the dressing room. I perused the pile but ultimately didn't find anything.

After a few minutes, she emerged with a smile on her face.

"I'm getting a few pairs!" she said, making her way to the long cashier line.

Shit. She got what she came for.

"I'm gonna go next door and see what they have. Come over when you're done," I told her.

I jetted to the other store and immediately found several pairs of pants I liked. I grabbed three, each in a different color, and went to try them on. I texted her to let her know in case she came by and couldn't find me.

I'm in the dressing room trying on pants.

Uh . . . Okay. Hope they fit.

I then noticed I had sent the message to Naked and Afraid instead of my non-date. I played it off.

She found pants already. What if she wants to leave now?

She won't. She also came to see you, dummy.

Well, these better fit. She's definitely not gonna want to stick around all night watching me try clothes on.

Maybe she will. Ha ha!

Ha ha! If we both finish shopping, maybe we could get dinner.

Always thinking!

While I had one leg in a pair of pants, a voice came through the door: "You in there?" It was her.

"Yep. Just finishing up."

"Okay. I'm heading to Calvin Klein. Meet me there when you're done."

Once I made it through the checkout line, I rushed over to Calvin Klein to find her. I wandered into the store, expecting to see her sifting through the racks. All I saw were three bored-looking teenage employees . . . and no customers anywhere. As soon as I walked back out front, my phone rang.

"You get lost?" she asked. "I'm standing outside Calvin Klein."

"So am I." I scanned the area but didn't see her anywhere.

"Calvin Klein next to Guess?"

"No. Next to Starbucks." I gazed around again. "Maybe there are two Calvin Kleins?"

"That's weird. Let's just meet over at Columbia," she said. "I promise I'll find it this time."

Despite our entire shopping adventure being filled with navigational confusion, we arrived at Columbia at the same time, right before closing. We each made a mad dash through the aisles, reconvening by the front door with one minute to spare before they locked us in for the night.

"Wanna grab dinner?" I asked, as an employee with a ring full of keys ushered us out.

"Yeah, I'm starving."

"Well, pants shopping will take a lot out of ya." I let out a small laugh, drawing attention to how awkward our evening had been.

We planned to meet at what we determined was the only Applebee's at the mall. The restaurant was packed, so we got takeout and headed to her SUV. She popped open the hatchback, and I ate in the very spot I had put my hiking gear just days earlier.

"How's the burger?" I asked.

"Good. How's your broccoli?"

"Tasty. Nothing like eating veggies in the trunk of a car." I stabbed my fork through a piece far too large for one bite and nibbled on it.

She laughed. Then there was silence.

We continued with small talk, followed by a lull, then more small talk, and another lull.

My stomach fluttered. It wasn't from butterflies, as those never really came. Instead, it was from the pressure I put on myself to make this whole experience feel like our text exchanges *and* the hike—fun and witty.

After finishing, we managed an even more uncomfortable goodbye than the one outside the pizza place. No hug . . . just a "See ya." This time, I knew we would never talk again.

As disappointing as our farewell felt, I was thankful to be avoiding an unrequited crush. I did not want to fall in love with someone who wasn't going to love me back.

Later that night, she sent a message thanking me for meeting up and checking to see if I made it back safely. Just as fast as the butterflies had disappeared, they returned with a vengeance. Was this *pow*, *boom*, *bang*? If so, I was in trouble.

Over the next few days, the non-date lady, whom I now more aptly referred to as Pants, and I exchanged silly banter and updates on our lives. There was no awkwardness, and the chemistry absent at the outlet mall was in full force . . . at least on my end.

Maybe if we spend more time together, she will reconsider her friendship-only request, I thought. So, I sent her a text.

> I found out the lottery for The Wave is tomorrow for February dates. I didn't want to miss the chance if you were up for it.

Sure!! Will it have snow in February?

It may. When are you available? On a weekday?

Yes. I can take time off if we get it.

Luckily, she couldn't see me jumping up and down in the tiny apartment over what she probably thought was a mundane text exchange.

Later in the day, I submitted my application for The Wave lottery and crossed my fingers . . . not just for the permit but that maybe something great was in store for us.

Big-Girl Pants

I returned to Arizona feeling more inspired, thanks to Eminem, Pants, and Law of Attraction Lady. Maybe The Plan was working.

I only had a few days to settle back in before East Coast was coming. We had squeezed her three-day visit in between my California trip and upcoming Grand Canyon trek.

The day before her arrival, I was chatting with Naked and Afraid during my morning walk. She asked if East Coast was staying with me or getting a hotel.

"With me. Why would I make her pay for a hotel?"

"What if one of you is like, 'Yuck!'?" she asked.

"I'm not worried about that. If we don't like each other, well, I have a guest room. What I *am* worried about is finding time to text with Pants." I started to dash across the street.

"You shouldn't be thinking about Pants. East Coast is the one who's traveling all the way here to meet you. Give her your full attention!" she yelled.

I came to an abrupt halt, thankfully having already made it to the sidewalk. "Won't Pants think it's weird if I don't text her for, like, three days?"

"Who cares? You two are only friends."

I knew she was right. I needed to focus on East Coast; she could be the soulmate I had been searching for. But even I wasn't sure I believed that.

For the two and a half weeks I was in California leading up to her visit, East Coast would send a text each morning saying, "Only X number of wakeups before we see each other." She would also include a sweet message and a link to a different Brandi Carlile love song.

I liked the attention, although her budding feelings for me were starting to make me uncomfortable. At first, I figured I was just nervous, so I stuffed my discomfort into the vacant space where all my relationship trauma liked to hide. But my unease grew with each passing day. *And* it didn't help that I had been developing feelings for someone else.

On the morning of her flight, East Coast sent her boldest message yet—about having a full heart and feeling fortunate to have crossed paths with me. She ended with how much she had been missing me all her life.

When I read it, I didn't feel warm and fuzzy; instead, my stomach flipped. I buried my uneasiness and wrote her back a nice text—absent the lovey-dovey stuff.

If only Pants had sent me that message instead . . .

I'm here.

You ready for this????

As ready as I'll ever be. 😊

Good! I'm wearing an orange hat and am by far the hottest lesbian in the waiting area.

I was sure my flirtatious message would help me get psyched up for East Coast's arrival.

Of course you are!

I waited by security, pacing and looking at every exiting passenger. I was hoping that once we met, my anxiety would melt away and I would have *pow*, *boom*, *bang*.

I finally saw her walking toward me. She was taller and stockier than I had imagined. Her sandy blond hair fell to the shoulders of her gray cardigan sweater, which she was wearing over a collared dress shirt, not quite the fashion I was attracted to.

She flashed a glowing, wide grin. As she came closer, I felt nothing . . . literally nothing. No *pow*. No *boom*. And certainly, no *bang*. The heavy rock sitting in my stomach smothered any butterflies that might have been there weeks earlier. *Shit. What did I do?* This lady just flew across the country for some romantic rendezvous with me, and I was so uncomfortable with my own guilt for feeling uncomfortable that all I wanted was for her to get back on the plane.

She gave me a huge hug, during which I jerked my head to the side to avoid any opportunity for the first kiss we had planned. *I am not feeling it, even a little bit.*

Once we were on our drive to Tucson, I droned on and on about anything and everything about the history and culture of the area. "Now, Arizona became an official state in 1912, the same year the *Titanic* sank. Isn't that weird?"

She nodded while eating the peanut M&M's I brought for her.

"And I love how we have six seasons here—two summers, a dry one and a wet one; fall; two winters, a dry one and a wet one; and spring. Most people don't know that!"

I wasn't blabbing because I was nervous. Instead, I knew if I didn't fill the airspace with constant chatter, she might ask me what I was thinking or feeling. Then I'd have to fess up about my lack of chemistry with her and how I wished Pants was here instead. So, I kept talking while repressing my internal angst and guilt, and she kept popping candy into her mouth and nodding.

As soon as we walked in the door, she followed me to my bedroom and sat her bag down. Weeks earlier, I'd sent a text, joking about us not being able to keep our hands off each other once we got to my place. At the time, I hoped that might be the case, but now I couldn't even imagine holding hands.

We changed into our pajamas since it was nearly midnight, and she got into my bed like we were already a couple. My heart was pounding as the awkwardness consumed my entire being. I climbed under the covers and said, "Um, I'm kinda nervous about all this. I think I just want to go to sleep."

"Uh . . . okay." She sounded disappointed.

"Night." I then rolled over and gripped the edge of my mattress until the sun came up.

I had gotten up early the next morning and snuck outside to text Naked and Afraid.

You awake?

Of course.

No chemistry. We hugged, and she slept next to me. Nothing else.

Well, just let things settle today. Then you can decide.

Should I keep saying I'm nervous? I don't want to do anything physical.

If that is still the case later, then I think you need to be honest.

I couldn't imagine letting things settle or waiting until later. I knew. I just had to convince Naked and Afraid.

I'm super disappointed.

Just see how it unfolds before you say something.

What if she tries to hold my hand or kiss me?

Well, at least try that. It's not gonna hurt you.

I did not want to hook up with this lady. Instead, I needed to figure out what to do to get out of the situation.

Yes, it will. There is zero attraction.

Is it really that obvious to you?

100 percent.

Did you discuss beforehand what you would do if there was no attraction? Why don't you call me?

I walked around to the front of the house, far away from any doors or windows that might carry my voice inside. She picked up on the first ring.

"Are you sure?" she asked.

"Yes," I said in an unnecessary whisper. "I'm totally sure." I paced up and down the street.

"How did you know so fast?"

"I could tell the moment I saw her. Something didn't feel

right. Maybe it's that I'm thinking about someone else, or maybe it's those Brandi love songs she kept sending me . . . kinda freaked me out. I really wanted to feel a connection, but I just don't."

"Well, then . . ." she said. "Put on your big-girl pants and talk to her."

"I feel awful. She flew to the other side of the country hoping to find her soulmate. And I'm just not her."

"You can't let her think you are."

I went back inside. She wasn't up yet, so I tiptoed past my bedroom, went into my office, and hid for the next ninety minutes. Thankfully, I had a meeting I couldn't get out of. Afterward, I found her on the patio reading Brandi Carlile's memoir.

"Oh good. You found the coffee I got you," I said, looking at the mug on the nearby table.

"Yep. Made a whole pot and been hanging out, waiting for you."

"Wanna go on a walk?"

"I'd love to!" She put down her book, drank one last sip, and stood up.

For the first three miles, I spewed Arizona factoids again, this time about desert plants and mountain ranges. Just before mile four, and only steps away from the house, I finally took a breath.

During the millisecond absence of my voice, she squeezed in a question. "So how are you feeling?"

The voice in my head started shouting, "Put on your big-girl pants, Corey, and get yourself out of this situation. You have nothing to be afraid of!"

My silence must have been too long. "About us," she said.

I took a deep breath and then blurted out, "I feel like this is more of a friendship for me."

She slowed down her pace. "You already know that? We've hardly spent any time together."

"I'm sorry," I said.

"Well, I really like you and want something more."

"I'm just not there." I exhaled. "I'm so sorry."

Our slow walk turned into a stop, even though all I wanted to do was speed off as fast as possible.

"Could that change?" She stared into my eyes.

Her hope burned right through me, and I had to look away. "I'd rather just enjoy our few days together doing all the fun things we have planned." I offered a small smile, trying to show some excitement for her visit.

"No pressure or expectations. But if you change your mind . . ."

"I'm really sorry." There were simply no other words I could say to make this situation not feel so awful.

When we got home, she settled back into the patio chair and picked up her Brandi memoir. I headed to my office to reply to a message from TikTok, who had been waiting for an update.

I hope things are going well. Send me one emoji face that shows how you're feeling right now.

☹ No chemistry.

C'mon. It's been less than twelve hours.

I'm 100 percent sure. I'm very uncomfortable, and it's awkward.

Oh no.

She asked how I was feeling, and I told her I felt more like friends.

Oh jeez. You don't think it's too soon to make that call?

Like Naked and Afraid, it seemed she needed some convincing, too.

Not at all. No chemistry, no spark. I want to find my soulmate, and I just know deep down it's not her. I don't want to fake it or try it out. I just know.

Well, just act how you would want others to if you were in this situation.

I will be the best host I can be.

I would expect nothing less from you. ☺

While I was texting with TikTok, I got a message from Naked and Afraid.

????

Had the talk.

How did it go? You're still alive, so that's good.

I told her I was overwhelmed and anxious. I didn't say anything about the chemistry but more about how I only wanted to be friends. She felt differently but appreciated my honesty.

Great! Good job. Did she leave?

She's still here. I put on my big-girl pants.

Yes, you did! Hooray!!

Maybe East Coast and I should have met up in Nebraska after all.

Despite the heavy vibe, we headed out for a jam-packed day of activities, including a city tour and hike, during which I continued to inundate her with Arizona trivia.

Later that evening, we put on *Snapshots*, a lesbian flick she suggested. I waited until she sat down on the couch and then promptly sat as far away from her as possible. About halfway through, we hit pause, and I dished us each a bowl of honey cluster ice cream.

I took a bite, ready to savor the rich sweetness. Instead, one of the clusters clung to my bottom molar like glue. In a frenzy to unstick it, I quickly opened my mouth and felt what I thought was a small pebble on my tongue. I spit it into my hand.

"My crown just came off!" I shouted, looking at my palm. I rubbed my tongue over my stump of a tooth.

"What?"

I held it up. "And it's all covered in honey."

I hurried to the kitchen to wash it off. When I was nearing the sink, I could sense East Coast right behind me.

"Let me take a look," she said over my shoulder.

I spun around, and there she was, inches from me.

"Open your mouth."

I'm not sure why, but I did, and she peered inside.

"I can't really see back there."

She then pulled on the sides of my mouth and leaned in. Trying to be polite, I gave her three seconds and then stepped back until her fingers fell out of my mouth.

"I'll call the dentist in the morning. I can't go to the Grand Canyon in a couple days without a tooth!"

I washed the crown off and flushed my mouth when she wasn't looking.

We called it a night. This time, she stayed in the guest room, and I slept like a starfish spread out on my bed.

The text from Naked and Afraid was already in my messages when I woke up.

Well, what's happening now?

Things are super awkward, and my crown came off. Living the dream!

Focus on the present and the positives. You invited this woman to your house. So be kind and patient and loving.

I hear ya. I'm being an excellent host, and we are having lots of fun.

"Fun" might have been a stretch.

I took my time getting ready for the day. At the stroke of 8:00, I called the dentist and then tiptoed out to the kitchen.

East Coast was already up, sitting at the table with her laptop and a mug of coffee.

"Morning," I said. "I was able to get an appointment in an hour. Are you cool if we go on our hike a little later, after I get back?"

"I'm flexible. Just get your tooth fixed." Her tone, though, made it sound more like, "I wish you felt the way I did, but you don't, so I'm just gonna pretend I'm okay with all of this."

She fixated on her computer and started typing.

"Alright, I'm heading out. I'll text you when I'm on my way home."

"See ya in a bit," she said, glancing up.

I gave a small wave and walked out the front door.

After the appointment, I sent her a message.

Just leaving the dentist. Be back in a few.

Almost immediately, I got a reply telling me she thought it was best for her to go home. She ended by offering good wishes to me and my daughter.

I read it a second time, then called her, but I hung up when I got her voicemail. I sped across town and barreled through the front door. She was nowhere. The guest bed had been made, and everything of hers, including the worn Brandi Carlile book, was gone.

I called Naked and Afraid in a frenzy. As soon as she answered, I yelled, "She left!"

"What do you mean, she left?"

"She packed up everything and snuck out while I was at the dentist. Didn't tell me, other than some 'Thank you for having me' text, and now she isn't answering her phone."

"Holy shit! It makes sense. It would suck to be in her situation, traveling out here to meet you, and then you reject her. I'd be super embarrassed if I were her. I'm surprised she didn't leave earlier!"

"Still, she could have told me before she took off."

After I sifted through my confusion, I realized the situation had no good answers, and no matter what, I felt awful about it.

But at least I lived my truth, *and* my crown was fixed.

The Sun Always Rises

"He flew all the way in from Italy," the presenter shared, "and walked across the entire canyon wearing a nice suit, fedora, and fancy shoes."

The audience hung on his every word.

"As the story goes, he came out the other side with his tie barely loosened and only a mist of sweat on his forehead. If an eighty-year-old can do it, so can you."

Shortly after attending the "So You Want to Hike the Grand Canyon?" seminar at the local outdoor shop years earlier, Zion and I embarked on our adventure, hiking from the South Rim to the river at the bottom and back out—17.2 miles over three days. A few years later, we did the longer rim-to-rim hike, with an overnight stay at Phantom Ranch midway to break up the trek.

But I had never tried to conquer the canyon in one day. Now, I was about to tackle this 17.2-mile, single-day, round-trip rim-to-river "bucket list item" with no lodging and minimal gear. And Naked and Afraid would do it with me. Hippie and Speedy weren't able to come, but my friend Peace Corps, who I had met at a lesbian karaoke Meetup event a few years earlier, would be joining us. She was the perfect addition to the team, exuding confidence with her short, spiky orange hair and a "no one would ever mistake me for straight" look.

I knew this adventure was meant to be. *Thanks llama.*

On the morning of the hike, Peace Corps and I woke up at 3:30 a.m. Naked and Afraid had driven several hours through the night to meet us at the hotel at departure time—anything to save a few bucks on a shared room.

The three of us carpooled into the very dark and very quiet park, taking our pick of spots at the visitor center. We boarded the first shuttle with a handful of other die-hard hikers and were dropped at the trailhead around 5:20 a.m. We wandered over to look at a sign with an enlarged map of the trail when a cold burst of air whipped at my face. I yanked my beanie over my ears and put on my gloves. I wasn't sure how Naked and Afraid planned to stay warm in her khaki shorts, one of the many pairs she had bought from Kohl's to avoid having to make apparel decisions on a daily basis.

We started down the pitch-black, steep, dusty path, with only headlamps to guide us. Naked and Afraid forged ahead, with Peace Corps and I nearly running to keep up with her. I couldn't help but worry about Naked and Afraid slipping on the gravel rocks and plummeting into the vast canyon as she bounded down wearing her ratty old hiking shoes wrapped in duct tape to keep the soles on. I never had to concern myself with Peace Corps's clothing decisions. She always seemed to come prepared and didn't tape her gear together.

When we arrived at a rest stop just a couple miles down, the sunrise had begun cresting over the top edge of the canyon.

"Hey, can you take my picture?" Naked and Afraid handed me her phone and morphed into a yoga pose. "Take it now before I fall over!"

I snapped a photo.

"How would you all feel if I met you at the bottom?" she asked after regaining her footing.

I looked at Peace Corps. Her mouth curved up in a slight smile, and she let out an exhale.

"Sure," I said.

"Works for me," Peace Corps said.

Within thirty seconds, Naked and Afraid was on her way, trotting down the trail in the dark. Peace Corps and I decided on a more moderate speed, at least until the sun fully rose.

The rest of the downhill was just a peaceful saunter, with a nice breeze and epic views. If healing ever felt like anything, it was this. Our conversation flowed, from East Coast's recent visit to my budding feelings for Pants.

"That's exactly why I don't date," Peace Corps said.

We both laughed.

We finally passed through a stone tunnel and emerged at the swinging suspension bridge spanning the Colorado River. I held both hiking poles in one hand and used the other to slide along one of the metal rails on the side of the bridge. With each step, we swayed back and forth.

"Hey!" Naked and Afraid's voice echoed from below.

"Hi!" I yelled. "We'll be right down!"

The three of us met up at the bottom, and in no time, were on our way to start our ascent. Our pace was more of a quick scoot than the run that Naked and Afraid would have preferred. But we had decided to stick together for the rest of the hike.

"I'm so glad we're doing this in November," she said. "Can you imagine how hot it would be if it were summer?"

"When I did rim-to-rim, it was in July," I said. "I thought we were going to cook when we were walking in between the huge canyon walls. They call that area The Box . . . because you can roast inside like a box oven."

"I want to do that!" Naked and Afraid said. "Not the dying-of-heatstroke thing but the rim-to-rim."

We all trudged on, making our way to Havasupai Gardens, about four and a half miles from the top. The sunshine was now nearly blinding, and the temperature rising.

After turning a few corners, we could smell the stench of fresh manure and had to shoo away the circling swarm of flies.

"Oh my God! How can they eat their sandwiches sitting right there?" Naked and Afraid pointed to the day riders having lunch next to the mule stop.

I covered my mouth and nose and kept walking.

We finally found a picnic table in a quaint spot, far away from the flies and mules, and downed our lunch. After twenty minutes, we were on the trail again and made it to the three-mile rest house in no time. We all agreed to forgo the stop and keep trekking before we were sure to lose steam. I kept my focus on the ground, avoiding even the slightest gaze with the upcoming switchbacks, which looked like zigzag carvings on a wall.

"My calves are tightening up!" Naked and Afraid yelled to me as I rounded a bend.

"Drink water!" I yelled back.

"Got it, Commander Corey!" Naked and Afraid shouted, using the name she called me when I would kick things into gear.

We made another turn, and a small building came into view.

"Mile-and-a-half rest house!" I announced. "Wanna stop?"

"Keep going!" said Peace Corps. Her bag was hanging off one shoulder, and she was trying to guzzle from her water bottle while walking.

"I'm good. Let's do it, people!" Naked and Afraid said.

Few words were spoken during our last leg. Instead, we concentrated on tackling the steep switchbacks while avoiding tourists strolling down in flip-flops with their coffee cups and gift store bags.

Within minutes, we reached the top. While I was hot and tired, I was overwhelmed with pride. I couldn't remember when I had ever felt this full of life. And after having had my emotions scattered about the past several months, trying to heal from the breakup while venturing out into the dating world, this trek showed me I had the strength to overcome any challenge.

We walked over to the Bright Angel trailhead sign and took plenty of pictures for Naked and Afraid to post on Facebook.

"I read somewhere about a group of men who hike the Grand Canyon a lot. They call themselves the Coconino Cowboys," Naked and Afraid said. "We should be the Coconino Cowgirls."

"I love it!" I said. "What's next for the Coconino Cowgirls?"

"Rim-to-rim-to-rim," Naked and Afraid said.

I couldn't wait to add that to The Plan.

"I haven't shared this with anyone. Not even Naked and Afraid," I said, stretching my legs across my hotel bed.

"Well, she's halfway back to Tucson by now," Peace Corps said.

We both laughed.

I picked up my phone from the nightstand and opened "Love Manifests." "Okay, here's the first one. It's dated for the future so I can give the universe time to respond." I squinted as I read the tiny words out loud.

It is Thanksgiving, and I feel an undeniable powerful romantic connection with and attraction to a potential partner who is physically, emotionally, and geographically available to me. This feeling is equally reciprocated.

I paused. "That's it." I fell back on the pillows behind me.

"Cool. What about the other one?" she asked, turning toward me and propping herself up on her elbows.

"It's pretty long." I sat up and zoomed in to read her the first line. "It's February, and I am grateful to be in an intimate partnership with a woman in her forties who lives in or near Tucson." I continued, going on and on about adventure, chemistry, and spending quality time together. "So, which one do you like better?" I asked.

"Well, it depends on who or what you want to manifest."

I leaned forward. "What do you mean?"

"The shorter one seems like it's about *who* you want . . . Maybe Pants?"

Mic drop and then silence on my end.

"The longer one is more like *what* you want. I think you should write about what you want, and the right person will come into your life . . . even if it isn't Pants."

Second mic drop.

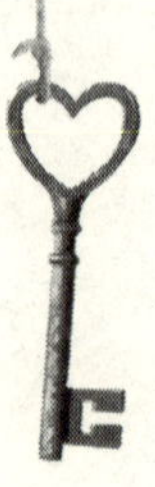

You Complete Me

East Coast checked my LinkedIn profile forty-one minutes ago. So weird.

Naked and Afraid texted right back. She was up early even after having made the drive back to Tucson the night before.

She was very enamored with you, if not in love. Not weird.

Just got on the dating app, too, and she clicked on my profile. I'm kinda creeped out.

Okay. That is a little weird.

Two days later, a text from East Coast popped up on my iPad while I was watching one of my fall-asleep-to shows. I took a deep breath and then opened it.

The message reiterated how much she had enjoyed our connection but that she had let herself get in too deep.

A wave of nausea came over me as the discomfort and anxiety around the whole situation—Brandi songs, Arizona factoids, and honey cluster ice cream—came surging back. I did not want to respond. It would just be me having to say, yet again, I was sorry, and then her telling me the terrible thing I did to make her run away.

Big-girl pants, Corey. You hate ambiguity, and this is your chance to get closure.

I responded and asked if she wanted to talk, even though it was quite late, especially for her.

The phone rang. I felt like patio-pacing again, but instead I was curled up under my comforter, swirling a lock of hair around my fingers.

"Hi," she said. Her voice sounded shaky. "Thanks for talking. I'm really sorry about what happened. I didn't know any other way to handle the situation than to just leave."

"Why didn't you talk to me about it?"

"I was just so embarrassed and uncomfortable about the whole thing. And talking to you about it would have been even *more* embarrassing. So, I ended up taking an Uber to Phoenix and getting a hotel."

That's a lot of trouble to go through to get away from me, I thought. "I would have driven you to the airport, you know."

"I know you would have. This had nothing to do with you, though. Again, I was just embarrassed."

I exhaled. *At least she didn't think I was a terrible person.*

"Just so you know, I was disappointed I didn't feel a spark," I told her.

"You were?"

I got up from my bed and started walking circles around my room. "Well, yeah. But I had to trust my gut."

"I'm glad you said something. It would have been worse if you hadn't."

I didn't share that if it weren't for Naked and Afraid's push for me to put on my big-girl pants, I would have spent the entire trip spouting Arizona trivia tidbits.

We processed for a while longer and then she shifted the conversation.

"How was the Grand Canyon?"

I filled her in on the trip and texted her a few photos.

"So where do we go from here?" she asked. "I would love to have a friendship with you."

The words seemed innocuous, and a friendship could be an easy compromise. But I couldn't get over the ghosting, even though she had a good reason for it. Her leaving only reiterated that the people I care about leave. I had to endure my dad starting a new life, First Love moving on with someone else, Zion leaving unexpectedly with Kiddo, and Runner blindsiding me by not getting on the plane. I knew I couldn't keep people in my emotional space who have a history of walking out.

"Maybe down the road, after all this has settled. Right now, I'd rather take some time." I could feel the lump in my throat and tried to clear it with an "ahem." But it didn't go away.

"I understand. I'll leave the ball in your court. If, and when, you are ready to be friends, feel free to reach out. I'll be there. Have a good rest of your night."

And just like that, it seemed as though East Coast's chapter had closed.

Despite the finality of our call, two days later, East Coast sent a text wishing me a good weekend with my daughter. She also said something about how as single moms, spending time with our children makes us whole.

The message came while I was out trekking through the neighborhood. The sun was shining, and the breeze was just perfect. Except now I had a big rock in the pit of my stomach. After reading her text a second time, I made my way to a shady spot and sent a screenshot to TikTok. Thirty seconds passed without a response, so I just called her.

"Hey, hey, hey," TikTok said, picking up on the first ring.

I started walking again, this time at an even faster pace.

"Did you read this? We talked the other night about the ball being in my court. This doesn't seem like the ball's in my court."

"Let me read it." There was silence for a moment. "Okay. I wouldn't respond. Or . . . you tell her you don't need someone to make you whole, and you are not a single mom, and—"

"Exactly! Technically, Zion and I co-parent, so I'm not really a single mom. And I've never seen myself that way. But the bigger point is that I don't need someone to complete me! I want someone who sees me as complete already and wants to connect on a profoundly deeper level."

Twelve hours passed before I finally replied.

Thanks. Have a nice weekend as well.

No response.

A few days later, my phone rang.

"Hello?"

"Is adfkjkdfjsdlfja;slfjka;sdfj there?" the voice asked.

"Who?"

The person repeated the same inaudible sound and then said, "I have the wrong number" and hung up.

After sifting through my recent calls, I figured out the number was East Coast's landline. Within minutes of solving the mystery, I got a text from her admitting to the misdial and apologizing. I never responded.

Later that day, I saged my house with my five-star-rated spray and vowed to never again invite someone from a dating app to stay over.

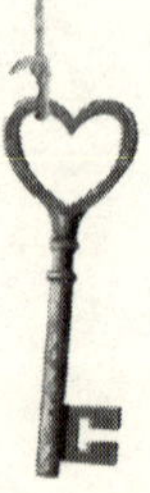

For Now

I need to figure out where she stands so I can move forward either way. This little cat-and-mouse thing is confusing me.

Naked and Afraid was growing tired of this conversation—all about my incessant messaging with Pants, filled with silly banter and daily check-ins, how I would get butterflies whenever a message came in, even if it was, "Walked the dogs and gonna make dinner," and whether our friendship-only pact was really still a thing.

Yes, just talk to her. And be clear.

While I agreed, only one thing was clear to me. The thought of talking to her about this was terrifying.

You can't keep avoiding this.

Two days had passed, and Naked and Afraid's patience was growing thin.

I'm in this weird limbo, and it sucks. But I'm freaking out just thinking about it.

It's better to know.

While I believed that to be true, and I had sworn I would never live in a state of ambiguity again, I was sure rejection would feel even worse.

The following weekend, Naked and Afraid and I went to a Meetup event at a local park where hordes of lesbians were eating barbecue, playing kickball, and trying their hands at a variety of lawn games. All I could talk about, though, was my predicament with Pants.

"I just don't know if she's changed her mind. What if she hasn't? What if—"

Naked and Afraid interrupted me. She put one hand on each of my shoulders, squeezed tightly, and stared into my eyes. "You have to put on your big-girl pants and find out! She probably feels the same way and hasn't said anything. Rip the Band-Aid off! . . . Now, let's go play cornhole."

The next day, I went for a walk along the river path, the same one where I hosted the Meetup event months earlier. Once I was cruising along, I shot Pants a text to chitchat about the weekend.

I went to that kickball thing yesterday. I didn't play but ended up in a very serious game of cornhole with some women who thought they were professionals.

😂😂 Any cute prospects for you?? Why didn't you play?

Yes!!! Some seventy-five-year-old woman asked to be introduced to me. Apparently, she is some rich lady who tries to find younger women. She came on strong. I politely excused myself and went to the snack table and ate like five pieces of watermelon. By then, kickball had already started, and I was super full.

😂 That is hilarious!!! You didn't see anyone who interested you? Fifty-nine-year-old Ron messaged me today on the app to tell me he liked me and wanted to get to know me better. Stupid app let this guy slip through. Ugh!

😂 No prospects for me. Lots of nonathletic older women wearing jean shorts!

I feel ya!!

I pulled off to the side of the path, bikes whizzing by, contemplating my next move. "Put on your big-girl pants," Naked and Afraid's telepathic voice whispered in my ear. "This is the perfect moment."

I took a deep breath and then pasted the prewritten message saved in my notes app into our text thread. Another deep breath. Send.

I know we established this "just friends" thing a while back, which has been great for me since the online app thing was a bit overwhelming and my dates up to that point had been real doozies. I wanted to check in to see if you were still good just being casual friends and adventure buddies, or if you were interested in seeing if there may be a connection beyond friendship.

The world's longest pause . . . Finally, three little dots showed up on the screen. I was shaking.

For now, I'm still good with being friends and adventure buddies. I really enjoy our conversations and hearing your stories. You crack me up. And I would still like to do The Wave. And come out and see Arizona.

I tried to stuff my hurt and embarrassment down into the place where my trauma hid. All I could muster up was a casual reply.

Sounds good to me! I, too, get a kick out of our conversations and am looking forward to some cool adventures.

And that was it. The buildup, the questions, the anticipation . . . gone. My hands were still trembling as I typed a message to Naked and Afraid.

I texted Pants. Got the rejection.

What? Are you joking? I did NOT see that coming.

Totally serious. And it sucks.

You did the right thing. Now you won't waste any more time or energy.

I'm disappointed. Maybe I should have just lived in la-la land for a while longer.

La-la land is not a good place. Better to live in reality.

Deep down, I agreed. The ambiguity had disappeared. Except now there was a massive elephant in the room, *and* I had to contend with my disappointment, embarrassment, and unrequited feelings. That was my new reality.

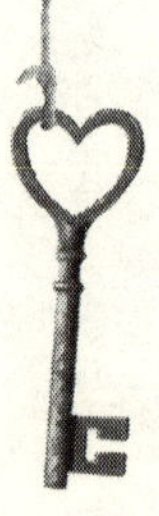

Back Out There

Hi. I hope you are having a great day!

The message took me by surprise. I had been so fixated on the situation with Pants that I had nearly forgotten about the dating sites. I clicked on her profile. Hmm . . . an attractive and successful woman who lived in Phoenix.

Thanks. It has been great. How is your day?

Wonderful. I spent some time in my garden, and the weather is just lovely.

She seemed polite and used proper grammar. I wondered if she repeatedly proofed her profile like I did with mine.

Our friendly exchange began only hours before the "for now" rejection from Pants, but once everything imploded with that, I sank into a space where all I could focus on was my embarrassment and disappointment, and certainly not the nice lady from the dating app.

The next evening, though, the lady sent another message right as I was getting into bed. Before I knew it, we fell into deep text conversation. She didn't hold back on asking me intriguing questions.

What exactly do you teach about emotional intelligence?
And do you believe you practice it yourself?

Basically, how to have more productive relationships.
While I use many of the practices, there are definitely
areas I could improve on.

What would you most like to develop?

I want to learn to be more forgiving of myself when
I make mistakes.

We went back and forth for nearly an hour as we explored our thoughts and opinions on a wide array of topics. And I never once thought about Pants.

A few days later, the lady called . . . right when she said she would. Again, I was curled up in bed in my pajamas—this time with my kitty snuggled up next to me. Our conversation ranged from discussing personality types to how we show up in relationships. Her pontificating nature helped me reflect in ways I wasn't expecting, and two hours flew by.

At the end of the call, I told her I would be spending Thanksgiving in Phoenix the following week and asked if she wanted to meet for a walk by the lake on Friday before I headed back to Tucson.

"I would love to," she said.

Just like that, I had a date planned. This time I wasn't rejected.

You're right. This happy hour is weird. All guys with glow sticks. Lots of pot.

Gross. Get out.

There were limits on Naked and Afraid's offer to be my wingwoman. Even she wouldn't go to this gay happy hour with me. But I didn't want to pin all my hopes on my upcoming date with the pontificating lady. So, there I was, solo and searching.

I made my way over to a tall table and leaned on the slightly wet top, scanning the room. Ignoring my damp elbows, I fired off another text to Naked and Afraid.

I'm gonna die alone.

No, you won't. But I told you not to go to that stupid event.

I glanced at my phone—7:00 p.m., the start of the witching hours.

After being squeezed out of my table by a group of stoned guys who looked like contestants at a Jerry Garcia look-alike contest, I decided to leave.

Naked and Afraid was right. Anything would be better than this.

So, I drove across town to the used bookstore, hoping my soulmate would be there this time.

When I went inside, everything seemed still—not because people were standing by the stacks, silently skimming old paperbacks, but instead because the place was empty, minus a handful of employees.

I did my usual lurking around the gay section, where I spent twenty minutes sifting through the crusty romance paperbacks again. It looked like not one had been taken off the shelf since I was last there.

My soulmate no-showed again.

The General and The Zen Master

"Have you always been a control freak?" Naked and Afraid asked as we trekked up the steep and rocky trail toward Romero Pools.

We had been discussing my Type A, controlling, overanalyzing nature for quite some time now. But she continued to be fascinated with it, as it stood in stark contrast to every fiber of her being.

"Pretty much," I said. "I can't remember a time I wasn't. Even when I was in elementary school, I would march through the neighborhood as the self-proclaimed general of my own army and boss the neighbor kids around."

She laughed.

"I wore a uniform I got from the military surplus store. I even covered it in medals and patches."

"I can totally picture it," she said.

"When I told them to line up, the kids would dash into formation. But it didn't take long before everyone got tired of it, even the little ones, and no one wanted to be in my army anymore."

We sped up to pass a couple hiking in front of us.

"What did you do with no one to boss around?" she continued, once we were ahead of them.

"Well, I became my own general. I would set super high expectations for myself and then rigid procedures for meeting them. If I went off track, my general would make sure I got right back on."

"That sounds exhausting."

"Like, if I got a bad grade, my parents didn't ground me. They always said nothing they could do would be worse than what I did to myself."

"What would you do?" she asked.

"Create some ridiculous study plan, pull all-nighters, and do whatever it took to not get a bad grade again . . . things like that. You know, I don't like to fail at anything."

"Wow. That explains so much." She laughed.

"My therapist and I have been talking a lot about how I've probably been like this since I was little. Maybe it was from my mom's incessant need to have everything in its place . . . or my dad being a workaholic. Whatever it was, needing to feel in control seems to be hardwired in me at this point."

She stopped at a bend, turned to face me, and then said, "So weird I've been calling you Commander Corey."

I came to a halt right before crashing into her. "Very weird."

"But now it's like your little general is on overdrive, and you're forcing your healing and forcing finding your so-called soulmate."

"Well, the only thing that got me through the first few months after the breakup was my ironclad 'get-over-her-in-no-time, get-ready-for-my-soulmate plan.'" I let out an awkward laugh. "I know it was a bit of a haphazard list but having that plan has made me feel more in control."

She took a swig from her water bottle. "But your general can't *actually* control how fast you heal . . . or *when* you'll find love. You're manifesting, doing Law of Attraction . . . everything is aligned perfectly for you to be more Zen. But you're still holding on so tight to some set of specific outcomes on an arbitrary timeline. Let go and see what the universe brings you."

"But I like taking charge of my life."

We started back up again, with the lush pools of water finally in sight.

She didn't press. "Well, I finally get why you track every lady who you message with on the apps on some color-coded spreadsheet. And your rules, you have so many—like waiting seventy-two hours to respond and not clicking on a profile more than once. Your general is totally behind all of that."

"Exactly."

"Except you apparently missed one very important dating rule."

"Which one?"

"The 'Don't have someone you met online fly across the country and stay at your house for three days' rule."

We both laughed.

"I have to admit, though, as much as doing all this stuff helps me feel in control, part of me wants to be the kind of person who doesn't have rules and just lets the process flow more naturally." I let out an exhale. "Maybe I can summon my inner Zen Master to keep The General in check."

"Well, I'd love to meet The Zen Master," she said.

"Me too."

We rounded the final bend and found a large rock near the pools where we could sit and have a quick snack before heading back. Naked and Afraid rifled through her bag, pulled out a squeeze pouch of some goo-like substance, and began sucking from it. I, on the other hand, tossed a few nuts in my mouth while contemplating summoning my inner Zen Master. As the warm sun beamed down, it came to me. All I had to do was add "Be more Zen" to The Plan, and I would find a way to make it happen.

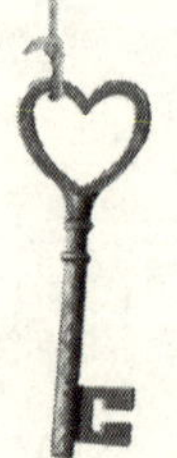

The Love Manifest

"Does your potential partner need to like cats?" the older gentleman from my manifesting group asked. I had just finished reading the *what* I wanted and not *who* I wanted version of my love manifest to everyone.

"Uh, yes, that would be good," I said.

"I saw your kitty on the webcam earlier," he said. "You may want to add 'Likes cats.'"

Others also offered suggestions, which I typed into the manifest as they shared them. By the time we finished discussing, I ended up with some in-text edits, notes at the bottom of the page, and yellow highlighted marks over phrases I wanted to revisit.

With their feedback, I completed my final version just a few days before Thanksgiving, as usual, dated for a few months into the future.

It's February, and I am grateful to be in an intimate partnership with a woman in her forties who lives in or near Tucson. I feel appreciated, connected, loved, and supported, and I love reciprocating those same feelings and behaviors. We have amazing physical and emotional chemistry, and

I feel fulfilled. Our relationship is passionate and exciting. Our values, ethics, and political views are in alignment, and we have a similar lifestyle, sense of responsibility and integrity, ambitious nature, love for hiking and the outdoors, commitment to fitness, spirit of adventure and travel, innovative mindset, professional drive, level of education, love for family, desire for healthy living, quest for intellectual banter, and a curiosity about events, history, culture, and other perspectives. We have so much to talk about, and our amazing conversations flow easily and seamlessly. She is affectionate and loving, and our connection feels deep. She is emotionally, physically, and mentally healthy; financially stable; attractive; athletic; worldly; smart; in a career she enjoys; supportive of my work and goals; and we bring out the best in each other to achieve our individual and collective ambitions. She is kind, thoughtful, honest, faithful, and loving. And she has a great sense of humor, both making me laugh as well as enjoying my charming wit. We love spending time together and make sure we prioritize each other in our lives. She is also emotionally and physically available to me and has healthy boundaries with technology, being able to easily detach from her devices to give others her full attention. While we enjoy spending time together and have mutual interests and friends, we also have our own friends and hobbies that we continue to engage with. We share similar views on the level of commitment and pacing of the relationship, and life with her is easy and filled with deep contentment, enjoyment, and physical intimacy. We love each other deeply and get along well with each other's families and friends. She loves spending time with my daughter and being around kitties, recognizing the importance of both in my life. Her kids, if she has any, are grown and live on their own or only live with her part-time. I am so thankful that she and I are experiencing big, grand love that is deep, respectful, healthy, sustained, whole, intimate, fun, and magical . . . one in which we both feel passionate and excited about sharing a life together.

I read my manifest aloud several times over the next couple days. I had a feeling she was on her way.

I Love Classical Music

Thanksgiving Day was a blur. And before I knew it, it was Friday evening—finally time for my date with Pontificator from the dating app.

I arrived early to the lake and was reading the "History of this walking path" sign when someone came up behind me.

"Are you Corey?"

I jumped a bit and then spun around. "Yes. Hi!"

A woman about my height with chin-length brown hair gave me a nice, tight hug. "You ready to walk?"

"Definitely."

We started down the path, weaving in and out of the crowds of slow walkers. Although kids on electric scooters zipped by, almost taking us out a few times, I hardly noticed as I was absorbed in our conversation.

"What kind of music do you like?" I asked at one point.

"I love classical."

I nodded as if I could hear concertos in my head.

"I mean, the famous composers are great," she said. "But the lesser-known ones are just as amazing."

I almost blurted out how I won a karaoke contest at a bowling alley rapping "The Humpty Dance," which I thought was a beautifully crafted, lyrical masterpiece. Instead, I kept nodding as she went on about this composer and that composer.

She then talked about all her volunteer work, growing her own vegetables, and reading thought-provoking books. *At what point do I tell her I watch reality dating shows, sometimes eat standing over the sink, and only dress professionally from the waist up for video calls?*

Despite my imposter syndrome, I must have appeared somewhat sophisticated enough for her because at the end of our walk, we stood by my car and talked about seeing each other again in two weeks.

"I could come down to your place on Sunday around five and stay the night," Pontificator said. "We'd have all day Monday, and then I would head out Tuesday."

As she ran through the hourly agenda, the awful vomit-splashing-up-in-my-throat, stomach-flipping thing set in. Images of East Coast curled up in my bed with me clinging to the edge flashed through my mind. And this lady saw it in my eyes.

"If it's too much, I can stay with friends."

"How about dinner on Sunday and then we reconvene on Monday for a hike or something?" I asked. "I recently had a weird experience with a woman I met on the app who stayed with me. I'm not sure I'm ready to host someone again just yet."

I wasn't sure if I was ever going to let anyone in my house again at all.

"I totally understand."

We hugged, another tight embrace, and both got into our cars. As soon as I pulled out of the lot, it occurred to me: I only had a couple weeks to get more cultured. I would definitely need to download opera and eat some kale.

Birds

Hey, can you let everyone know I'll be like five minutes late?

I shot the text to Speedy from a stoplight.

Sure. There's just a bunch of folks standing under a ramada. You'll be fine.

I pulled up to the already-full lot and had to make a U-turn to find street parking. I grabbed the first available space, jumped out of the car, and started hustling down the road with the strap of my pack draped over one shoulder.

I saw a group up ahead and figured it was them, since lesbians can be easy to spot. Once I got closer, Speedy and the hike leader, who I knew, came into view. I made my way over, slightly out of breath.

"Sorry I'm late."

"No worries," the hike leader said with a slight drawl.

She then turned her attention to everyone. "Glad you all could make it. I wasn't sure what the turnout would be the weekend after Thanksgiving. And so many new faces!"

I scanned the group and noticed all the ladies were considerably older, except for Speedy and a petite woman wearing hiking attire, sporty sunglasses, and a worn backpack. She had slight gray streaks barely visible in her long, tied-back brown hair.

I had hiked this trail before and remembered it was fairly short and flat with miles of the same scenery—some might say uninteresting. It would make for the perfect monotonous backdrop to give all my attention to chatting with this new lady.

Once we lined up to start walking, I situated myself right in front of her. "Is this your first Meetup event?"

"Yeah. I just moved back to Tucson. I lived here years ago, though."

The group slowly meandered down the trail.

"It's funny. I've lived in a few different places over the last decade but have always found my way home to Tucson," I said.

"Yeah, I love it here."

There was a pause. After a few more steps, I asked, "So what do you like to do besides hike?"

"I go birding when I can."

"I don't know a lot about birds, other than I had a few parakeets as a kid."

We both laughed.

I talked for much of the hike—this time, engaging in witty storytelling rather than the nervous chatter I sometimes used to avoid tough conversations. I didn't bring up one single Arizona factoid.

Instead, I shared about my upcoming sabbatical and how I love to walk up Tumamoc Hill, or as Naked and Afraid called it, Tu-MAAM-ick, a pronunciation I've never repeated. The lady talked about her love for travel and adventure, the perils of trying to buy a home, and how her kitty liked to perch in the window to cackle at the birds.

Once we made it back to the ramada, the group circled up.

"Anyone interested in a hike next weekend?" I asked. "I'll post one if you all are up for it."

A few women raised their hands.

I glanced over at the bird lady. "I'm not sure what my plans are yet. I'm a maybe."

Panic shot through me. *If she didn't come, would I ever see her again?*

When everyone dispersed, I walked alongside her toward the parking lot. "Hey, let me know if you ever want to hike Tumamoc." The words came out far more chill than I felt inside.

"Sure. I haven't done it since I've been back."

Before I could celebrate my smooth move, a car sped right up to us, kicking up dust. It then screeched to a halt.

"You all talking about Tumamoc? I want to go!" Speedy called out from her rolled-down window. *Had she been eavesdropping?*

I wanted to say "Nope," have her drive off, and then secretly plan to go alone with Birds, which I had already nicknamed her in my head. Instead, I said, "Yep."

After Birds shared that group texting wasn't working on her phone, I said I'd reach out to each of them separately and coordinate a time. They both agreed, and Speedy took off. Birds then gave me her number.

"I just texted you," I said to Birds. "Reply when you get a chance."

We said goodbye, and I headed back to my car to call Speedy.

"What did you think of her?" I blurted out as soon as she answered.

"It'll be awesome to do Tumamoc and see if she'll be a new friend," she said.

"You know, though, I could date her if she's cool. She seemed cool."

"Hey, did you hear from Birds yet?" Speedy asked later that evening as we watched a swath of old lesbians dance to an '80s medley.

"Not yet."

"You should text her right now and invite her here."

"Uh . . . no. That would be so weird. She hasn't even responded to my text from earlier. I'm not going to ask her to drop what she's doing and come to a lesbian dance."

"What's her number? I'll text her." Speedy pulled out her phone.

"Seriously? Do you want to ask her out?" I asked.

"No. No. That's not it. I just think she's someone we might wanna hang out with."

"Well, I'm kinda interested. Can you give me a head start before you swoop in and the whole thing becomes a huge friend zone for me?"

"Okay. Okay."

Birds messaged me the following day. She suggested we meet on Thursday at five to hike Tumamoc.

I sent a text to Speedy, who replied nearly instantly.

Oh, bummer. I have something then. You two have fun, and I'll catch you on the next one.

That is a bummer. I'll keep you posted.

I loved Speedy, but I wasn't really bummed at all.

Apple of Everyone's Eye

Just a few hours before getting the reply text from Birds, Naked and Afraid, Peace Corps, and I had begun training for our rim-to-rim-to-rim trek planned for June. We met at Pima Canyon for a four-mile hike where we would traverse through a lush valley, a surprising find in a desert climate.

Our first hour of conversation meandered from one current event to the next and catching up on everyone else's business. Then we had to listen to Naked and Afraid drone on about her amazing love life, before turning our attention to my floundering one.

"So, how's your dating spreadsheet?" Naked and Afraid asked, speeding ahead of us as usual.

"Ha ha." I rolled my eyes, although she couldn't see. "You know I'm trying to be more Zen now."

"How's *that* working out?" She laughed.

"So strange. Over the last week, all these women have come out of the woodwork on the apps—a Reiki healer from LA and another lady who is coming from Colorado to stay in Arizona for a few months. Not to mention Birds, who I met on the hike."

"What about Pontificator?" Naked and Afraid asked.

"Her too!" I paused. "Go with the flow, right? Well, it's flowing!"

"That's good!" Naked and Afraid said as she rounded a bend.

"All this is probably from my manifest."

"Which manifest? The love one?" Peace Corps asked from behind me.

"No. This is the 'I will be the apple of everyone's eye' manifest I created to bring in more dating prospects. I wrote it last month and postdated it for November so the universe would have time to make something happen."

"You seriously wrote that? I wanna hear it!" Naked and Afraid pulled off to the side of the trail and waited for us to catch up.

We all stood on the ridgeline while I pulled out my phone, zoomed in on the text, and read them the manifest word for word. I made sure to emphasize the line, "I am being healthily pursued by several viable potential partners who are emotionally, physically, and geographically available to me."

"Really," Naked and Afraid said rather than asked.

We began hiking again, hurrying past a group gathered by a giant boulder.

"Right? I have calls scheduled with both Reiki and Colorado this afternoon, a date with Pontificator coming up, and hopefully Tumamoc with Birds. I'm not sure what I summoned."

"Hello?" I had been looking forward to my call with Colorado, especially since our banter through the app over the past week had been quite playful and fun.

"Hey!" she said, a bit aggressively. "So sorry, but I'm in a horrible mood. Actually, I'm pretty pissed off. Maybe this isn't the best time to chat."

"Do you want to talk about it?" I leaned back on the pillows propped behind me and stretched my legs across my bed.

"I'm supposed to leave in a few days to come to Arizona." Her voice was booming. "I got a lease like a year ago, but the landlord just cancelled it. I know my rights, though!"

After ten more minutes of her rant, she suddenly shifted gears and asked, "What are you looking for in a relationship?"

I was still overwhelmed from her angry monologue.

Before I could answer, she said, "C'mon. You must have something in mind."

"Um . . . Honesty, fidelity, and someone who has good boundaries with technology—like not on their phone all the—"

"Did you not have these with your ex? What happened there? Obviously, that's a trigger for you," she said in a loud voice.

I leaned forward and crossed my legs. "I'd rather spend our time learning about each other than talking about exes."

She continued to press. "Why don't you want to discuss this? Are you not over her?"

After a deep breath, I responded. "It just wasn't very healthy toward the end."

She fired more questions at me, but I dodged divulging anything private. I finally said, "We didn't see eye to eye on things."

"You know what I do in those situations? I just say, 'Hey, babe, what's triggering you?'"

The hair stood up on the back of my neck, and the blood rushed to my face. What I wanted to say was, "You know what triggers me? A stranger telling me what to do without knowing anything about the situation!" Instead, I said, "I did check in with her triggers early on, but these issues were more serious."

"Sounds like maybe some mental health stuff going on. My mom was a psychotherapist, you know."

I said nothing. She then spent the next thirty minutes sharing details about her own mental health issues. We finally hung up, thankfully with no plans to chat again.

⟷

As soon as the call ended, I headed to the kitchen table, anything to get away from the negative juju that had now overtaken my bedroom.

I took a few deep breaths and dialed Reiki's number.

"Hi," she said, answering after the first ring.

"Hi," I replied, leaning forward on my elbows and putting my chin in my hands.

"I'm so glad we're getting a chance to talk." Her tone was gentle.

"Me too." I exhaled and settled back into my chair.

We went on to chat about our careers and hobbies, with no discussion of exes, relationships, or triggers. Two hours flew by. And she never once suggested saying "Hey, babe" to anyone.

My Happy Place

Tumamoc is my happy place, filled with countless memories of trekking the steep, three-mile-round-trip paved path, a true desert oasis right in the middle of Tucson. Sometimes, I would meander up with others, catching up on life among the majestic saguaros and lush green Palo Verde trees. And other times, I would race up, rap music blaring through my earbuds, trying to beat my record time.

When I arrived at the bottom of the hill, I could see Birds about thirty feet away, stretching her legs on an empty bench. My heart raced a bit, although I was merely strolling over to meet her. She was cute—track pants and T-shirt . . . just my type.

"Hi," I said, once I got within earshot.

"Hey." She looked up and waved.

"You ready?" I zipped up my fleece and put on my gloves. Probably a little overkill for the weather.

"Yep." She pulled her leg down from her bench stretch, and we took off.

"Tell me more about your job," I said as we started up the incline.

She went on for a while about a project she had been working on. Given I had talked her ear off on the group hike, it was nice to listen. And learning about how conscientious and dedicated she was to her work made her all the more attractive to me.

After an hour or so, we made it back down to the base of the hill, just as dusk was rolling in.

"Um, do you want to do this again next Thursday?" I asked as a gust of cold wind whipped at our faces. I pulled my beanie further down over my ears. *I don't know how she's not freezing with just a T-shirt on*, I thought.

"Sure."

"Now I'm gonna go home and defrost." I let out a small laugh.

She smiled. "See ya later."

"Bye," I said. And just like that, she was gone.

As I walked to my car, I already knew she wasn't a product of my quest to be the "apple of everyone's eye." Instead, she seemed to be the epitome of my love manifest.

"How was it?" Naked and Afraid said. "Did you feel *pow*, *boom*, *bang*?"

I paused. "Not yet. But we're going again next week."

I pulled into the grocery store parking lot across the street from Tumamoc.

"Like a date?" she asked.

"No. Just as friends." I said, still sitting in the car. I was not about to have this conversation while trying to buy bananas.

"Are you gonna ask her out?"

My neck grew hot. "I'm too nervous . . . plus, there's a lot going on. I have a date with Pontificator and another call with Reiki soon." My voice started speeding up. "I'm still texting with Pants, even though *that* isn't going anywhere. Anyway, I just have a lot swirling in my head."

"Go with the flow," she said. "If it feels natural to ask her out, then just do it."

"Nothing about this whole dating thing feels natural. Plus, I *have* been going with the flow."

"No, you haven't. It's like you've been rushing to find this elusive soulmate."

"I'm not rushing."

"Yes, you are. It took you no time after East Coast and Pants to get a whole new slew of ladies lined up to be considered for your role of soulmate, *even* after you said you wanted to summon your inner Zen Master and just go with the flow. Whatever is happening here is *not* flow."

"Maybe if I knew where I was flowing to, I could be more Zen about it."

"You can't plan Zen! That's the whole point!"

I let out a sigh. "The anticipation is killing me. I just want to know who I end up with."

"Well, you can't see into the future. So, you're gonna just have to let things unfold."

Divine Interruption

The next morning, I still couldn't get the conversation with Naked and Afraid out of my head. *What if I could see into the future? What if I could just* know *who I'm supposed to be with?* No more ambiguity, angst, worry, speculation, overthinking . . . none of it—just clarity. There was only one way to find out. And it would be the perfect addition to The Plan.

I grabbed my laptop, settled in at the kitchen table, and took a deep breath. *Here we go, Corey.* I then typed, "Psychics near me."

Three names popped up. The first one linked to a Facebook page with the word *psychic* and a phone number. The second went to a vague overview of mediumship on a plain website. The third opened to a purple page with tiny white writing and a clip art picture of a stereotypical-looking fortune teller with a crystal ball. I called her.

"Hi. I'm looking to have a reading done. Are you available today?"

"No. But Sunday morning at eleven, honey," she said in a thick Eastern European accent. She then gave me her address and promptly hung up.

I texted Naked and Afraid.

Going to a psychic on Sunday.

Seriously? Why? What about your date with Pontificator? Isn't that the same day?

I need answers. And my date isn't until later.

I'm not sure if I believe in all that stuff. But I want to hear what you find out. Come over when you're done.

You'll be the first to know.

On Sunday morning, I drove across town and parked in front of a small nondescript house that had a sign in the yard with big, bold letters that said "Psychic." I knocked on the door, and a woman who looked just like the clip art picture from the website answered.

"Come in," she said, ushering me in with urgency.

As I scurried through the doorway, I noticed her long, brown hair was tied in a tight bun, drawing attention to her dangling silver earrings. *Do all intuitives wear dangling earrings?*

She led me into one of her bedrooms, which was filled with crystals, cards, candles, and ornate decorations. They looked like they came from the shop where I bought my love crystals.

"Sit down, honey," she said.

We sat at a card table covered in a fancy tablecloth with a crystal ball on top.

"What is your question?" she asked.

I was trying to focus without being distracted by the kids' voices coming from the other room where they were watching cartoons.

"Um . . . I'm curious to know what's going to happen with my love life," I said.

I imagined her saying something like, "It's dark and dismal. There is no hope for you, child. I see a burning tower." Instead, she said, "Ooh, there's a karmic partner in your life. Did you end a relationship about six months ago?"

"Yes," I said. "What's a karmic partner?"

"It's someone who we have unresolved business with from a past life. Often, karmic partnerships are very toxic and short-lived because they are only meant for us to connect to resolve our issue. This one was very unhealthy and ended horribly."

"Yes," I said. "Horribly."

"This person moved on quickly after your breakup too. That must have been difficult. Don't worry. It won't last."

Strangely, after all my heartache about Runner and the breakup, I really wasn't interested in talking about her. I simply wanted to know what was in store for me now.

"What about the present?" I asked.

"Oh, you've met someone recently who has feelings for you." She stared deeply into my eyes. "Do you know who it is?"

"I have no idea."

She leaned forward and paused, which seemed to be more for effect than anything.

"This is your divine partner . . . the strongest of the soulmates," she whispered. "You've known each other for about two months."

That eliminated Birds, Pontificator, and Reiki since I had only recently connected with them. And I met East Coast earlier than that. Plus, I was absolutely certain she was not my divine partner.

"The timing isn't right. And your communication is quite confusing. But you enjoy each other and get along really well. It's like you have known each other a lot longer." She leaned back in her chair. "I'm also picking up a water sign . . . Cancer, maybe."

She paused while I contemplated.

Oh shit.

It could only be one person—Pants.

I wasn't sure of Pants's zodiac sign, but everything else lined up. We had met within the last couple months. Our communication was frequent but sometimes confusing for me—exhibit A: the "for now" text exchange. And she had felt oddly familiar to me from the get-go. Plus, we still texted nearly every single day. So, she was an option. Actually, she was the only option.

In a fit of desperation, I asked, "How many divine partners do we have?"

"Most people, around fifteen. For you, only five. You haven't met any of the others."

Given I had been rejected by Pants twice, I wasn't keen on putting my cosmic bets on her. "Could I just pass this one up and wait to meet the other four?"

"You can. But you might never cross paths with any of them." She had a serious look on her face.

"What am I supposed to do?"

"Focus on this divine partner. Know that your timing now is off, and you won't communicate much in January because of a situation she will be dealing with. You'll both then have time to do your own self-work and put closure on any lingering business you need to tend to. Something will happen in three months, though. Pay attention to the timeline." She jumped out of her chair and then pointed me to the door. "Our time is up."

I left feeling somewhat bewildered and went straight to Naked and Afraid's, where I recapped the entire story while pacing through her living room. She sat on the couch, listening intently and petting one of her dogs.

The moment I finished, she grabbed her phone and called to set up her own reading for the next day. "This will be the true test. We'll see what I find out."

"I need to call and cancel my date tonight with Pontificator," I said.

"Probably a good idea."

"What do I say, 'I saw a psychic who may have been a fraud, but she told me a woman I met on a dating app who rejected me, technically twice, is my soulmate'?" I let out a laugh, masking my unresolved hurt and embarrassment from the whole situation.

"Well, maybe not in that much detail."

I drove home, scripting every explanation I could give. As soon as I walked in the door, I called Pontificator.

She answered with a warm greeting, as always.

"Hey!" I said.

"I'm gonna head out in an hour and should be at your place around seven."

It felt like a pound of bricks landed on my chest.

"I'm so sorry to do this, but I need to cancel our date for tonight. I'm really, really sorry for the last-minute notice."

"Is everything okay?" she asked, in her kind, inquisitive way.

"Well, I got some news that's really throwing me off. I just know I'm not in a place to date right now."

"I'm glad you told me. If you want to talk about it, just let me know." If it were me, I would have said "No worries" and then gotten off the call as quickly as possible.

After offering many more apologies to her, we finally hung up. I was expecting to feel a sense of ease, knowing I had cleared the path to my destiny. Instead, I was all-consumed with guilt and anxiety. I spent my evening eating the enchilada casserole I had planned for two while scouring the Internet for anything I could find about divine partners.

HOLY SHIT

The text from Naked and Afraid came in just like clockwork—one minute after her session with the psychic was supposed to end.

Right?!

She totally described my relationship. She said we were twin flames.

Twin flames?

Two people who share one half of the same soul who spend lifetimes trying to find their way back to each other to be whole again. They are like mirrors, reflecting each other's weaknesses, which can make things turbulent between them.

That made sense given their relationship was hot and cold, intense and tense, and so on fire that I believed the Earth spun better on its axis when she and her girlfriend, now rightfully referred to as Twin Flame, were in sync.

Do you believe her?

It explains so much. Plus, she knew a ton of other things she couldn't have known.

The whole situation seemed absolutely absurd. But something about this psychic felt so real. If she was right and Pants was my soulmate, I would have my answer. But then I might spend the rest of my life pining for someone who didn't realize our supposed soul connection, which would be worse than not finding my true love at all.

I needed assurance. So, I did what anyone would expect after getting advice from a clairvoyant they found online. I made an appointment with another . . . for a second opinion.

—

"What is your question?" she asked, leaning toward me.

Psychic number two didn't have the thick accent, nor did she look like a clip art fortune teller, as she instead had on jeans and a T-shirt. But the huge "Psychic" sign posted out front led me to believe she was the real deal.

I, too, leaned in, trying not to knock any of the crystals or candles off the card table. "What's going to happen with my love life?"

She shifted in her chair. "I must first tell you about a karmic partner who you split up with maybe six months ago. Sound familiar?"

The hair stood up on the back of my neck. "Yes."

She shared much of the same information about Runner that the first psychic did.

"As for the present, there is someone who has romantic feelings for you," she continued. "But the timing is off. You need to wait and work on yourself. Look for a shift within three months."

I gasped. *Three months? That's exactly what the other psychic had said.*

"Who is this?" I asked.

Without giving me a name, she too went on to describe Pants.

"Is she my divine partner?" I took a deep breath.

"It's unclear. The universe will know more later on. You may be together, or not. But likely not because you won't want to wait for her and might just move on. More will be revealed in three months."

As soon as we were done, I called Naked and Afraid and filled her in.

"Should I sit tight for the next three months . . . see if Pants changes her mind? Should I reach out to a third psychic? Maybe the tiebreaker one says there is no future relationship with anyone and that I'm gonna die alone. Then do I consult a fourth?" My voice sped up as the questions poured out.

"Just live your truth, and everything will unfold as it's supposed to. Remember . . . Zen."

Yeah, right. That whole Zen thing again.

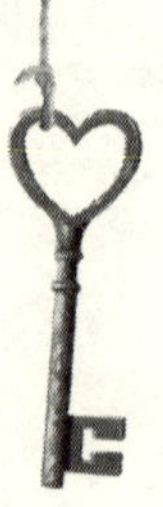

Hanging On

"Thank you for applying to the Coyote Buttes North (The Wave) Permit Lottery. The lottery drawing recently took place and, unfortunately, your application wasn't selected for a permit at Coyote Buttes North Advanced Lottery (The Wave)."

Oh no.

Shortly after, I got a text from Pants. She had gotten the same email.

I scrambled to try to salvage the situation and pitched her my wild idea—head out to Utah for our original dates in early March and try for a walk-in permit.

She was on board. We set up a time to talk a few days later to discuss logistics.

Right before 6:00 p.m. on the night of our call, I went to my office and settled into my desk chair so I could take notes as we chatted.

I stared over at the phone, waiting for her name to pop up on the screen. It finally did. But I let it ring twice before answering.

We caught up for a few minutes and then jumped into trip planning.

"How long do you want to go for?" I asked. "I mean, it's a long drive to Utah for both of us to hang out for only one day."

"Yeah, longer than a day, for sure."

All I could think was, *I'm planning a trip with Pants. Breathe, Corey.*

"Maybe get there Monday and leave on Friday? We try for the permit and then do other fun stuff the rest of the time?" I asked.

"That sounds good. Do you like rappelling?"

"Yeah!" The word came out, and I couldn't unsay it.

Terrifying images of my only experience rappelling flashed through my mind. The guides had to deal with my constant delay tactics with each descent, and the tears . . . so many tears. I think they cried, too.

"Let's definitely add that to the list," she said.

"Sounds good!" I summoned my repressed enthusiasm for getting to vacation with Pants and channeled it into fake excitement for scaling cliffs.

We finalized the schedule, which I typed into my meticulous notes, and we decided to divide and conquer the planning. After the call, I added the dates to my calendar . . . They were right before the end of the three-month psychic window.

Over the next week, despite my abhorrence for marriage, I began having fleeting daydreams of what appeared to be my future wedding. I was dressed in white, rappelling down the side of a mountain with my elusive partner, saying our vows in front of friends and family. Perhaps rappelling was top of mind from my conversation with Pants, or maybe it was just a symbol for doing something that terrified me. I wasn't sure. What I was sure of, though, was that in this vision, I couldn't wait to marry this person.

While hanging from the side of the cliff, I would say, "You are everything I have always dreamed of. And I can't imagine life without you."

Our eyes would lock, and we would know we had discovered an extraordinary love. There would be no fear, no regrets, and no hesitations . . . simply anticipation. We would then zip to the bottom and embrace, feeling as though we had saved each other's lives.

Around the same time these visions started, I also noticed a weird sensation on my left-hand ring finger. It felt as though something was missing. While I wore a ring when I was with Zion, nothing had been on that finger for years. Was I longing for something I finally realized I wanted? Had I watched too many Hallmark movies? Or was I ready to receive all the good that would come from being with the right partner? I had no idea.

If all of this wasn't odd enough, for days, a marriage mantra had been playing over and over in my head as well. One night, it wouldn't stop, so I wrote it down on an index card, slid it into an envelope, and signed across the seal. Once I stashed it in my nightstand drawer, the visions, phantom ring sensation, and mantra stopped. I had declared my feelings and intentions, and only the universe and I knew what was on that manifest.

It's That Time of Year

"You will never believe this!" I blurted out. "Runner sent me an email!"

It was late on a Monday night, and I was sure my call had woken Naked and Afraid from couch dozing.

"Well, what did it say?"

"Something about me blocking her from talking to Kiddo." I paused. "Let me just read it to you. Here's the greeting—'Hello' . . . no name included."

"Seriously?"

"Right?! And the rest of it looks like a template copied from some 'How to Send a Stern Email to Your Ex' book."

I then read her every line, some over again for emphasis. "I thought she would have sent an apology and not this, whatever *this* is."

Then, it occurred to me: The holidays were right around the corner, and feelings of nostalgia or even the need to complete unfinished business before the new year can set in.

"That is ridiculous. Do *not* write her back!"

"I'm not," I said. "I'm still doing no-contact."

"Good. You don't need to bring that negativity into your life."

"Exactly! You know what's funny, though? The anticipation of hearing from her was way worse than actually getting this message. Maybe I'm finally being a little Zen."

"I doubt that," she said and then laughed. "You've just moved on."

"Come over here," a short brunette from my lesbian Meetup group shouted from across the patio. She ushered me to a tall, round cocktail table where several other Meetup people were gathered. They were all wearing either silly Christmas sweaters or scantily clad Santa's-helper attire. No one could see my holiday llama shirt I had bought shortly after my vision that was now buried under my heavy coat. It was the perfect tribute to the tentative Christmas spirit I was feeling.

"Do a wall sit with me for two whole minutes." She walked a few feet over to the patio wall and pretended to sit in a chair propped against it. "Just like this."

"Count me in," Peace Corps said. She had come as my wing-woman. Thankfully, this happy hour was not at a marijuana bar.

Hippie pulled out her phone to start the timer. "First one to two minutes wins," she said as the three of us lined up to take a seat on our imaginary benches.

Peace Corps, with her long legs, went down right away, followed a minute later by the lady whose brilliant idea it was to squat for an extended period of time.

"How much longer?" I asked. My legs wouldn't stop shaking, and my quads were on fire.

"Thirty seconds," Hippie said.

Despite being the last one standing, I had to finish the entire challenge. And I did. My competitive spirit had lured me in. Perhaps I was channeling my seventh-grade self, who wanted to impress my new friends. Or maybe I just wanted to prove to myself I could accomplish whatever I set my mind to. Either way, I could barely walk the next day.

"All this dating stuff is ridiculous. It's like all I'm doing is overthinking. I analyze every message with Pants for psychic clues and reflect on every conversation I've had with Birds to see if she lines up with my love manifest. I've even been fixated on trying to figure out why people on the apps aren't messaging me back after all that apple-of-my-eye stuff. I mean that Reiki Lady texts every once in a while, but no new prospects." I let out a huge breath.

I heard Naked and Afraid laugh through the phone. Meanwhile, I was completely exhausted with myself.

"You can't keep going on like this," she said. "How many times have I told you to go with the flow?"

"I know. I'm gonna use the Law of Attraction to help me release this death grip on my dating life. When my mind kicks into overanalysis and I go into controlling mode, I'll divert my attention to other things, like those that bring me joy."

"So, you want to control being controlling? I'm not sure that's how the Law of Attraction works."

I found a book about not overthinking.

Naked and Afraid responded right away.

I like that, taking a studied and researched approach.

I have to overthink how I want to stop overthinking.

I let out a laugh when I sent the text. But then I thought, *Overthinking and trying to control everything isn't funny; it's painful.*

I knew in that very moment I had to be done with it. No more dating apps; no more fixation on specific outcomes; no more overanalyzing everyone else's behavior. I *had* to just let life unfold, healing and finding love however it was meant to happen.

After my revelation, I looked at the calendar and noticed it was December 18, a unique anniversary date for me. That same day, at age fourteen, I gave up chocolate to prove I could conquer my obsession with Girl Scout cookies and Twix bars. Here I was, thirty-four chocolate-free years later, abandoning another obsession—my relentless quest to find my one true love. The Zen Master buried deep inside of me finally exhaled.

The Holiday

> My mom is going to ask if I've seen The Holiday, like she does every year, to which I will respond, "Yes, like 25 times, and all with you." She will still suggest we watch it again on DVD, which she owns. Then she will tell me she doesn't know how to switch over the TV to watch the DVD. She will make me get the whole thing working and then fall asleep 10 minutes into it, leaving me to watch this ridiculous heterosexual rom-com alone!

While I joked about it with Pants, I knew it was only a matter of time before Mom dug out the DVD. Regardless of how many times I had seen this movie, I always rolled my eyes, thinking about the completely nonsensical holiday flick that reminds us that we too can have magic if we just have enough money, time, and trust in strangers.

It was almost Christmas, and Mom had yet to mention watching it. So, I kept quiet. The idea of having to sit through a movie about magical love seemed hollow. I hadn't experienced *pow*, *boom*, *bang* during my six-month stretch of singlehood. And no visions of sugarplums danced in my head, only ones of llamas and my rappelling wedding.

"Check this out!" I sifted through the bin and pulled out a headband with two springs sticking out from the top, a reindeer head on each. I slipped it on and shouted, "Come dance with me!" and then began rocking out to "Carol of the Bells" while both Rudolphs bobbed around.

Kiddo and Mom just watched and laughed.

After my solo dancing, I decided it was time to face the real music—decorating the Christmas tree without Runner. I took a deep breath and opened the box of ornaments. As soon as I began rummaging around, I remembered she had taken all of hers, including the little plush wolf that resembled her . . . albeit in wolf form. The matching fox ornament that looked remarkably like me, if I were a fox, still sat in the box, along with others that held great backstories of our time together. I felt a little twinge in my heart.

"This one," I said, as I held up a tiny Louisville Slugger bat, "is from Kentucky when we did that epic cross-country road trip. Remember?" I asked Kiddo.

She nodded.

I then took out a small plastic plate ornament with "Las Vegas 5K" written on it.

"You all don't know this story. It's from a race Runner and I did one New Year's Eve when it was freezing." I laughed, a welcome relief from what was starting to be a sad journey down memory lane. "We were, like, the only people who showed up."

They both let out awkward laughs.

We finished decorating the tree but not absent all my grand tales about each of the many ornaments I had collected over the years.

While sitting on the couch admiring our work of art, I handed Kiddo a bag. "I got you a couple of new ornaments."

She pulled out a wad of tissue paper and gently unwrapped a miniature glass poodle.

"It's just like Grandma's!" She ran over to the tree and hung it right in front of one of the twinkle lights.

"There's another in there," I said, as she sped back to the couch.

She rustled around in the bag and out came a small, furry black-and-white cat. "Wow! It looks just like Phoenix!"

The kitty ornament found its place next to the glass poodle. As I stood back and looked at the tree all decorated and lit up, I was reminded that Runner would never see these additions to the collection. Tears filled my eyes, but I quickly wiped away any evidence that Christmas wasn't cheery.

We all headed to the kitchen to prepare the fondue dinner, our tree-decorating-night tradition. Kiddo started getting food out from the fridge while Mom set the table.

"Why don't you move that placemat down closer to us?" Kiddo asked her. "There's a weird space between you and Mama."

I looked over and saw the emptiness.

"No one is sitting there anymore," Kiddo said.

We all froze. Mom then slid her placemat next to mine, and we all ate dinner as if that space had never been filled by someone else. But I knew it had, and even with Mom there, it still felt a little vacant.

The next day was Christmas Eve, and the three of us made the drive to Mom's condo in Phoenix to continue the festivities.

After the obligatory white elephant gift exchange with my brother and his family, we all went to the clubhouse to count the number of uninterrupted volleys my brother and I could do on the Ping-Pong table. It was nice to be out of that funk that got in the way of playing eight-ball with him on our trip months earlier.

We finished out the night eating dessert and playing the game I won during the gift exchange. Although everything seemed fun, lively, jovial, and all the other festive Christmas words, I felt like a dark cloud was hovering over me. Unlike the lightness of magic, this was the heaviness of unmagic. And I just couldn't shake it.

"Why does Christmas just suck?" I bawled into the phone, barely able to catch my breath. "It's not that I miss Runner. I just want to feel magic. I want someone to love me. And I want someone to love back. And that isn't happening." I wiped my runny nose across my sleeve as I scurried along the walking path near Mom's condo.

"It's gonna be hard, this first one," Naked and Afraid said. "Keep doing things that bring you joy. Like walking,"

"I know, but it still sucks," I said, tears running down my face.

"Just get through today. Now, did you see that link I sent you?"

"What link? You send me like ten a day."

"The one from this morning—about that new Netflix movie."

I slowed my pace so I wouldn't trip while scrolling back through our text thread. "Uh, yeah. I haven't opened it yet, though. What's it about?"

And, from there, our discussion meandered from the movie to holiday traditions to mundane current events. We never revisited how much Christmas sucked.

After we hung up, I had a cold sweat on my forehead, five miles on my tracker, and no tears left to cry. It wasn't the Christmas magic I'd imagined, but at least I could feel the dark clouds clearing and the unmagic lifting. And that was a start.

Maybe a love story like *The Holiday*, where characters travel to the ends of the earth to find magic, was hokey. But it also made a lot of sense. Perhaps ending my relentless quest for love had been a *bit* premature.

What's in a Date?

Thursday was filled with constant drizzle and frigid temperatures. I was sure I would get a text from Birds saying, "Terrible weather. Not gonna make it tonight." But with no message ten minutes out, I grabbed my jacket, hat, and gloves and made the drive over to meet up for our third Tumamoc walk.

When I got there, not a soul was in sight, except for her. She was stretching on the bench, seemingly unbothered by the rain.

She looked over at me. I smiled, and she smiled back.

We started to make our way up the hill, picking up where we left off during our second walk the week before when we exchanged funny grad school stories and online dating woes. Just when it seemed we had the place to ourselves, a shirtless man, huffing and puffing, jogged up the steep incline, passing us. She and I swapped smirks and then went back to our conversation.

By the time we had returned to the bottom, the rain was coming down harder, and the temperature had plummeted. We stood there anyway.

"Hey, as much as I love chatting on our walks, do you maybe wanna hang out sometime outside of Tumamoc?" My voice sounded shaky as I uttered the words, but I was proud I had the guts to ask.

"Sure," she said. "What did you have in mind?"

"Maybe dinner?"

"I'm not going out a lot with the pandemic, but we could eat at one of our houses."

"That sounds good. I'll be in Phoenix this weekend for New Year's. But how about Sunday night after I get back? I can make enchiladas."

"Works for me."

We said our goodbyes, and I walked away with a huge grin. *Only three days until I see her again.*

⟷

"Do you think she's assuming it's a date? Or maybe she sees this as just being friendly? And what does 'hang out' mean? Like, I hang out with people all the time and don't want to date them. Should I have said, 'Do you want to go on a date with me?'?" I had called Naked and Afraid in a frenzy on the way home to process.

She cut me off mid-spiral. "Chill out! Who knows? Just wait and see."

"You always tell me that."

"Because it's what you need to do!" She paused. "I thought you were gonna stop obsessing about your love life and finally embrace your Zen."

"Yeah, easier said than done."

⟷

A few days later, I had settled into the fact that my date proposal with Birds was unclear. Regardless, I was still excited about the chance to see her outside of Tumamoc. *What would she be wearing? What would we talk about? Could she really be everything on my love manifest?*

I couldn't stop thinking about her . . . that was until an interesting news story appeared in my feed. The headline read: "Most

Common Zodiac Signs of Serial Killers." *Pants loves crime shows.* So, I forwarded her the link with a message.

What's your sign? Just need to know if I should bring my coyote siren to Utah. I'm Virgo. Pretty harmless!

😂😂 You better worry . . . I'm a Cancer!!!

My stomach dropped, not because her sign topped the list as most likely to murder me, but because of the faint whisper in my ear. "I'm also picking up a water sign . . . Cancer, maybe."

Oh shit. The psychic.

A Lot Can Happen in a Year

On New Year's Eve, Kiddo and I drove to Phoenix for New Year's festivities. I was excited to have a bit of a reprieve from my revived soulmate search and just enjoy time with family.

Shortly before the ball drop that night, there we were, all of us . . . attempting to do the Cupid Shuffle in my brother's living room. Although the instructional video had us repeating the same few steps, none of us seemed to figure out the choreography.

Memories of us attempting this dance the year before flashed through my mind. We had followed the online tutorial in much the same fashion—my brother kicking out of unison, Mom spinning the wrong way, and all of us crashing into each other—all of us except Runner, who instead sat on the couch.

"Hey, come show us your moves," I said to her.

"I'm good. Just going to watch and take pictures."

But she wasn't watching or taking pictures. She was barely present.

"No, seriously. It's fun!" I said.

"You all dance. I'm just gonna do my thing." I could see her thumbs pounding away as she typed on her phone.

Only days earlier, we had started the Marriage Fitness boot camp program and recommitted to reconciliation after our "I know how much you love warm tortilla chips" break. This did not look like reconciliation to me.

A darkness came over me, like a heavy, sopping-wet blanket of despair and regret. Looking back, I realized that was my intuition, and it was saying, "She's not in this, Corey. What are you doing? You want better. You want more." Apparently, my intuition wasn't broken after all. I just didn't want to see the red flag.

After we got into bed that night, I asked her why she hadn't danced with us. She went on about how she had to text with her new lesbian friend who was going through a breakup.

My face grew hot; it felt like *Fun Home* all over again.

I lay there, angry and hurt, with major doubts swirling in my head. But I ignored them and instead followed the advice of my alter ego, The General, who had been pressing for me to work things out with her and save this relationship. Giving up would be a sign of monumental failure.

Now here we were, one year later, my first New Year's post-breakup. My family was again trying to master the Cupid Shuffle. I didn't sense a dark despair overhead or horrible feeling in the pit of my stomach . . . because no one was there to remind me of what I didn't want.

I climbed into bed that night and thought about how last New Year's Eve, I was heartbroken and empty with Runner next to me. But now, I felt empowered and fulfilled, even though I was alone. I stretched out like a starfish and fell fast asleep.

A lot can happen in a year.

I woke up the next morning and saw the sunrise peeking over the horizon through the window. The house was quiet, as the late-night dancing had seemed to wear everyone out.

I slid my laptop out of my backpack, waited for it to boot up, and then opened the spreadsheet where I logged my miles.

My walking quest began years earlier, in 2020, when Runner, Kiddo, and I signed up for the 52 Hike Challenge. It involved walking or hiking for at least thirty minutes on fifty-two different occasions . . . in theory, once a week. However, by early May, we had completed them all, having logged 128 miles.

After finishing the challenge, neither of them wanted to continue. But I did. So nearly every day, I would make the loop around the neighborhood by myself. The distance was 3.14 miles, the same as the mathematical ratio pi. By the end of 2020, I had walked more than 1,000 miles.

I kept up with the challenge once 2021 rolled around. The more I walked, the better my body felt. My creaky knees creaked less, and my tight back loosened up. My cardio health skyrocketed, and the extra weight started coming off. *Walk pi instead of eat pie*, I would say to myself.

Despite my fast pace, I would always stop and snap a few photos of a beautiful skyscape, the desert scenery, or the many critters out and about. Then, I would send them to TikTok out in Ohio.

Here's a cool picture of a javelina.

What's a javelina?

It's like a big, hairy pig.

Why on earth would you walk with oversized wild pigs?

I love the desert. I couldn't imagine it any other way.

And I couldn't.

While the health benefits and scenic views offered quite the draw to my die-hard routine, logging miles provided me with an unparalleled sense of achievement. Some days I baked in the sun, drenched with sweat. And others, I wore three layers of clothes. When it was pouring, I put on a jacket and let the drops roll off my sleeves. I walked no matter what.

Many people kept me company on my quest in 2021—political pundits bantering about the latest issues and musicians playing their tunes. Later on, I added breakup podcast hosts with horrible relationship stories, and authors, like Gabrielle Stone, who wrote *Eat, Pray, #FML*, and John Kim, who authored *Single on Purpose*.

I also enjoyed the nice lady on my Law of Attraction podcast, along with all the narrators from the manifesting audiobooks I binged—particularly those from *The Secret* and *The Secret to Relationships*. Sometimes, though, I found my walks were best spent catching up on the phone with Mom, TikTok, or Naked and Afraid.

Walking saved me, in every way I could imagine.

As I sat there in bed on the first day of January, two years after the start of this challenge, I looked at the total on my spreadsheet for the past year: 1,823 miles, 623 more than my initial goal. But I wanted something more ambitious for 2022. I got dressed, tiptoed through the house, and snuck out the front door for my first walk of the new year. I only had 2,022 miles to go, and I couldn't wait to get started.

Part 3

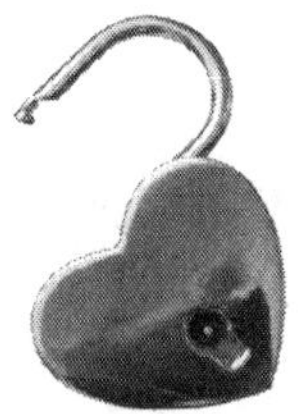

Getting Through

Little Glass Bowls

"Delayed until four." *That will put me back an hour, but I can still make it to Tucson in time to make the enchiladas.*

Ten minutes later, I refreshed the flight status screen. "Delayed until four thirty."

I gasped and then fired off a message to Birds.

My daughter's flight is a bit delayed. I have stuff for enchiladas if you want to come over around seven instead.

This situation did not feel like an opportunity to "go with the flow" or be Zen. The whole thing just felt stressful.

Well, since you are coming from Phoenix, would it be easier to come here? I don't know how to make enchiladas but could make tacos or burritos.

I exhaled. Relieved, but still not Zen.

Thanks! That would be great. I'm not sure if I mentioned it, but I'm a vegetarian. I eat just about anything except meat. So, beans, cheese, veggies, rice, etc. are all awesome.

I'm veggie, too.

Check another item off the love manifest for Birds—vegetarian. Pants, on the other hand, could wolf down a rack of ribs in no time. *Cancer sign or not, would my divine partner really eat meat off the bone?*

As soon as Kiddo's flight took off, I raced to Tucson and parked in front of what the GPS said was Birds's house. I darted through the gate, past her yard, overflowing with trees, plants, and succulents, and tapped on the door. Within moments, it opened, and she greeted me with a huge smile.

As soon as I walked in, I noticed the walls were decorated with pictures of animals, mostly birds, and her shelves were filled with travel and wildlife books. Several potted plants were placed throughout, precisely located to soak in the sunlight from her large windows.

She had on a T-shirt and jeans, along with slippers adorned with embroidered birds. Her long hair was pulled back in a loose bun, like she usually had it.

We immediately made our way into the kitchen, where the wafting aroma of grilled peppers and onions filled the air. I noticed several little glass bowls on the counter with various toppings, including cabbage, avocado, and all the other fixings. Nobody had ever put out glass bowls for me before.

"I picked up some cheese too." She opened the fridge to show me the package. "I'm not a huge fan, but I remember you saying you like it."

"I do! Thanks!"

"I like cheese on pizza, though."

After discussing our shared love of pizza, I talked about New Year's with my family while she finished cooking.

Once dinner was ready, she handed me a plate, and we each filled our warm tortillas with a mound of veggies and all the goodies from the little glass bowls. She doused her burrito with hot sauce, which I opted to pass on.

I followed her into the living room, and we both sat on the couch.

"So, what was it like studying all that science stuff in grad school?" With the coffee table as our dining hub, I leaned over and took a bite. The spicy veggies offered quite the kick, even without the hot sauce.

"Hard, but fun. I love figuring out why things are the way they are."

"That's so interesting," I said. "I study how people *feel* about why things are the way they are."

We both laughed.

She talked more about her research, then I shared about mine. She understood what I did, and that was refreshing.

"So, why Tucson?" I asked. "When we were on the hike, you said you loved it here. What do you love about it?" I took another big bite.

"The warmth and the sunshine. I just didn't like driving in the snow or freezing to death."

"Me too! I know it's hot here in summer. But I'd take that over the cold. You know, you never have to dig your car out of sunshine."

She let out a small laugh.

While finishing off our burritos, we went on to talk about our dream jobs. I told her I'd always wanted to be a professor, so I *was* doing my dream job.

"Mine would be working on the set of a David Attenborough show . . . You know him, right? *Please* tell me you know him."

"Isn't he some wildlife guy?" That was my best guess.

"Yep. I'd want to do some behind-the-scenes stuff for one of his nature shows."

Hours passed, and we hadn't even taken a break to bring our dirty dishes to the kitchen. But around nine thirty, I noticed her heavy eyelids.

"You look tired," I said. "I should get going."

"Oh, I'm good." She sat a little more upright on the couch, took a drink of water, and shot me a big smile.

We continued to chat for a while longer. But I, too, was getting tired. So, we wrapped up our conversation and headed to the kitchen with our plates.

"Here," she said as she put out her hand. I gave her my dirty dish. She took it over to the counter and set it next to hers and all the little half-empty glass bowls. "I can clean up later."

She then turned around and began walking toward the doorway where I was standing. The General was yelling in my head, "Ask her out—for real this time!"

"Tumamoc on Thursday?" came tumbling out of my mouth. *Oh no!* I gasped inside. That wasn't asking her out. I just confirmed plans we already had to go on the walk we usually went on.

"Sure. Works for me."

I scurried back into the living room, realizing I couldn't salvage the situation. So, I said a quick goodbye and ran out the front door. So much for my big-girl pants.

The next morning, I woke up kicking myself for missing my chance with Birds. So, I wrote her a text. And then I rewrote it . . . and rewrote it again. Finally, I landed on what I thought blended a little wit and a tad of flirt.

> Thanks for dinner last night. It was fun to chat and eat some good food—not too spicy, by the way! You up for some enchiladas Thursday after Tumamoc? Or maybe this weekend? I can definitely go easy on the cheese and heavy on the spice.

After an hour passed with no reply, I needed Naked and Afraid to talk me off the ledge.

I texted Birds about dinner a while ago.
Waiting for a response.

Just chill out. This lady has a life.

I waited a bit longer and then messaged Naked and Afraid again.

No word from Birds. Texted three hours ago. ?????
Maybe tomorrow . . .

Yes. Tomorrow.

The next day, I started into a small tailspin with Naked and Afraid.

Crickets—sent at seven last night.

Sometimes I fall asleep that early on the couch or whatever. Don't take it personally.

Okay. Hopefully, I hear back from her today.

I'm sure you will.

I hadn't heard from my supposed divine partner, Pants, in days. And now Birds, the epitome of my love manifest, was ghosting me. Maybe neither were "the one."

Twenty-four hours after my initial text, I finally got a response from Birds. She apologized and let me know that between work and crashing early the night before, things had been hectic.

Enchiladas would be lovely, and Thursday after Tumamoc would work great.

I let out a sigh, both because I wasn't ghosted *and* because she used the word *lovely*. I couldn't wait until Thursday.

"Maybe she thinks we're just friends," I told Peace Corps as we strolled down Tumamoc. "I mean it did take her twenty-four hours to respond to my dinner invitation."

"You have to let it play out. Sometimes you just don't know."

I still wanted to know. So later that day, I called TikTok. *Surely, she'll have some good insight.*

"When she comes over, be direct," TikTok offered. "Flirt a little. Say this: 'I think you are really attractive. I'd like to take you out on a date.'"

"Um, that's too forward for me."

"Okay. Okay. Just practice on me. We'll role-play."

I would have rather died than do a role-play. "Oh . . . I'm good."

The day before my dinner, I met up with Speedy at Tumamoc for an early morning walk. We had spent much of the time deconstructing the situation when she finally said, "If you don't know if it's a date, make a move and see what she does." She then laughed.

I stared at her, eyes wide open.

"I mean, you have to read the situation. If she looks interested, go in for the kiss."

My face grew warm, more so than it did on the uphill we tackled earlier. "I couldn't tell you what 'interested' looks like. So, there is no scenario in this world that would involve me doing that."

"How about this then? 'Might you be interested in exploring possibilities beyond friendship?'"

I gasped. The awful memory of the "for now" text exchange

with Pants came flooding back. Even The "take-charge, get rid of ambiguity" General cringed hearing those words. But I knew I had to ask.

I spent the next twenty-four hours practicing the line—in my head and out loud to the kitty. "Might you be interested in exploring possibilities beyond friendship?" I hated the sound of it. But I hated ambiguity more.

I finally took a break from rehearsing and sent a text to Naked and Afraid.

Only eight more hours.

Seriously? You're counting down?

I count down every time I get to see her.

I looked at the clock. Seven hours and fifty-six minutes to be exact.

Shortly after, a text came in from Speedy.

Don't forget . . . be bold!!! Play the Rocky theme song or "Eye of the Tiger" on your way to Tumamoc.

On my pre-dinner Tumamoc walk with Birds, I decided not to broach the subject of dating and instead kept the conversation light. Once we got to the bottom of the hill, we agreed to reconvene at my place forty-five minutes later.

I hadn't been home for long before Naked and Afraid started blowing up my texts.

Did you brush your teeth? Shower? Put on clean undies?

Doing that now! House is spotless, too. She went home to change. Heart pounding.

Ha ha . . . did you get any vibes?

Some. We'll see.

Good luck!

When Birds arrived, she took off her coat and draped it over the arm of my couch. She was wearing a striped sweater, jeans, and a pair of what looked like red bowling shoes. I wanted to make sure I asked her where she bought them. Her hair wasn't tied back as usual; instead, the thick, brown waves fell beyond her shoulders. She smelled good, like just-got-out-of-the-shower good.

We walked into the kitchen.

"So, I made veggie enchiladas. They should be about done." I pulled the pan out of the oven and piled a huge portion on each of our plates. I added a scoop of spicy black beans and a handful of tortilla chips.

We sat at the table for well over an hour, eating and delving deeper into conversation about school, work, and travels. The more we talked, the more obvious it became that she checked off every item on my love manifest. Plus, I found her quite attractive.

"I'm not sure if you need to head out or not. But if we want to keep chatting, my couch is a lot more comfortable than these hard wooden chairs." The words came out with more wit and flirt than I had expected.

"I'd love to stay for a bit."

I donned a huge grin.

We went into the living room, where she sat on the far end of my very large sectional. Without wanting to presume anything, I settled down on the other side. I had seen people at bus stops at the height of the pandemic sit closer than we were.

I made small talk, trying to drown out the line overtaking my thoughts. "Might you be interested in exploring possibilities beyond friendship?" The General wanted me to ask and ask now. The Zen Master hoped I would let things unfold naturally, even if tonight wasn't the night. But "naturally" in my book likely meant never as I had grown a little apprehensive of putting on my big-girl pants after the few instances that doing so blew up in my face.

"Well, I better head out. I have an early morning." She stood up and walked toward the end of the couch where I was still sitting. She then grabbed her coat and put one arm in the sleeve.

The General was screaming in my ear, "Just ask her!"

Instead of saying, "Might you be interested in exploring possibilities beyond friendship?" my hand gestures flew out of control, and I did what looked like several karate chops in the air. "So, what's going on here?" I nearly shouted, hands flailing about.

She stared at me. Momentary silence. "I don't know."

Oh my God! Why did I say it that way? Obviously, she was confused. And I was too.

"Is there something going on between us?" I asked. *Oh, no. That sounded demanding. Why am I messing this up?*

She tilted her head. "I don't know," she said again.

"You don't know if something is going on between us, or you don't know if you want something to go on between us?"

Semantics . . . important, but still highly confusing.

"Um . . . I'm good either way," she said.

I took a deep breath, and The Zen Master came to the rescue. "I like you and would love to go out on a date with you. Might you be interested in exploring possibilities beyond friendship?"

I did it! I put on my big-girl pants! Suddenly, though, I was overtaken with worry. *What if she isn't interested? What if she says, "for now"?*

Before I went into a complete tailspin, she said, "Okay. A date sounds good."

I let out a huge exhale, hoping she didn't notice. "How about Saturday? Maybe dinner again?"

"Sure."

I got up from the couch and went over to her. She was standing by my front door, coat on and zipped up now. More silence. *Am I supposed to kiss her now?* "Can I hug you goodbye?" I asked.

She came closer, wrapped her arms around me, and gave me a long, warm, tight embrace. As we were both pulling away from the hug, she went in for a kiss. It was soft and sweet, ushering in the kind of chemistry that says, "You will be safe and loved with this person."

Before I knew it, she left. When the door closed behind her, I noticed I was shaking. But the adrenaline rush was tempered by the feeling of her warmth still lingering in my body.

I actually did it. I pulled it together and asked her out. The General and The Zen Master both showed up, and they were a good team.

Both, And

After kicking off the new year with a lofty walking goal, I knew my baggy thrift-store workout pants weren't going to cut it. So, I ordered two pairs of track pants in the hopes that at least one would fit. As soon as they arrived, I tried them on. Both slid off my hips onto the floor. Return. My pants-buying exercise continued with two more orders of the wrong size and then their subsequent returns. After finding one more pair online, I made my purchase and went into another waiting period for their arrival.

During the week and a half of my track pants pursuit, things were quiet. I had ended my phone chats with Reiki a couple weeks earlier after my chocolate anniversary revelation, and I hadn't heard a word from Pants in over a week. It was the perfect opportunity for me to give a hundred percent of my attention to Birds. We had gone on a few dates—a hike, another dinner, and our weekly Tumamoc, and they were all "lovely."

> Going to the store tomorrow. Getting ice cream with toppings! I'm counting the hours until Birds comes over. ☺

TikTok responded right away.

Oh hell. #crushing

After the date, I regrouped with TikTok.

Best date ever. Wow. Amazing and really connecting. She is the real deal. Lives in Tucson. Has like every quality on my manifest. And she likes me. What more could I ask for? #donewithpants

Love a good hashtag.

I'm on day ten and nothing from Pants. The timing couldn't be better. I'm all in with Birds.

And all in I was.

That night, I rifled through my nightstand drawer, looking for the envelope I had signed and dated over a month earlier. I ripped it open, pulled out my handwritten marriage manifest, and tore it up. A sense of relief came over me. I wanted a fresh slate for Birds.

Hey, how's your new year going?

On day twelve of the text hiatus, a message came in from Pants. I paused my favorite medical drama and responded right away.

Awesome. Lots of hiking and catching up with folks after the holidays. How about you?

Ugh. Sucks so far.

I scooted up in bed and propped the pillows behind my back. The kitty, who was curled up next to me ready to turn in for the night, didn't seem to be bothered with all the commotion.

What's going on? Are you okay?

She continued with a few details about her dad having gone into the hospital for some ongoing medical issues.

I sat with him in the ER for six hours.

That sounds terrible. I'm so sorry to hear that. You want to pause Dateline or Survivor or the Celtics or Dexter or whatever and call me? We haven't chatted in a while.

Within one minute, the phone rang. We talked about how stressful everything had been. My heart sank, and I shared about what it was like when my dad had lung cancer six years earlier. While her situation was different, I knew how it felt to watch a sick parent go in and out of the hospital, never knowing if each day would be the last.

This conversation struck a chord with me—and not because I was talking about my dad. I had processed his death with many people over the years. Instead, it was the first time Pants and I had talked about anything serious like this. But before I could savor the depth of our discussion, she was onto a story about a patient vomiting in the ER.

"You know, I have second-hand vomiting issues. Like, if I see someone puking, I feel like I also have to," she said.

"I do too! I actually have an intense fear of it. What are we gonna do if one of us gets sick in Utah?"

"I'll get another hotel room and leave you in ours."

We both laughed.

"Fine, I'll do the same, then!"

We finally hung up, and the cosmos seemed to be back in alignment. I texted Naked and Afraid and filled her in.

Heard from Pants. She had some personal stuff she was dealing with and that's why she hasn't been texting.

Didn't the psychic say you two would be out of touch in January because of something she needed to take care of?

Oh my God. She did. What do I do?

Just be there for her. Be a good friend.

Why do I have tears in my eyes and feel like bawling? What the hell?

You like her.

Part of me was hoping we might just fade out. It would make things easier with Birds.

That doesn't look like it's gonna happen.

The new track pants arrived the very next day.

"Do they fit?" Naked and Afraid's voice boomed through the speakerphone.

"Yeah. I'm wearing them now." I looked at myself in the mirror. "It's weird, though. I looked for dress pants for months, and as soon as I meet Pants, *boom*, I find the perfect ones. Same thing with these track pants. It's like her presence summons pants into my life." I laughed.

"Or," Naked and Afraid said, "she is the force that brings you what you've been looking for."

Pants texted and told me she thought of me when her dog barfed in her bed this morning. She wanted to know how I felt about animal vomit. Definitely not the same kind of chemistry I have with Birds!

I was back at it, overanalyzing everything with Pants for any clues about our soulmate connection and filling Naked and Afraid in on all the details.

I think it's equally special and cute.

What should I do?

Cut things off with Pants and go all in with Birds.

When I read those words, it was like a boulder landed in the pit of my stomach.

No way. I'm not there yet.

Well, then stop seeing Birds to make room for Pants when she's ready.

I don't like that idea either.

I was overcome by the urge to pace, so I stepped outside onto my patio to continue our conversation on the phone.

As soon as Naked and Afraid answered, I jumped right in without even a "hello." "If I'm supposed to leave this stuff up to the universe, then why am I getting mixed messages? The psychics pointed me in one direction and my love manifest in another."

I started making circles around my patio furniture.

"You have to shift your mindset. What you are going through is a journey with yourself, not a quest to find someone else. Once you let go of that expectation, you can truly enjoy this time of self-reflection and growth. Focus on being the best version of you." She paused and then said, "Ooh, that's good. Like therapy-level, pay-me-the-copayment kind of good."

I stopped pacing. "Hmm, that's an interesting theory. I'll have to type it into a spreadsheet, overthink it, and then confirm it with a psychic."

She didn't laugh.

Oh, hell. Girl, ask her.

TikTok's boldness was both terrifying and motivating. She would have already shot off a text saying something like "Coming to town in a couple weeks. Let's hang out." *I wish I could be that forward. And, even if I was, after her "for now" text rejection, I'm not sure I could ask Pants anything ever again.*

Whispers of "big-girl pants" started repeating in my ear. I wasn't sure who was saying it, but I think this time it was me. So, I sat at my kitchen table for the next ten minutes, crafting and then repeatedly editing a message until it struck the perfect balance between a clear invite and a witty request.

So, I'm coming to CA next Friday for 8 days to spend time with Kiddo. Wanna hang out? I already have pants, so I'm good there. But I'm game for whatever—hike, gentle mountain-bike ride, Ping-Pong game, etc. What's your schedule like during the week when my kid is in school or either weekend on the front or back end?

I hit send and waited. No immediate response. I got up, put my dishes in the dishwasher, and started wiping down the counters. Minutes went by. No word back. I couldn't handle the anticipation and finally messaged TikTok.

Texted Pants. Radio silence. That was five minutes ago. That's forever in Pants's world to wait for a reply.

Now I had to wait for TikTok to respond. After a few minutes, she finally did.

Oh boy.

If she takes too long or waffles or makes some excuse, I know my answer.

Okay . . . give it fifteen.

Now it's been twelve.

Is it odd she didn't respond right away?

When I asked if she wanted to explore something beyond friendship, she wrote me right back. That seems like a much more difficult text to reply to than "Wanna hike in a couple weeks?"

I don't know, hon.

I started scrubbing an area of the counter I had already cleaned.

I might reach out to her . . . "You still there?"

I put the sponge down and took a breath. I knew right then I needed to turn my focus to Birds, who, unlike Pants, did seem interested in seeing me.

I'll check in with her tomorrow. I'm heading to bed soon. Then, when I wake up, it will be only twelve hours until I see Birds, which makes me super happy to think about. I'm so confused.

A few minutes later, Pants replied. I texted TikTok to fill her in on how the saga ended.

She wants to hang out. She even suggested two days, stopping there on my drive back to Arizona. Woohoo!

You are on fire.

Shit. What am I doing?

Babe. You need to pump the brakes on Birds. Figure out Pants first.

As I read the words, I felt the boulder again, right in the pit of my stomach. *I don't want to lose my chance with Birds. But I also don't want to cut things off with Pants.*

I finally had to face the reality that the universe had a plan that would unfold in its own time—because no matter how much I tried to get clarity, I only made things worse.

Right after the breakup, I subscribed to every astrology, soulmate, tarot, and horoscope email list I could find. But that meant that every day, there would be hordes of messages from the universe, ready for me to peruse and glean all sorts of insight from.

After a few days of carrying around my uncertainty boulder, I woke to my normal barrage of emails from the cosmos to find one that described the romantic compatibility of Virgo with different astrological signs.

Whose do I click on first? Pants or Birds?

Given all the hoopla with the psychic around Pants's sign, I went with Cancer. It said: "Consider an act of kindness to enhance your connection, like buying cupcakes for one another."

Cupcakes? What kind of weird advice is that?

I read it again. *Oh my God. The Suns game.*

Back in early December, Pants took me up on a proposition: loser of the Suns/Celtics game would buy the winner a cupcake. On the night of the game, we feverishly exchanged texts as she watched on TV and I sat at my kitchen table refreshing my phone for the latest score, given I was too frugal to invest in cable.

This game is like Dateline. Just like the victims in your crime shows, the Celtics are getting murdered. Ha. Took me two whole minutes to come up with that one!

😂😂 Except not murdered yet! On life support. Right now, attempted murder charge.

Laughed my ass off on that one. If the game ends with more than a twenty-point lead, I think I deserve this . . .

I sent a picture of a dozen cupcakes.

Nope. We bet one. LOL

Alright. I'll double down for the next game.

I'm turning this crap off.

On New Year's Eve, the teams squared off again, and we had another bet.

Celtics up by twenty-three at the end of the third. ☹

Woohoo!!!! All I'm winning is not having to buy you a cupcake. LOL

Nope! I still want mine. I'll have to suck it up and get you one too.

I was so overwhelmed about the horoscope cupcake message, I forgot to read about Birds's sign.

Spinning Sisters

"Am I just holding out for some fairy tale that's never gonna happen with Pants? Be honest."

Naked and Afraid and I huffed up the long beginning stretch of Tumamoc. She always started off too fast on the easy incline, leaving us out of breath just moments into the hike.

"No! You are literally going on two trips with her over the next few weeks," she said. "And she's your supposed divine partner . . . which I totally believe."

"But what if I'm just sabotaging any possibility with Birds by clinging onto this fantasy? I mean, here's Birds, someone who may very well move mountains for me." I gasped for a few breaths. "And Pants, who has had every opportunity to and hasn't. It's just like what I did with Runner—hanging onto false hope in a situation that doesn't serve me."

Naked and Afraid began weaving in and out of the slower walkers, one of which was a lady trying to usher her toddler up the hill. I zigzagged around them as well, staying on Naked and Afraid's heels.

"This is nothing like the Runner thing," she shouted over her shoulder. "Just keep moving forward with both of them and see what happens."

We then skirted past a man pushing an empty baby stroller up the path. I glanced back at the mom with the toddler. *Lady, just put him in the stroller*, I thought. Then, flashes of the years I spent doing this hill with Kiddo in my baby backpack sent a wave of empathy through me.

"You have a ton of time left in the three-month window," she continued. "And a lot is going to happen between now and then."

"I still need to figure out at least what *I* want. Maybe if I add some new things to the plan."

She nearly cut me off. "Tell your little general to be patient. You'll figure it out . . . in time."

"Okay, but until then, you know this is all we'll be talking about. And I'm gonna want to process the same stuff over and over."

She threw her hands up to the sky. "I know. *That's* why we have Tumamoc!"

I smiled. I had finally convinced her of the correct pronunciation, making it a lot more tolerable when she said it.

"I know it can be annoying sometimes," I said. "But talking about all this as much as we do is actually super helpful. I learn something new every time."

"Well, good. I'm not annoyed yet."

"I have an idea," I said, slowing my pace just a bit, both for a dramatic pause and to breathe.

She turned her focus from the path over to me. "Uh oh. What's your idea?"

"What if we recorded our conversations—like on a podcast?" I asked.

"Sign me up!" She started bounding up the incline with newfound energy.

I sped up too. "We could talk about everything! It could be more therapy for us. Well, maybe not the intimate details about the psychics and my torment between Birds and Pants."

I laughed. "But what we've learned through our heartbreak and healing so other people could avoid making the same mistakes."

She jumped in. "We should do an episode on the witching hours . . . and one on dealing with friends and families when you're dating someone. Also, one on the no-contact rule."

"We could be the Spinning Sisters," I said, already thinking of branding. "We spin around and around, processing different issues . . . kind of like we do when we talk for real."

As we approached a group of teens taking a water break on the steep curve, several turned their attention to our loud chatter. I didn't care. My adrenaline was flowing, and I was now cruising up, hardly out of breath.

"Let's do it!" she said. "But I definitely think we should bring up the psychics."

While I wasn't sure about that, I was sure that "Do a podcast on relationships" had to go in The Plan.

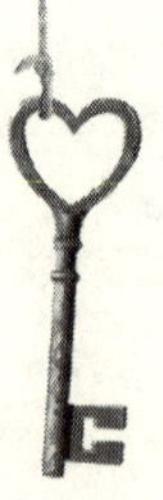

Pickleball Chicks

"What exactly is pickleball?" one of the women from the Meetup group asked.

We had just circled up in the parking lot after finishing yet another amazing hike. I was able to squeeze this one in just before my trip to California.

"It's like Ping-Pong, but on a miniature tennis court," I said, as I sat my pack on the ground.

"I'm training to play competitively. I think I can win some tournaments. Corey's gonna be my partner," Naked and Afraid said.

"I've only played once. Naked and Afraid has high expectations for me."

Everyone laughed.

After several expressed interest in playing, one of the women said, "I'll put together a text for all of us so we can connect. I'll label it the Pickleball Chicks."

The next day, the "Pickleball Chicks" all met up, ready to go.

"You just drop the ball and swing the paddle straight on," Naked and Afraid said.

"Like this?" someone asked. She sent the plastic pickleball flying way over the back court line. We all laughed . . . except Naked and Afraid, who looked like a frustrated teacher with a child who wouldn't listen.

"No. Just soft and flat." Naked and Afraid demonstrated the proper swing. "Let's just start, and it will make more sense."

While Naked and Afraid was conducting her clinic, Hippie and I walked across the court to get some water.

"Guess what?" I leaned in and said in a loud whisper, "I'm dating someone."

"Really? Who?" she asked.

"Remember the hike we did back in December?" I grabbed my bag from the bench and rustled around in it to get my water bottle.

She looked up, as though trying to recall which of the many hikes it could have been.

"The one where the lady fell," I said, and then took a big swig.

"Are you dating the falling lady?" she whispered.

"Yeah." I smirked. "That seventy-year-old who had never hiked!"

She laughed. "I didn't want to make any assumptions."

"No! But it's someone who was on *that* hike."

A ball soared over to us, and we both glanced at the court.

"No, no, no!" Naked and Afraid shouted over the chatter and laughter.

Hippie turned back to me. "I know! The bird lady!"

I nodded and smiled.

"That's so cool. I'm really happy for you two," she said. "You know—I've met so many new friends through Meetup. I don't even have time to date."

"Break's over, ladies!" Naked and Afraid yelled in our direction.

Neither of us responded. At this point, she had everybody lined up on the baseline practicing their serves.

"Good grief," I mumbled and then shot Hippie a wink. "Anyway, I couldn't agree more—about the awesome people in Meetup, not the 'no time to date' part." I laughed. "Truly, though, I'm not sure how I would have made it through these last six months without all of you, and especially Naked and Afraid."

Signs, Signs Everywhere

Lauren's son has COVID. I had dinner with them on Friday, and I know you and I hung out this weekend. I booked a test for tomorrow morning.

My blood turned cold, and the hair on my neck stood up. I ran my dinner plate to the dishwasher and then texted Naked and Afraid.

Birds might have COVID. You and Twin Flame will want to test since we all hung out on Saturday night.

I'm sure we're fine. Are you sick? What about your trip this weekend?

I feel okay. But if she's positive and I'm negative, we can't see each other for two weeks. And if I do have it, I won't be able to go to California, which means no Kiddo or clarity weekend with Pants. Oh, the universe . . .

The next afternoon, I heard from Birds.

Results were positive 😨. Hope you are okay.

I gasped for air. It was like an elephant had just stepped on my chest . . . and right before I had to teach, no less. That felt familiar.

My mind went into a spiral. *What if I have COVID too? If I do, I can't see Pants or my kid . . . not to mention, I could get sick and die. If I don't, I won't get to see Birds before I leave at the end of the week. And what if she gets really sick while I'm off hiking with Pants?*

I texted Naked and Afraid with the update. She responded immediately.

COVID does not scare me!

Well, it scares me.

The next morning, I drove across town to take my COVID test and then spent the afternoon hiking with Naked and Afraid, who didn't care in the least whether I might be positive. Despite her lack of worry, *I* had a lingering fear in the back of my mind that the results would come back, and I'd have to call off my trip to California.

That evening, I got the email in my inbox. I stared at it for a while before opening it. Finally, I did.

"NEGATIVE."

I let out a huge exhale. The visit with Kiddo—and Pants—was still on.

There wasn't much time to celebrate. The next morning, I got a message from Naked and Afraid.

Shit.

In came a screenshot of her positive COVID test.

When did you take that?

Tuesday.

That was two days ago. And you just got your results? I spent the whole afternoon with you yesterday, unmasked—in your car, in your house, hiking.

Twin Flame has it too.

There is no way I'm dodging the COVID bullet twice.

"Negative again! I don't know how that's even possible," I yelled, staring at my swab kit on the bathroom counter. "I'm literally supposed to leave in two hours."

Naked and Afraid's voice came through my earbuds. "It's a miracle. The universe is telling you to go on this trip so you can get clarity."

Suddenly, a text came across my screen.

"Hold on," I said. "I just got a message from Pants."

It was a meme of a tiny dog, bundled in a fleece, with the caption, "Me . . . as soon as the temperature drops two degrees, and I feel a little breeze." She then added:

So you.

"How did she know to text me right when I got the results—results that would determine whether or not I would see her?" I asked Naked and Afraid.

"You know why."

"I don't want to let go of the possibility of Birds, but the signs for Pants are relentless. Remember when I saw that exit sign with her last name on the way to my stepmom's? I mean, I had never seen that exit before and then she texts me as I'm passing it. That's just bizarre . . . And the fact that she's a Cancer, just like the psychic said . . . And the whole cupcake astrology email."

"Well, you should pay attention to these signs. Obviously, you were meant to go on this trip."

After hanging up, I looked at my COVID test once more, just to double check, and then tossed it in the trash. I wandered back into my bedroom. As I stuffed clothes into my suitcase, I heard Naked and Afraid's voice in my head: "You should pay attention to these signs."

I was just minutes out from leaving for California, two negative COVID tests later, ready to exchange cupcakes with Pants. I guess the universe finally decided to stop being subtle.

"Say yes to a project" was Thursday's advice. "Weigh your decisions about money carefully" was the guidance for Friday. But on the morning of Saturday, February 5, the day after arriving in California, I received an unusual email from my favorite astrology site. It said, "A 'five' date is part of a surprise future."

Minutes later, a different horoscope email came in. It said, "555 signifies a time of significant changes and opportunity for you, Corey. Have you been thinking about starting a new project, business, or even relationship?"

I felt an unsettling wave come over me. *Wasn't the breakup with Runner on the fifth day of the month?*

I opened a Word document and began typing every significant event I could think of associated with the fifth of the month.

- July 5—the breakup.
- November 5—the beginning of the Grand Canyon trip.
- December 5—the meeting with the first psychic.
- March 5—the day I was planning to return from my adventure trip with Pants and the close of the psychics' three-month window.
- June 5—the date my second Grand Canyon trek was scheduled for.

In my bout of reflection, I recalled an event I had recently attended where a medium singled me out among a crowd to deliver a message. She told me I was about to have an experience that would "make me feel alive." Her prophetic words were spoken five weeks before my five-day trip with Pants, which just so happened to be five months after she and I connected on the dating app.

Then, I remembered I supposedly had five spirit guides, according to the intuition coach, and five divine partners, according to the first psychic.

After learning more about numerology, I found out that five is a lucky number for Virgo and represents transformation and change, as well as love and marriage. It also symbolizes excitement, adventure, energy, curiosity, fun, and magic. There it was—the love and magic I'd been looking for. All in the number five.

My first week in California had proven to be relatively uneventful. Kiddo and I had been hunkering down in a tiny studio we had rented for a couple weeks. During the day, I would work from a small end table I had turned into my office. In the evenings, we would binge the winter Olympics. Birds was still home with COVID, and Pants was prepping for our hike the next weekend.

Both had been texting me nonstop. Despite my torment about the situation, I kept my tailspins at bay. That was, until I opened one of my tarot card emails.

"Meeting someone who resonates with the Two of Cups could feel like reconnecting with someone you've known for a long time, even from a previous life. Your conversations could feel electrified while strangely comfortable. While the Two of Cups can indicate a soulmate kind of relationship, it's also a reminder to take things slow."

I sent a screenshot of it to Naked and Afraid.

What is this?

Wild shit. That's what it is. Every day, it's something about Pants.

Switchbacks

"Hey, which one is your house?" I said into the speakerphone. "I can't find it."

"The one on the corner with the lights on. I'll come out," Pants said.

"Okay."

I pulled into the first corner house I saw that had a light, speeding up to clear a huge curb at the entrance of the driveway.

Pants was still on the phone. "I'm literally watching you, and you are at the wrong house. I'm across the street. The one *with* the lights on." She laughed. "Can't you see me standing in front, waving?"

"This one has lights too." I then started backing out, and something under my car crunched.

"I heard that," she said. "Mine has actual porch lights on, not some dim streetlight."

"Ha ha. I see you now. Your driveway also looks like it has way better pavement."

I finally pulled in, and we hung up.

As I got out, she was laughing. "Your GPS skills suck."

"Hey! You were the one who couldn't find the Columbia store." I laughed.

She ushered me inside, and I dropped my bag on the guest bed. After a quick hug, we went into the living room, which was filled with two large couches and a huge TV. I could imagine her sitting there alone at night, eyes fixed on some serial killer documentary.

She sat down on a worn cushion on the far couch. I opted for a spot on the other one where I could prop my feet up on the built-in adjustable recliner. As soon as I settled in, two of her dogs jumped up and snuggled on my lap. They fell fast asleep.

Nothing remarkable stood out about our conversation, except it felt familiar and comfortable—and the déjà vu was overwhelming. I knew Pants, I knew her dogs, and I had lived this moment before. Maybe she wasn't just my divine partner in this life—maybe she was in a past one too.

The next morning, I heard her up and about. I wandered into the kitchen and saw her toasting bagels and making eggs with veggies, which was surprising given her strong disdain for healthy food. She told me she would make an exception and eat vegetables since I was there. I helped set the table, and we ate before getting on the road for a day of hiking in Yosemite.

As soon as we were in the car, she opened the music app on her phone.

"I know you like rap. I have a bunch on here," she said while tapping on her playlist.

She played the role of DJ much of the ride while we chatted nonstop about concerts, favorite musicians, and other get-to-know-you stuff.

The two hours flew by, and before we knew it, we were at the park.

"Wow, this is so beautiful," I said, looking out the window. "I haven't been here in forever." The views of the towering rock cliffs were almost overwhelming.

"Yeah, I love this place. I've never hiked to Upper Yosemite Falls before, though."

"It's weird that you mentioned that trail in one of our first text exchanges. And I talked about The Wave. Now we're doing this *and* going to Utah."

"That is strange," she said.

We pulled into a parking spot near the trailhead. She put on two layers, and I, my usual four, including a child's hat with built-in ear covers and braids coming down each side.

"You look like a fool," she said and then burst out laughing.

"Ha ha. Look who will be warm. And I'll be sure to photobomb all your pictures now!"

I unfolded the map the park ranger had given us. "Okay, it' 7.6 miles up and back. And it looks like there are maybe ten switchbacks. Not bad. The Grand Canyon has around a hundred!"

We started up the trail, continuing our chat about my hat, which devolved into sharing other silly stories. After about thirty minutes, she came to an abrupt stop.

"We've done more than ten switchbacks." She was huffing from the climb.

"I know. I think we only have a few more," I said, trying to channel the positive Law of Attraction Lady.

Four hours later, trudging through the mud and snow, bend after bend, we emerged at the top.

"Finally," she said. "What the hell was that?"

"It would have been nice if it hadn't been so icy and steep . . . and had a whole lot less switchbacks."

We could hear the rushing water down the side of the rocks and walked around until we could get a glimpse of the waterfall below. I had Pants take a picture of me "on the edge." I took a few of her, and we got some selfies of both of us.

"Do you know how many switchbacks there were?" I asked a couple taking photos nearby.

"I think it's 135," the guy said.

"Seriously?" Pants asked.

"Well, that park map isn't to scale," I said.

Everyone laughed.

"You all going to the fire waterfall tonight?" the woman asked. "It happens when the sunset shines perfectly on the waterfall and makes it look like fire. You can only see it a few nights a year."

"That's so cool! I guess it depends on whether we make it down these 135 switchbacks," I said, then smiled at Pants.

After snapping a few pictures for the couple, we slogged through more snow to a big flat rock and got out our lunches. We ate, took a few more photos, and then started our descent.

Other than the last hundred yards or so, during which Pants opted to sprint down solo after popping ibuprofen, we stuck together the whole trek. We discussed past relationships, home buying, and everything in between. It felt natural and easy, like we had been here before . . . not on this hike, per se, but in this connection.

Once we both got to the bottom, Pants asked if I wanted to stay to see the fire waterfall.

"Definitely!" I practically shouted. "I mean, it only happens a few days a year."

So, instead of heading to her SUV to take off our hiking shoes and crank up the heat, we trudged our sore and tired bodies a mile down the paved road to the viewing site.

Once we arrived, we heard a booming voice announce, "It'll be about forty-five minutes before you can see anything. So, just hang tight." The park ranger then went back to ushering people into the roped off area.

I wandered over to an old, rotted log and sat down. The small branches poked into my back, which is probably why there was a spot available on the log to begin with. Pants planted herself next to me, seemingly less bothered.

"I'm freezing," I said.

"I bet you are. You're always cold, even when it's warm!" She slid a bag of candy out of her pack. "Want a Valentine's heart?"

I pulled one out. "Love," I read aloud. "What did you get?"

"Be mine."

"Did you buy yourself your own Valentine's candy?" I asked.

"Of course I did! I love candy, and I'm not waiting for someone to buy it for me!"

We both laughed. That could have been our moment. But I didn't feel any romantic chemistry. Instead, I felt like I was commiserating with an old friend about Valentine's Day. Maybe it was because I was dating Birds and unconsciously blocking any butterflies. Or maybe the butterflies only came when we were apart, kind of a "longing for the idea of her" rather than "longing for her." I was confused about being confused. But I ate her Valentine's candy anyway.

By the time the fire waterfall was visible, even she was cold. We took some photos and then booked it back to the car.

Our return drive was filled with as much music and chatter as the ride there. Although it was late when we got back, we decided to stay up talking and indulge in our cupcakes. She took a spot on her couch, and I on mine.

"So, any leads on the app?" I asked while unwrapping my dessert.

"Nope. You?"

I took a deep breath. "Yeah. I met someone."

After what seemed to be at least a ten-second pause, she said, "I'm really happy for you." Her voice was unconvincing. "What's her name? What's she like? Where did you meet? How long have you been dating?"

"Only a few weeks. And not online. Go figure . . . We actually met on a hike. She's really nice, and we have a lot in common." I went on and on about how amazing Birds was and how excited

I was to date her. About two minutes into my monologue, I realized I had blown any chance to find out if Pants's feelings for me had changed since the "for now" text.

I crawled into bed that night, and my mind started going into overdrive. *Since I don't plan to pursue anything with her, does it really matter how she feels?* I pondered for a second and then answered my own question. *Absolutely it matters. And now I will never know.*

The next morning, I woke up early and replied to a message from Pontificator. After having finally confessed to her about the psychic situation, we had developed a nice friendship. I enjoyed her even-keeled thoughts, which often sat in stark contrast to any conversation I would have with either Naked and Afraid or TikTok.

Did you see Pants? What do you think?

Spent the weekend with her. It was great. It definitely felt more like a friendship, though.

Hallelujah! Clarity. And how wonderful to have discovered such a connection!

I feel a sense of relief. She is definitely a soul connection. It might not be romantic. But it makes sense why I continue to be drawn to her. Just so familiar, like we have known each other our whole lives. But that makes for a great friendship.

For sure! What a gift.

I got dressed, packed up, and, after a brief hug with Pants, made my way straight to Birds's house. The ten-hour drive left plenty of time to process with TikTok.

"I didn't feel anything romantic. It was like we were old friends who were really comfortable and familiar with each other," I said.

"Girl, comfortable and familiar are right out of the soulmate and past-lives playbook."

"There was no *pow*, *boom*, *bang*, though."

"That doesn't matter," she said. "Sometimes the connection doesn't come with fireworks; it's just gut-level. That's what you have."

After TikTok and I hung up, I called Naked and Afraid. Our incessant processing would surely help pass the time on my boring, unscenic drive.

"You so want this situation to be resolved that you're blocking your feelings," she said. "That's respectable, since you're dating Birds. But it doesn't mean you don't have feelings for Pants deep down."

"I'm sure I want to be with Birds and not Pants. Isn't it a good thing I got clarity?"

"I don't believe you have clarity. I think you want to believe you have clarity to make your life easier. Remember what both psychics said . . . three months. You still have a few weeks, and you're going to Utah with her soon. Just wait and see what happens."

I didn't want to wait and see. I was sure I already had clarity.

Stopped in My Tracks

A few days later, on my way to pick up Naked and Afraid to go hiking, I started replaying the conversations with her and TikTok.

What if they are right? Maybe I want certainty so bad that I'm convincing myself Pants is not "the one."

With this sudden revelation, tears began to well up, and I could feel a tailspin coming on. The more I tried, the more the confusion and angst trapped inside me wanted to escape. But if they did, I'd finally have to deal with how awful I felt having been rejected by Pants *and* admit I was still pining for her—not to mention having to contend with the guilt I was carrying keeping this divine partnership obsession from Birds.

I started huffing for breath, knowing the buckets of tears were right behind. So, I scrambled to find Eminem on my playlist. *Surely, he will help fend off this meltdown.* I cranked the music up so loud my speakers started shaking. And I sang along, the volume of my voice competing with the thunderous thumping of the bass. Adrenaline was rushing through my blood, so much so I was sure my Zen Master was going to have a heart attack.

And then it all came out—sobs so hard I almost had to pull the car over. Even Eminem couldn't stop this. I cried and cried. "What am I supposed to do?" I shouted to the universe. "I just don't know what I'm supposed to do." My voice trailed off as I pleaded.

When I had finished yelling into the air, I duly wiped my eyes with my hand. I thought maybe this cathartic moment would trigger a sense of liberation and perhaps even clarity; instead, my soul ached from the agony and hurt finally being released.

I pulled into Naked and Afraid's driveway and lowered the volume. She jumped in the passenger seat, looked at me, and said, "Something's wrong."

I could barely say anything before another tear streamed down from under my sunglasses. "I'm so confused." The tears started pouring out again. "I just don't know what to do, and I feel like crap. I'm sad, angry, disappointed, ashamed, embarrassed. The list goes on. Why did I let myself get into this?"

She didn't gloat. And she didn't say, "I knew you didn't really have clarity." She just sat by my side while I cried.

Once we got to the trailhead, I'd calmed down a bit.

"Ready?" she asked as her finger was about to press start on her timer.

We took off.

I rambled on and on as we bolted up the rocky trail. "I don't understand why I can't let this idea of Pants go and be with Birds. All I'm doing is torturing myself and getting in the way of my own happiness."

Naked and Afraid came to a screeching halt, spun around, and stared into my soul. "You are with the wrong person. Go be with Pants!" She didn't flinch. "You have an energy with her. You light up when you talk about her. It's obvious."

Another tear rolled down my cheek. And then buckets more just poured out.

Wife from Another Life

Shortly after the "Go be with Pants" hike, I went to see Tarot Lady for some guidance. My catharsis of emotions emphasized yet again that I was confused, not just in the conscious mind, but also at an intuitive level. And how better to get clarity than by having Tarot Lady tap into the universe's prophetic messages?

Naked and Afraid came along to get a reading, too. She wanted to know if she and Twin Flame were in it for the long haul.

I had been to Tarot Lady's before. It was exactly as I remembered—an everyday home with art on the wall and knickknacks on the shelves. No wafting patchouli aroma, crystal balls, or funky music that might be expected.

She led us to a room toward the back of the house with a small card table and three folding chairs. On top of the frilly tablecloth were a few burning candles, several decks of tarot cards, and three pendulums.

Tarot Lady and I sat across from each other, with Naked and Afraid next to me.

"The card I'm about to select will frame your entire reading."

Please don't let it be the Tower card.

She shuffled, drew one, and set it on the table. "New partner."

Naked and Afraid shot me a glance.

"Hmm, there's more to know here. I'm gonna pull another," Tarot Lady said.

I held my breath as she took a card from the top of the pile and flipped it over. *Please don't let it be the Tower card.*

"Clarity."

The blood felt like it rushed out of my face, leaving me stark white. But no one said a thing about my zombie appearance or the cards on the table. Naked and Afraid, though, was still giving me a piercing stare.

After a deep breath, I was able to regain my composure. *At least no one was jumping to their deaths.*

Tarot Lady then handed me the deck. "Shuffle as many times as you would like. Then, split them into three piles."

I followed her instructions. She then stacked all the cards and drew five to lay out in my spread.

After pausing, she said, "You are torn between two paths of possible love; you are mentally stuck. One isn't ready but will be in the future once you develop a trusting friendship. Contemplate and sit in this space for a while; things will unfold how they should . . . Keep waiting."

Waiting . . . that sounds familiar.

Before I had a chance to ask anything, Tarot Lady looked at me and then at Naked and Afraid—then back at me.

"Eww. I'm not her path of possible love!" Naked and Afraid shouted.

"We're not a couple," I said, in a far more polite way.

"As soon as you walked in today, I felt your souls were connected, so I assumed you were in a relationship. But now I'm sensing you might have been married in a past life."

Naked and Afraid gave me a puzzled look.

"I feel like maybe you were both women in the early 1900s,

perhaps in France, and were artists or creatives of some sort. Of course, such relationships were forbidden back then."

Naked and Afraid and I both leaned in.

"You've been in each other's lives several times and are in this one together for a reason."

"Wow, that's interesting," I said.

I wanted to hear more, but Naked and Afraid jumped in. "Everyone thinks we're dating. But we both get grossed out thinking about it."

There was an awkward pause.

"We've never been attracted to each other," I said, trying to more politely chime in. "Just good friends."

Tarot Lady shifted in her seat. "Let's move on to the pendulum. Pick whichever of these three is calling to you."

I pointed to the rainbow one. She held the pendulum in the air by the chain at the top, and the crystal hung motionless in front of me.

"What is your question?"

"Am I supposed to date Birds?" I asked.

The pendulum whipped back and forth.

"Yes," Tarot Lady said.

"How about Pants? Am I supposed to date her?"

It swung in a circular motion. "Unsure," she said. "Maybe down the road. But not now."

"How far down the road?" I asked.

"Let's ask. Will Corey be dating Pants sometime during the next ten months?" The crystal again made a circle. "Unsure."

"Well, then, probably not within a few weeks like the psychics said," I whispered to Naked and Afraid.

"Between the cards and this, it seems you should be with Birds now and see where that goes. Just know you and Pants may end up together later on."

My time was up. And my head was swirling.

Naked and Afraid and I swapped seats, giving me the next thirty minutes to ponder.

After her reading, we headed to Tumamoc to walk and process.

"It's so weird she thought we were dating," she said while speeding along. "You know, maybe I was Gertrude Stein, and you were her wife, Alice. They lived in France in the early twentieth century."

"I've always had a fascination with Paris . . . well, the Eiffel Tower," I said, trying to catch my breath from scurrying uphill.

"I'm going to order a book about them. That was totally us."

I laughed. "Okay, so what about the Birds and Pants thing?"

"I'm not sure she provided any more clarity about who you're supposed to be with . . . in the long run, that is. I just know it's not me . . . at least not in this lifetime."

Playing Games

"You nervous at all? I don't want you to be nervous, but I'm just asking."

As the words came out, I could tell I was likely making Birds *more*, not less, nervous. Despite my incessant confusion about the soulmate situation, she and I had been spending a lot of time together, and things were progressing as one would expect when dating.

"A little bit. I mean, I'm meeting your daughter," she said.

Kiddo was in town for her spring break, and she and I had a week's worth of adventures planned, one of which was to meet Birds.

"I'm sure she'll love you."

Right at six, the bell rang. After I introduced the two of them, Birds set the table, as she had been used to doing, while Kiddo poured herself a glass of milk. We all then dished up our food and sat down.

Silence.

"So, Birds brought a fun game for later . . . after we do some conversation cards." I pulled the lid off the deck I had brought to the table.

"Do we have to do those?" Kiddo asked.

"She makes you play them too?" Birds smirked at me.

"Hey, now. Those cards are awesome," I said. "Plus, who wouldn't want to know someone else's favorite smell?"

They both laughed.

We ate while I read from the deck. Once Kiddo wolfed down her food, she scooted the pile of cards near her and took over asking the questions. Deep down, I knew she loved them.

After finishing, we cleared the dishes and set up the game Birds had brought over.

"So, there are these little eggs." Birds pointed to the pile on the table. "You collect the chips, play a bird card, and then you can earn one of the eggs if you have a certain number of points."

"Wait, how do we get chips?" I asked.

Kiddo was halfway listening and halfway organizing the various game pieces.

"I think you get the chips when you put down a card with a chip symbol on it," Birds said.

My blank expression gave away my confusion. After ten more questions on my part, we all realized we had no idea what we were doing, despite the saintly patience of Birds in trying to decipher the rules. So, we decided to play a different game . . . one with a tiny instruction book. And we laughed the entire time.

I exhaled. The night was a win.

"So, how do you think things are going between us?" I said to Birds as we snuggled up on the couch. Kiddo had gone to bed, and we finally had some alone time, which I was hoping to use to get some clarity.

"Good," she said, leaning down on my shoulder.

"What do you mean by 'good'?"

She lifted her head and turned to me. "I don't know . . . good."

This isn't giving me clarity. What does "good" even mean? I sat there, waiting for her to expand on her thoughts without my prompting. But she didn't. She just smiled.

Here we were, at the couch again, and I needed to not fudge my words this time. I finally blurted out, "Well, I want something real and lasting . . . with a future, not something casual and low-key."

Good job, Corey! Maybe a little brusque, but at least clear.

"I hope what we have isn't casual. I just met your kid," she said, in a soft, sweet tone.

"True." I squeezed her hand. "So, then, tell me more about what something real and lasting looks like to you."

And she did. We stayed up until nearly dawn talking about all the possibilities between us. She had so much love bottled up, and it was clear she was ready to move mountains for me.

It was a total turn of events. And it *was* good.

The Secret

"You know, today may be our first date in the daylight," I said to Birds as we stood in the kitchen waiting for Kiddo.

"You're right. It's like we only hang out in the dark."

I laughed.

Birds reached out her hand to grab mine and gave it a tight squeeze.

"So, what do you want to do . . . in the daylight?" I asked.

"I want to do all the things with you."

I smiled. "Me too."

After dropping Kiddo off at a friend's house for the day, Birds and I drove to the river path for a bike ride. She was definitely more of an avid biker than me, but she never sped ahead. Instead, we glided along together, chatting and laughing.

When we finished, we wandered around the nearby farmer's market, perusing fresh vegetables and artisan crafts. The warm sun and gentle breeze continued to remind me why I liked Arizona so much. And this date reminded me why I liked Birds so much. It was always so easy and fun with her.

Before we knew it, it was time to pick up Kiddo.

Once she hopped in the car, I asked if they both might want to stop at the bookstore on the way home. I hadn't been there since my last soulmate search excursion but was hoping to *really* shop for books this time. They both jumped at the offer.

As soon as we walked in, Kiddo sped over to the reference area. She had been trying to teach herself how to speak Italian to prepare for her summer immersion program in Italy. Birds wandered off in the other direction, and I beelined for the spirituality section to bury myself in books about cosmos, horoscopes, and tarot cards.

After roaming the store, Birds finally made her way over. She peered at me from the other side of the bookshelf over the tops of several thick Zen paperbacks.

"Come here often?" she asked, grinning.

I laughed, gazing back through the racks. "All the time."

She came around the shelf and reached for my hand.

I then said, "I'm not sure if I told you, but I may have hung out here searching for my soulmate . . . on a few occasions."

"Really?"

"Yep. I would linger by the gay area and browse crusty novels—you know, the ones that have been here forever? I thought perhaps an attractive, career-minded, single lesbian would show up."

She snickered. "How'd that go?"

"Not even a prospect. When I moved to the self-help area during another visit, all I saw was a straight-looking lady wanting to improve her life. But today, you approached me . . . in the spirituality and intuition section. Maybe I should have seen that coming!"

We both laughed.

I knew the bookstore would be where I'd find some amazing, attractive woman. And there she was. I finally got a sign for Birds. *Thank you, universe. I needed that.*

We linked arms and made our way around the corner toward a nearby display stand.

"Hey, check this out." I pointed to *The Secret* perched on the top shelf. "This book changed my life."

She pulled a copy off the rack and read the back cover aloud. "As you learn *The Secret*, you too will come to know how you can have, be, or do anything you want."

"Sounds interesting." She tucked the copy under her arm, along with another book she had been carrying around. "I'll read it while you're on your trip," she said.

A wave of guilt moved right through me. Birds knew nothing of the psychics, my divine partnership with Pants, and my intense confusion about the whole situation. And now she would be reading *The Secret* while I was in Utah with my very own secret—seeing if there was any truth to the psychic prophecy.

"Hold on. I need to get something."

We all came to an abrupt stop. Naked and Afraid and I stood there while Twin Flame swung her pack off her shoulder and rifled through one of the pockets. Birds, being a few steps in front of us, hadn't noticed and trudged on. Kiddo was even further ahead.

We had squeezed in one last hike before Kiddo and I were heading out to Phoenix. I was planning to drop her off at the airport and then continue on to Utah to meet up with Pants.

As we stood there waiting for Twin Flame, I gazed around at the scenery. "Look! Do you see that?" I pointed at a huge boulder.

Naked and Afraid spun around. "What the . . .?"

Twin Flame looked up. "I definitely didn't notice that when we passed by earlier."

"The universe couldn't be any clearer," Naked and Afraid said. "Why would *her* name be written in huge letters across that rock?"

"I don't know." My voice started shaking. "Things have been going great with Birds. I even got that sign in the bookstore about her."

Twin Flame then shouted, "Aha. There it is!" as she pulled her sunglasses out of her pack. "Well, this is definitely a sign for Pants," she continued.

I took a deep breath. "What am I supposed to do? As soon as we're done, I'm leaving for my trip. I can't say goodbye to her when I feel like all the blood just drained from my body."

"You're gonna have to," Naked and Afraid said. "Whatever you do, don't bring it up."

We all started trekking along again.

"Well, obviously. What did you think I would say? 'I'm headed out. By the way, a psychic told me Pants was my soulmate, and I just saw her name written on a rock on our hike. Wonder if it's a sign that she's the one. Off to see her. Have a great week'?"

"Yeah, not that." Naked and Afraid laughed.

The three of us picked up the pace, hopping over trickles of flowing water and traversing the rocky terrain until we caught up to the others.

Once back at the lot, Kiddo ran to our car, and I walked Birds to hers.

We leaned against the driver's side door, our arms wrapped around each other, like teenagers lingering after a school dance.

"I hope you have so much fun on your trip. But I'm gonna miss you," she said.

"Me too."

Although the words came out, my mind was distracted by images of the boulder, and my gut was filled with the heaviness of the guilt of everything this secret had become. While I wasn't eager to let go of my embrace with Birds, all I wanted to do was get in my car, listen to Eminem, and cry. Except I couldn't . . . at least not with Kiddo in the passenger seat. I would just have to hold it in.

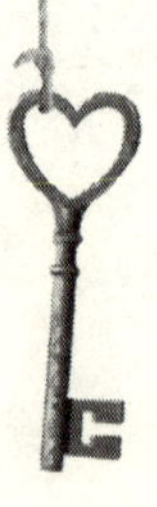

Noise Machines and Jelly Beans

How close are you to your destiny? Oops, I mean destination. No, I don't . . . I mean destiny!

At the hotel. She will be here in twenty-five minutes.

After a little more razzing from Naked and Afraid, Pants called. "Hey, I just pulled in."

"Great. I'll grab a cart and come down."

Once I exited the lobby, I could see her across the lot, sifting through her stuff in the hatchback . . . which reminded me of eating Applebee's with her in that very spot. I didn't feel any butterflies or romantic attraction when we exchanged a hug, but there was also no awkwardness.

We loaded the cart and headed to our room. After she unpacked, we went to dinner, where the conversation flowed like a reunion between old friends. In no time, we had devoured the two entrees we split and then ended the evening in the hotel hot tub, chatting with a friendly couple about their hiking adventures. Everything felt easy.

Once we returned to the room, I said, "So, I have the perfect show for us—*Love Is Blind*."

"I thought we were going to watch an episode of *Dateline* for me and one of *My 600-lb Life* for you."

"Well, since we both like *Married at First Sight*, I was thinking this could be a good compromise. Plus, your crime shows freak me out."

"Okay. But someday you're gonna watch *Dateline* with me. And I get to pick the episode." She stretched out on her bed and propped her head on two pillows.

"Fine."

I sat my laptop on the TV stand and pulled a cord out of my bag.

"You came prepared," she said.

"Yep. This way, we can stream onto the big screen.

"So, what's this show even about?"

"People speed date behind these walls for like a week. Once they narrow in on who they want to marry, the two meet in person."

I plugged in the computer cord so what was on my laptop projected on the TV. Suddenly, a text notification with the "destiny" message from Naked and Afraid appeared. I gasped and closed it out as fast as I could.

"Only after they agree to get married? That sounds ridiculous," she said.

"It's like *Married at First Sight*," I said, trying to divert attention from what she may have seen on the screen.

"No, it's not. That show has experts matching them. This is just a bunch of people saying whatever they want to impress each other. Who knows if they're even compatible?" She sat up.

"If you feel chemistry with someone, everything else can be figured out," I said.

"You have to have something in common with the other person. Chemistry can develop later on as you get to know each other."

I glanced up from my laptop and looked over at her. "Well, you can do it that way. But I want *pow*, *boom*, *bang* . . . the fireworks, from the start."

"What if the person isn't who they say they are? Or what if you really aren't compatible? You've now fallen for someone who isn't good for you."

"I wouldn't only be with someone because of the butterflies. I mean if that person was a jerk, then no way. But passionate love has to come first," I said.

Her conviction tempered a bit. "Do you have that with Birds?"

Why is she asking me this?

"I definitely have butterflies, but it's a slow burn . . . one-butterfly-at-a-time kind of thing."

She didn't respond.

I clicked on the episode and plopped down on my bed. While I watched intensely, Pants split her attention between scrolling through her phone and making comments about the ridiculousness of the show. Our banter ended up being far more entertaining than anything on the TV.

Once we finished, she stepped into the bathroom to shower. I ran over to my laptop and changed my text notification settings to avoid any future pop-up scares.

I then messaged Naked and Afraid from my phone, to be safe.

It's easy with Pants, like I've known her my whole life. No pow, boom, bang, but definitely a sense of familiarity, like when I was at her house.

Interesting. Gotta be past-life stuff.

As soon as Pants came out of the bathroom, I put my phone face down on the nightstand.

"Remember I told you I have to sleep with a fan on?" she asked, getting under the covers.

"Yep."

"Since there's no fan here, I have this app." She tapped on her phone, and a horrendous noise blared from the speaker.

"It sounds like someone's showering upstairs. What *is* that?" I asked.

"Rain. It's supposed to help you sleep."

"That thing is so loud. How am I supposed to sleep when it's like you left a bathroom faucet on full blast?"

She laughed. "Well, how am I supposed to sleep with the heat at eighty degrees?"

"Ha ha."

This was going to be a long week. And the least of my worries was the rain app.

"Twenty-three," I said out loud. That was the number the man behind the lotto wheel handed me. Pants and I had finally made it to the front after waiting in a line that snaked around the gym floor. I loosened my grip and looked at the number again. *Two plus three equals five, my supposed magic number. Maybe that's a sign.*

"There are a hundred groups here today trying to get a Wave permit for tomorrow, and we *only* draw four for the walk-in lottery," Lotto Man said to an eager crowd. "It doesn't matter how big your group is. We only pick four numbers."

He spun the wheel hard. Once it came to a stop, he pulled a ball out. "Sixty-seven?"

An older man ran to the front, shouting about how excited he was after having traveled all the way from Europe by himself.

Lotto Man then drew the remaining numbers, none of which were ours.

"Three solo groups and the number ninety-eight. Those people must have walked in one minute before the drawing," I said. "That sucks."

"Yep. No Wave for us." She started heading toward the door.

We left the packed gym with hordes of other disappointed hikers and went to the car.

The drive was just over an hour to Bryce Canyon, where we had planned to spend the day after the lotto drawing. Once we arrived at the visitor center, Pants hit up the restroom while I hunkered down behind a T-shirt display to text Naked and Afraid. I filled her in on everything from the night before and my speculative interpretation of it. As expected, she insisted I get some guts and talk to her to see how she was feeling about everything. I reminded her I was still recovering from the "for now" rejection and wasn't interested in being vulnerable again. She then told me to suck it up and put on my big-girl pants. It was an exchange right out of our usual playbook—I spiral, and she tries to knock some sense into me.

As soon as Pants started coming toward me, I shoved my phone in my pocket.

"You ready?" she asked.

"Yep. Let's do it!"

We drove to the trailhead where we immediately noticed no cars parked nearby, most likely because of the vast amounts of snow and ice on the ground. We strapped spikes onto the bottom of our boots and started down what we hoped was the path.

We hadn't walked for two minutes when I said, "Oh my gosh . . . I'm sinking! This isn't ice. It's like quicksand!"

"I know! My boots feel like concrete blocks!" She stopped for a moment to knock the mud off the bottom.

Despite the conditions, we decided to trudge on, hiking in and out of stretches of thick mud. We filled the time with constant chatter but still made sure to stop every couple of miles to take pictures of the hoodoos, the skinny rock formations that look like stacks of dripping sand.

After several hours of random banter, the conversation turned into a debate about what was more important in a relationship—chemistry or compatibility. It was essentially a more detailed version of our *Love is Blind* discussion, but not in a warm hotel room.

Right when it seemed we were at an impasse around the philosophical underpinnings of love, the trail sign came into view. I shifted my focus from arguing about the merit of chemistry and simply shouted, "Look!" while pointing up ahead.

"Thank God," she muttered. "I'm so done with this mud."

"Me too," I said. "We can finally walk on the pavement to the parking lot!"

Once we got to the sign, neither of us could see a paved path . . . just more mud. We both rattled off a few choice words and then regrouped at a nearby bench.

Pants reached into her pack. "Jelly beans?" she asked. "Maybe they'll give us the energy we need to make it through this muck."

"Yes! Jelly beans are my go-to in tough situations." I thought about the many bags I consumed during the chaos of my breakup.

She poured a few into my hand.

It took nearly an hour, but we finally trudged our way from the trailhead to her SUV, still the sole vehicle in an otherwise vacant parking lot. Our clothes were soaked and filthy, and our boots were layered with caked-on mud. We took off our spikes and slapped them together until pounds of wet earth fell to the ground.

When we got back to the hotel, I offered to shower after her. Once I heard the water come on, I texted Naked and Afraid.

Made it out of Bryce Canyon. Tons of clarity!!!

Please enlighten me!

We have such different views on love and relationships. I don't think it would ever work with us. Plus, I've been missing Birds.

Good. Let her go and focus on Birds then. Done.

I had no idea if Naked and Afraid had changed her mind and was now pushing me toward Birds or was simply exhausted from my teeter-tottering. I knew *I* was exhausted from it. But I still didn't feel done.

After another night of the rain app, we made sure to pack plenty of jelly beans for "The Wave Alternative," the back-up day trip we had booked in case we didn't receive a permit through gymnasium lotto.

We left for the tour company's headquarters before the sun was up. Once we got there, we loaded into an old Jeep with all our gear. Our lead guide, who was in his fifties, looked worn from hundreds of tours over his lifetime. A younger, heavyset woman who served as our apprentice guide also tagged along to learn the ropes. Once we were all buckled in, we sped off, weaving around holes and divots on several winding dirt roads. My head kept slamming against the roof, and I was certain my organs were being dislodged with every bump. It was the longest two hours ever.

We finally made it to a scenic set of colorful buttes, among terrain that appeared barely traveled by the public. After spending the day rock traversing and posing for photos taken by Apprentice, we drove back on the same bumpy, curvy roads.

Pants and I grabbed a quick bite to eat on our way back to the hotel and ended the night with hot tubbing and another episode of *Love Is Blind*, which was again flooded with her commentary about the questionable premise.

"Tomorrow is going to be my favorite day," she said after the show. "I've been excited about rappelling since we planned it."

"Should be fun," I said, feigning enthusiasm. *On the upside, though, perhaps doing something death-defying will make my love life confusion feel far less significant.*

"Ready for another adventure with us?" Apprentice asked.

"Yep! I've been waiting for this!" Pants said.

I managed a relatively convincing "Uh-huh."

After another rough two-hour ride with the same lead guide from the day before, we parked at the edge of the canyon and started unloading gear.

As we were putting on our harnesses, Apprentice asked, "So, how long have you two known each other?"

Pants and I both shot each other a stare.

"Five months," we said in unison.

"That's it?" she asked. "It seems like a lot longer."

"Yeah. Sometimes it feels like five years," I said.

Everyone laughed.

"How did you meet?" she asked.

"Online dating app," Pants said as she tightened her belt.

"Oh. So, you're a couple?"

Pants was quick to respond. "No. She has a girlfriend."

I leaned down to clip my helmet onto my backpack. "Well, that's not the only reason we aren't dating."

Before Pants had a chance to respond, the lead guide summoned us over. "You all ready?"

Crap. Now, I'll never know what she was going to say.

Pants shoved a newly filled baggie of jelly beans into her pocket, and we put on our packs.

After an hour of hiking, we came upon the canyon's edge where we would do our first drop. I looked down, which might have been a mistake. Pants went before me, and although she made it look easy, I could still feel my stomach doing flips in anticipation.

Once it was my turn, the lead guide clipped me in. "Grab the rope with your hand and tuck it behind you. It's like your gas pedal. It controls how fast or slow you go."

"Got it." I didn't think I got it at all.

I jerked myself downward, one step at a time, like descending a ladder. Once I got halfway, I picked up speed and glided to the bottom with little fanfare.

When my feet hit the ground, I yelled, "That was awesome!" My excitement was more an expression of relief that I survived rather than an exclamation of my overwhelming enjoyment. And there were no tears.

We finished the day with seven rappels and hundreds of pictures of slivers of sunlight peeking through rock crevices. Apprentice also took some good shots of Pants and me navigating our way down the slick canyon walls.

On the ride back, I asked the lead guide, "What's the coolest rappelling tour you've ever led?"

"I did a wedding once. The two got dressed up and rappelled off a cliff while exchanging vows."

The hair on the back of my neck stood up.

I glanced at Pants to see her reaction.

"That is so cool!" she said.

The universe had spoken. Maybe I shouldn't have torn up that marriage manifest after all.

The rest of the ride back from rappelling was uneventful. Everyone was exhausted and spent the time either staring out the window or making occasional small talk. I sat quietly, fixating on how tearing up my marriage manifest had somehow derailed destiny. It would have been a lot easier to stuff that distress down into the deep, dark caverns of my soul, but with all the other angst about this situation already renting space there, I knew there wasn't much room to hold anything else.

More importantly, though, I had two days before the three-month psychic window was set to close, and I needed to find out how Pants had really felt. If she had never seen me as anything but a friend, I could finally release the divine partner illusion I had been grasping onto and be all in with Birds. If not, I'd probably have to run off to a psychic in Utah for immediate guidance.

Once at the hotel, we dropped our bags and headed out to get ice cream. I thought it would be the perfect time to have the conversation.

We ordered at the counter and found a table outside. I scooped up a spoonful of my pralines and cream, knowing that the fifteen bites in my cup served as a countdown clock for our talk.

"So, you think we're gonna be friends after this trip?" I asked.

"Why wouldn't we be?" Her eyes widened. "Do you not want to be friends anymore?"

Yikes! The moment was unfolding like karate-chop night with Birds. *What in the world am I asking?*

"Yeah, I didn't know if we were just keeping in touch until Utah and then we'd sort of fade off," I said, doubling down on the confusion.

"I would hope not."

"I mean, you've gone on other trips with people from the dating apps. Am I, like, just a random person on your list of adventure buddies?" I sounded completely desperate, pathetic, and insecure. What I had planned to ask was, "Has there ever been something more to our friendship, despite the 'for now' text?" But that is *not* what came out of my mouth.

"I hope we stay friends," she said.

"Me too."

The fifteen bites were gone. My countdown clock had expired, and I hadn't had the conversation. If anything, I had just confused her and made her doubt our friendship.

"What an adventure!" I said. "I can't believe how many cool things we did. And there's still so much more." I opened a syrup packet and poured it on my waffles.

"Yeah. Even though we didn't get the permit, it was fun anyway." She chomped on one of the many pieces of bacon piled on her plate. "I'm definitely game to come back."

In between bites of all the breakfast fixings in the hotel lobby, we both went on and on about what our next trip might look like—more rappelling, some hiking, and even mountain biking. By the time we were done eating, we had an entire list of ideas for another week-long adventure.

It seemed like an innocuous trip-planning conversation. However, what Pants didn't know was that The General had been whispering in my ear the entire time, "Just ask . . . 'Did you ever have feelings for me?'" But casually sliding that in between "Pass the salt" and "Let's try for The Wave again" felt off. So, it never came out of my mouth.

After breakfast, we headed outside, stopping in front of the sliding doors to say our goodbyes.

"Keep me posted about Birds," she said, giving me a tight hug.

I gave the last squeeze and pulled back when it felt like we had hugged for too long. "Will do! Safe travels!"

I walked to my car—full of regret. I didn't get my answer. I didn't even ask the question. All I did was wolf down waffles in the hotel lobby and apparently agree to go rappelling again.

"Be done with this situation." Those were essentially Naked and Afraid's words after I spent nearly an hour on the drive telling her about how everything unfolded at the end.

My call with TikTok was just as insightful. Her summation was: "If Pants is your soulmate, it's obvious neither of you are ready. Go be with Birds for now."

My two trusty confidants, both of whom had been champions of the psychic, were getting off the "Pants is my soulmate" train. *Maybe it's time I do too.*

The rest of my trip home was filled with wise insight from Eminem and my own deep reflection, leading me to the only conclusion that made sense: like the situation with Zion and the saguaro cactus, the conversation with Pants didn't happen because it wasn't meant to.

By the time I arrived in Tucson, I was clear. I wanted to be all in with Birds. I drove straight to her place, wearing my Utah clothes and with gear and half-eaten snacks in my trunk. I pulled into my usual spot in front of her house, jumped out of the car, barreled through the gate, and knocked repeatedly on her door. The knob slowly turned, and then there she was, hair tied back and bird slippers on. She gave me a huge smile.

I threw my arms around her. "I'm so happy to see you!"

"Me too." She gave me a tight embrace.

"I missed you," I whispered into her ear.

"I'm so glad you're home," she whispered back.

I kicked off my shoes, and we laid down on her couch, where we snuggled, talked, and I shared some pictures from my trip. I made sure to swipe past the photos with Pants and me. Naked and Afraid had said they appeared too couple-y when I sent some to her the day before. Although I disagreed, I opted to focus on the solo ones where I looked like a hardcore adventurer.

That night, after Birds and I crawled into her bed, we scooted as close as we could, facing each other. I interlocked her fingers with mine and squeezed her hand.

"I know we haven't talked about it, but how would you feel about being exclusive?" I asked, looking into her eyes and donning a big smile.

"I mean, we're kind of doing that already," she said. "But I suppose it's good to be on the same page."

I made my choice. No more confusion, and no more torment. It was done. And I couldn't wait to move forward on this journey with Birds.

From Every Angle

"I finally get clarity, put my whole heart in, and she's moving forward like we're just casually dating," I said, a bit out of breath.

We rounded the bend, waving at a few Tumamoc regulars passing us on their way down.

"She's taking it slow," Naked and Afraid said.

"It's too slow. It's like she's not even into me."

"Really?" she replied, more so in disbelief.

"So, yesterday she told me she didn't want to sleep over. Then, right before leaving my house last night, she changed her mind, and I had to give her a toothbrush. I don't get it." I glanced at my watch and saw my heart rate skyrocketing.

"Well, I know you think you got clarity in Utah . . . but I'm not so sure," she said.

"What? I thought you were all about Birds now."

"You have doubts again," she said. "Plus, there's something there with you and Pants that won't go away. And you know it."

I wanted to say, "Please don't open this door. You told me to be done with this, and I finally made my decision." But instead, I leaned in. "Pants keeps texting me bird pictures and asking me how things are going. She said she bought me a bird birthday card, even though she knows my birthday isn't for six months."

"That's because she likes you," she said in a teasing sort of way.

"Not true. If she did, she would have said so in Utah."

"She couldn't say anything. You told her about Birds before your trip, even though I told you not to. If she had said anything, she would have just seemed like a jerk."

Okay. There's that.

"Maybe. All I know is that after all this confusion and torment, I chose Birds, and now it seems like she doesn't want to be with me!" The back of my neck was getting hot, more from my own frustration than the sun.

"She doesn't know what you went through. Cut her some slack."

We huffed our way up the last fifty or so yards and tapped the gate at the top of the hill. I looked at my watch to check our time.

"But what if she changed her mind?" I asked, turning my attention back to her.

We started strolling down. "Go read your plan—not the soulmate search stuff, but the other things on your list!"

"Where's your 'go with the flow' speech?" I asked. "Aren't I supposed to sit back and let life happen?"

"That's not what I meant by 'go with the flow.' Anyway, you have to do *something* to get out of this headspace."

"Well, this couldn't have come at a worse time. Birds has a friend coming tomorrow for eight days. We won't have any alone time and might not even see each other at all. And I don't think going to another women's circle or buying more love crystals is gonna help."

"Look at this flower," Birds said.

She and her friend squatted down and started taking pictures from every possible angle. I looked at the trailhead sign fifty or so yards back and let out a deep breath. *It's going to be a long day.*

We started up again, but two minutes later, they stopped.

"That one's really purple. Let me get a picture," the friend said. She crouched down and took a close-up shot. "Yeah, then she left and worked at this other lab."

"What? She told me she would never work there!" Birds said.

I wanted to shout, "How many times are we gonna stop? And why in the world am I here with you? I don't know any of these people or anything about labs." But I didn't. I just quietly strolled along.

After a couple of hours of the photography shoot disguised as a hike, we finally made it to Romero Pools. I laid on the warm sand next to several carved-out divots filled with water. I relished in the peacefulness of my own little beach while the two of them continued exploring the area and chatting about old friends.

When I got home after the hike, I called Naked and Afraid. "What am I doing?" I unzipped my backpack and started taking out snack baggies.

"What happened?"

"I felt like a third wheel. I mean, I get it. She has a houseguest. I really like her, but she doesn't seem like she's into me at all. I guess I'm just sad."

"Remember, if things aren't going the way you want them to, you can end it. Your relationship with her has nothing to do with the whole Pants situation. It's never been a choice between the two of them; it's a choice about what you want."

"That's exactly what my therapist has been telling me."

"Well, maybe you should listen to us."

Hey, we're about to get off the streetcar by campus. Be there in a few.

I didn't reply with a smile emoji or some sweet words of excitement. Instead, I texted:

Naked and Afraid and I had spent the morning at the Tucson Festival of Books, going from presentations to publisher booths to various exhibits, occasionally processing my dilemma. Afterward, I was planning to meet Birds and her friend for lunch.

I walked out from under the food tent so they would be able to see me, while Naked and Afraid held our table.

"Hey," I said as they strolled up.

"Hey," Birds said back, with what seemed like the same lackluster I was feeling.

No hug, no kiss, no nothing.

We made our way over to the table.

"I'm taking off," Naked and Afraid said as she started walking away.

All I wanted to say was, "Nooooo. I'm so uncomfortable. Don't leave me!" Instead, I said, "Okay. I'll catch up with you later."

And then there were three.

We grabbed lunch from one of the food trucks and ate while trying to have a conversation over the hundreds of loud voices echoing under the tent and then walked around the festival, stopping at booths I hadn't yet visited. On our way out, her friend made a quick restroom stop, which gave Birds and I our first alone time in days.

"What are you doing Tuesday night?" Birds asked as she sat down on a nearby stairwell.

I put my backpack down and joined her. "I have my writing group until seven. Why?"

"How about dinner and a sleepover?"

I couldn't tell if she sensed something was off and had decided to throw me a lifeline or if this was a true invitation coming from someone who simply missed me.

I took a deep breath and looked right at her. "But you have company until Thursday. Won't that be weird?"

"No. She's staying on the pullout couch in the other room. I really want to see you."

"Sure." As the word fell out of my mouth, I realized I had agreed to a sleepover date just days before I was planning to break up with her.

On Tuesday, I arrived at Birds's place with my overnight bag, ready for an awkward evening. As soon as she answered the door, I said hello and raced past her to drop my stuff on her bed before returning to the living room for a quick hug.

"Something smells good. What did you make?" I asked, taking in a deep breath.

"Veggie curry with rice," she replied, smiling.

She knew I loved her curry. *Shit. Now I feel even more terrible about breaking up with her later.*

We all wandered into the kitchen where Birds handed each of us a plate. The friend dished her serving first and then went to the living room. As I was scooping veggies, I looked through the doorway and noticed that she took one of the two places on the couch.

Birds ended up sitting in the other spot, and I parked myself in a wooden chair pulled from the corner of the room and staged for a third person. It felt like the hike all over again.

After we finished, we sat around having strained conversation for hours . . . with no end in sight.

At the stroke of ten, I yawned and stretched my arms into the air. "I'm pretty tired. I think I'm gonna head to bed."

Birds jumped up from the couch. "Me too."

After a speedy dinner cleanup, Birds and I went into her room and closed the door. It was our first private moment in almost a week, outside of the friend's restroom break at the book festival. In some ways, I was relieved to have escaped the dinner conversation but anxious about being alone with Birds, knowing what my intentions for the night were. Once I started getting into my pajamas, though, I realized I hadn't thought through what you do if you break up with someone just before falling asleep in their bed. *Do I just go home?*

I sluffed off my concern and walked toward the bathroom anyway. "I'm gonna take my contacts out."

"Okay."

As soon as I exited, Birds passed by me, like the next person in line would at a public restroom. I got into bed, nestling into the side I slept on, and she joined me a few minutes later. We laid much further apart than usual, making small talk.

The light conversation about our days made its way to an analysis of our friends' love lives, at least as they were portrayed on Facebook, when suddenly I blurted out, "What do you want . . . with you and me? I know we've talked about this before. But maybe things have changed over the last few weeks."

This is not how you break up with someone, I thought. But then again, I had never really broken up with anyone, unless you consider sending a breakup text to a partner who already ghosted you.

"Well, I love spending time with you. I wish we could be together more."

"Seriously?" I raised an eyebrow.

"It's just I don't want to pull you from everything you like to do. So, I've tried to back off," she said. "Plus, this week was so busy. I haven't had a houseguest in years."

I propped myself up on my elbow and looked her right in the eyes. "You want to spend *more* time with me?"

I was in unfamiliar territory. Zion walked out, and Runner didn't get on the plane—clear indications of wanting to spend *less*, not *more* time with me.

"Yes. And do more sleepovers."

I dropped down on the pillow. "You said last week you don't like sleeping over."

"It came out all wrong. The thing is, I hardly sleep because all I do is focus on trying to lay still so I don't wake you up. And then I'm tired all day."

"I didn't know that. I thought you just didn't want to spend time with me."

She reached out to hold my hand. "It's the exact opposite."

A voice in my head started shouting, and I was pretty sure it was The General. "You almost broke up with her, you idiot! Put on your big-girl pants, and say what's on your mind. Don't just walk away from this because you're too afraid to be vulnerable."

I cleared my throat, pushed The General's voice to the back of my mind, and said softly, "I've just felt so far away these past couple of weeks. Instead of talking to you, I made assumptions and pulled back. I'm sorry."

"I'm sorry, too. It's been hard these last few days since we haven't had any alone time together. I've missed you."

"I've missed you too." I paused. We could have ended on that amazing, lovely connection, snuggle all night, and move forward with our budding magical love . . . or I could go into full-blown big-girl pants.

"It's more than just the last few days, though," I continued, opting for the big-girl pants approach. "Since we started dating, sometimes we'll go twenty-four hours without exchanging a single message. I don't need a huge text exchange. But maybe a check-in would be nice."

She nodded and squeezed my hand.

"Or when I text something like 'good morning' and you do finally respond, it's mostly about work." I waited for her to say something, but she just looked lovingly at me. "I want more sweet, silly stuff. The 'I'm thinking about you' message and not the 'I'm thinking about this spreadsheet' message."

She laughed. "I do think about you . . . all the time. Just so you know."

"Really?"

She smiled and nodded. "*All* the time."

We laid there, looking at each other. The horrible dread I had been carrying was gone. Now I felt like I couldn't get close enough to her.

I scooted over until I was nestled in her arms, and we fell asleep cuddling.

After I got home the next morning, she sent me a text.

Thanks for brightening my day. ☺

☺ It was so nice to wake up with you. And I loved being able to spend time together last night.

We should definitely do that more often.

I was thinking the same thing!

I was also thinking that not every tough conversation ends up with a date fleeing while you're at the dentist or a "for now" rejection from your so-called divine partner. More importantly, though, I realized I don't have to leave at the first sign of discomfort for fear that I might stay in a relationship too long again.

The Universe Has Spoken

After the shift with Birds, I was reenergized to get back to my joyful, positive, not-spiraling self The Zen Master liked so much. I could feel I had been putting a lot of negative, worried, and anxious vibes out into the universe. So as Naked and Afraid had suggested, I revisited The Plan. The first thing I did was make an appointment with the energy healer to cleanse myself of all my recent internal chaos.

Before I knew it, I was back in the familiar dimly lit room. The soothing sounds of trickling water from the speaker stood in stark contrast to the rushing shower noise from Pants's sleep app. I laid on the heated table under a thin blanket and closed my eyes.

"I'm going to place my hands over your chakras, filling you with light and love," the energy healer said.

"Okay," I mumbled. "I could really use some light and love right now."

I tried to clear my mind and allow visions to pour in. But like my first visit, I started thinking about my schedule and the tasks on my to-do list.

My new mantra seemed to be "Get milk, pick up toilet paper." *Where is my cool llama?*

Just as I was finishing compiling my daily checklist, an image of Pants appeared in my head. Suddenly, I heard *Zap!* It reminded me of a bug zapper making that awful sound when the poor fly gets too close. Pants disappeared, and then "Get milk, pick up toilet paper" started circling through my mind as if nothing had happened.

Ever since Naked and Afraid visited the psychic, she had convinced herself Twin Flame was her destiny. And because they had finally found each other, all could be right in the cosmic world.

But with twin flames, one or both are bound to get burned. After a few false emergency breakups earlier, the fire was finally extinguished in mid-March. Twin Flame called it off . . . rather unexpectedly. Naked and Afraid was left with only a few of Twin Flame's items, a handful of love poems she had written for her, and the biggest broken heart imaginable. The Earth stopped rotating that day. Even I felt it.

Minutes after the breakup, Naked and Afraid called me to share the whole story. "Did she ever really love me? Do you believe we're twin flames?" she asked while sobbing.

I evaded the question about their imminent destiny but assured her that Twin Flame had loved her.

Day two post-breakup, I checked in with her.

How are you?

Sad, but okay. Went to the gym, but didn't go in. Just eating cookies, watching Netflix, and using my under-the-desk cycle.

She then sent a picture of an aerial view of her feet strapped into pedals. I could only imagine the tears pouring down her face as she cycled.

Day three, in came a screenshot of a quote: "I see happiness is mine to enjoy." No explanation.

Then, another message.

Send me Tarot Lady's number.

I shared her contact information.

Day four, another quote arrived: "I am ready to start the new chapter in my life." No caption. She was definitely not ready to start a new chapter. A few hours later, another quote: "I am very proud of the life I'm creating."

Day five, she sent a video of a cat as a 911 operator, several updates about work, her latest hiking time, another inspirational quote, and a screenshot of a comment Twin Flame made on a mutual friend's Facebook page.

As I witnessed her grief, reminders of my own heartbreak flooded back. I knew the pain of having unanswered questions, profound loneliness, and deep sorrow for a future that would never be. I hated those feelings. And while I was well on my way with my healing journey, I knew hers had only just begun.

"How's everything with Birds?" Pants asked. We were chatting on the phone while I was driving to Phoenix to get Kiddo from the airport.

"Great now, but things were off for a while."

"What do you mean?" she asked.

I wasn't sure how much to share but then opted to fill her in on the details . . . since we *were* supposedly friends.

"It's good you worked through it. You have to have open communication," she said.

"Yeah, I'm realizing that now." I sighed.

"Well, I have an update," she said, more as an announcement than a statement.

She paused, and my stomach did a flip. I knew exactly what she was going to say.

"I've been chatting with someone. She's a firefighter and is gonna visit in a couple of weeks, over Easter."

"That's awesome!" The words came out far too fast and enthusiastic to be believable. "That's the same weekend I'm taking Birds on her birthday trip," I said. "I'm assuming you met online? How long have you been talking?"

"Since, like, January."

I paused before blurting out, "We've hung out a ton since then, and you haven't said a word about her."

"I didn't want to jinx it," she said.

I could feel my foot pressing hard on the gas pedal. All I wanted to say was, "That's crap, and you know it. You obviously didn't tell me for a reason." But all I could muster up was, "Tell me about her."

"She sleeps with a noise machine on too. As soon as I found out, I thought of you."

Thought about me enough to not say anything about this person's existence? I let out an awkward laugh. "Well, then it's a perfect match."

After a bit more chitchat during which I slowed my vehicle to a more reasonable speed, we said goodbye, and I immediately called Naked and Afraid.

"Hello?" She answered on the first ring.

"She met someone. This lady is visiting her in a few weeks." The words spewed out of my mouth.

"Pants, I presume?" Her voice was unusually calm.

"Yes, Pants!" I could feel my grip tighten on the steering wheel.

"You knew the day would come. How are you feeling?" She sounded like my therapist.

"Ambivalent," I said, eyes fixated on the road.

"If you were ambivalent, you wouldn't be calling me." Okay, my therapist would not say that.

"I *am* ambivalent. I told you I decided to be done with all the confusion. So, I'm done!"

"You can't just declare it and make it so." She was still unusually calm.

"Sure, I can."

Only $19.95

"Get a personalized sketch of your soulmate. One hundred percent accuracy. Only $19.95."

I stared at the message and then closed my email. *Hmm. A hundred percent accuracy*, I thought, as I wandered into the kitchen to make coffee.

Over the next hour, I sipped on my morning brew and reread the message several times . . . until I finally pulled out my credit card and began entering the details into what looked like a shady website. Before clicking the "pay now" button, though, I paused, not because of any concern for identity theft. Instead, a booming voice inside my head yelled, "Do not go there. You have moved on. This will only make things worse."

I leaned back in my desk chair to contemplate when a quieter, more even-keeled voice popped in. "Wouldn't it be worth it to finally get an answer? And for only $19.95?"

"Yes!" I said out loud. "I need to put an end to this mystery."

Phoenix, who was curled up on the chair next to my desk, didn't even perk up with my definitive revelation. I then clicked the "pay now" button and off went my twenty bucks to a sketch artist from another part of the world who would validate or undermine my path to love.

Two days later, I received a lengthy email describing my supposed soulmate, listing many attributes like adventuresome, passionate, determined, and loyal. It ended with: "You may also feel a strong connection to her, as if you've known her forever."

I then opened the attachment. It was a black-and-white sketch, similar to a caricature drawing from the state fair, featuring a woman in her forties with brown, wavy hair, feathered in the front. She had a wide grin and appeared to be squinting, as though she was forcing her eyes open while staring into the sun.

I compared the drawing to photos of both Pants and Birds. Nope . . . neither. Not even one characteristic was similar. Either I hadn't met Sketch Lady yet, or I'd just blown twenty dollars on a bunch of nonsense after all.

I paid to have someone draw a soulmate sketch for me. I know it is total BS, but I was curious.

I shot the message off to Pants without much thought.

You have to send it to me!

I forwarded her a copy with my own caption.

Not my type. $19.95.

Suddenly, a wave of terror came over me. I hadn't told her about any of my cosmos stuff—not the tarot cards, love manifests, healing crystals, and certainly not the psychics. She would surely think I had lost my mind with this.

Looks like a drawing of a serial killer you'd see on Dateline. LOL.

Once her reply came in, I let out a deep sigh of relief.

Like she buried her husband in the backyard.

I couldn't help but laugh as I re-read my response to her. Three little dots popped up.

Or a Jane Doe body they found and are trying to figure out who it is.

We continued to banter with no pause between replies.

Total cold case files.

Ha ha! Maybe she's better looking in person. LOL.

I'm sure she's a hottie and hikes a lot.

LOL

The whole thing is ridiculous.

😂😂 We all have a little of that in us.

So true! What's yours?

That's a secret. LOL. Maybe you'll see it in real life sometime.

At least I knew I wasn't the only one with a secret.

The Zeneral

The following week was Kiddo's thirteenth birthday. I was ready to focus on anything other than my love-life saga. Instead, I intended to put all of my energy into baking her an epic cake, like I had done every year for the past decade.

The ritual started when Zion and I made three cakes, each a character from *Thomas and Friends*, for her third birthday. For her fourth, it was a 3D version of Mater from *Cars*, including donuts for wheels and an upside-down peanut butter cup for the nose.

By the time Kiddo's fifth birthday rolled around, Zion and I had split up, so Runner helped me make a 3D tabby cat. While all the cakes had been a hit at her parties, this particular one was a showstopper.

"Which piece do you want, birthday girl?" I asked after bringing the cat cake out to a patio filled with small children and their parents.

All the kids surrounded the table, leaning over each other to get as close as possible.

"The face," my daughter said.

I held up a huge knife. "This is incredibly morbid . . . defacing a cat."

The adults laughed.

I lowered the blade slowly and sliced off the face, pretzel whiskers and all. I set the piece on her plate.

"I want the tail," some kid yelled.

"I want the paw," another said.

Before I knew it, the kids were shouting out anatomical pieces. I imagined myself as a butcher and baker all in one.

The next seven cakes were a joint effort between Runner and me, with the surprise unveiling taking place at Kiddo's birthday party every year.

"Just tell me," she would say a few days before. "What flavor is it, at least?"

"I can't. But you'll love it."

This birthday, though, I was on my own. No Zion; no Runner. Just me and a box of Funfetti mix. My mind was feeding me motivational and inspirational messages to pump me up for the challenge.

"You nailed it with the tooth fairy situation," the voice said.

But despite the "You got this, girl" mantras, I could feel the anxiety bubbling inside. I didn't want to screw this up . . . for Kiddo or for me.

I pushed my nerves aside and decided on a 3D Baby Yoda cake, which seemed simple enough on paper. I coordinated with my brother to make everything ahead of time at my house and then do the assembly and decorating the next day at their place, right before the party.

The preparation went as planned, and I was able to sneak everything into my car for Kiddo's and my drive up to Phoenix.

The following morning, my brother and sister-in-law decided to take the kids to the aquarium so I could finish up. While my brother was getting the girls situated in the car, my sister-in-law lingered back.

"Here's a spoon and spatula. Oh, I got you some extra frosting too." She sat everything out for me.

"Thanks. All I have to do is stack the cakes for the body and put the Rice Krispies head on top . . . and then frost it. Most of the hard stuff is done."

"Here, these might help. Use as many as you want." She handed me a bag filled with wooden skewers. "We should be back in a couple hours."

"Perfect. I really don't need a lot of time."

She headed out. As soon as I heard the garage door close, I got out the rest of the ingredients and supplies.

I began by setting one cake on top of the other, gluing them together with a layer of pudding. This would be Baby Yoda's little body. I then attached the Rice Krispies head using two of the skewers.

"Perfect!" I shouted to no one. "That should do the trick!"

I hadn't yet finished frosting the body when I noticed one of the Rice Krispies ears starting to sag. I pushed the sticky hunk back on and continued with my masterpiece.

Plunk. The ear finally dropped to the plate. I repositioned it and then stabbed another skewer into the head to hold it in place.

Plunk. The other ear fell off. I did my skewer trick once again and went back to work spreading the remainder of the frosting.

Plunk! The head rolled backward onto the counter, like a football after a fumble. I gasped and caught it before it landed on the floor.

As I was standing there holding the sticky mess, the phone rang. It was my sister-in-law. I put her on speaker.

"Hey, the balloon delivery guy is out front. Can you open the door for him?" she asked.

"Sure."

I set the head down on the counter and ran to the sink to wash the thick frosting off my hands.

"Oh, and we'll be back in, like, thirty minutes. Is that enough time?"

I looked at the trail of green icing across the countertop and pile of broken skewers strewn about the now-shredded cake.

"Yep. That works."

After bringing the balloons inside, I returned to the kitchen and stood staring at the mess. I could hear the timer counting down in my mind—twenty-nine minutes. I paused, closed my eyes, and called on both The Zen Master and The General. I needed one to help me embrace the idea of a plan B and the other to make it happen.

A solution then came to me. I pressed the cake chunks into the shape of Baby Yoda's body from an aerial view rather than a 3D one. I then set the head at the top and used the extra frosting to cover the disaster. It actually looked like Yoda, if he were a bakery item.

Once everyone returned home for the party, we devoured the cake. And no one knew of the near catastrophe. They just saw that I made an epic creation . . . on my own.

But I wasn't really solo on this mission—The General and The Zen Master offered much-needed assistance. I hadn't seen them work together as "The Zeneral" since karate-chop night with Birds. It was nice to have them both back.

The Omission Condition

"Neither of them knows about any of this—the psychics, signs and symbols, manifests . . . none of it. I want to be open with both of them about everything. It's only fair."

"Yes, I agree." Tarot Lady looked deep into my eyes.

"Who should I tell first?"

She flipped over some cards, swung a pendulum, and urged me to start by confessing everything to Pants. "This makes sense. You two seem to be connected through a past life. So, there might be more you need to deal with when it comes to her. Get that resolved before talking to Birds."

I nodded.

"Then, when you tell Birds, you can fill her in on what you and Pants talked about too. It's the only way you can have an honest relationship with her."

While I had been able to summon the courage to ask Birds out *and* be more transparent on "almost breakup night," this situation wasn't at all about vulnerability like those were. Instead, it was about being open about what I had kept from both of them.

But first order of business—tell Pants.

A few days later, I finally got up the nerve to text Pants asking if we could chat about something important. I received a near-immediate response that she would call right after lunch, which gave me some time to overthink and go into a what-if tailspin. For the next hour, I kept glancing at my phone, not sure if I wanted it to ring after all.

Soon, it did. I felt a cold rush of fear run through my body, and my hands were trembling. I ran out to the patio, took a deep breath, and answered.

"Hello?" I said.

"Helllllloooo?"

I started the conversation with, "So, I have a funny story to tell you." I paused momentarily to get up my nerve. "Back in December, I went to a psychic. It was just hours before my second date with someone from the apps. But I got so rattled, I called off the date. More on that later." I could feel the words flying out, leaving barely any room for a breath. "Anyway, the psychic babbled on and on about my ex. Then I told her I didn't really care about the past and would rather hear about my current love life."

"A psychic?" she asked.

"Yep. She told me about my supposed divine partner, and after going into great detail, it was clear she was talking about you."

Silence.

By this point, I was circling around my patio furniture. *I should have put on my tracker and gotten miles for this*, I thought.

She finally asked, "What's a divine partner?"

"It's basically a soulmate," I blurted out. "I showed her two pictures—one of you and one of my ex. She picked you. She also said this person was a Cancer. Then, I found out later *you're* a Cancer. So weird."

I was whipping around the patio at record speeds waiting for her response. But there was nothing on the other end of the phone except more silence.

"The lady seemed legit," I went on. "And then Naked and Afraid got a reading from her, and she was spot on! But I wanted to double-check anyway, so I went to another psychic. She said nearly the same thing."

I started laughing out of nervousness. I could hear chuckling on the other end, which at least meant she was still there.

"Both told me that you and I would be together within three months. But that window ended when we were in Utah and nothing happened. And it couldn't have because I'm dating Birds."

Although my brain wasn't able to keep up with my mouth, what felt like nonsense kept flowing. "But there had been so many signs. Like I passed an exit for a road with your last name on my way to my stepmom's at Christmas. Never saw that before. And your name was painted on a big boulder I saw while hiking." I took a big breath. "Okay. I'm freaking out. Say something."

"This is hilarious!" she said and let out a huge laugh.

"Hilarious like 'Ha ha, what a fun story' or hilarious like 'You have lost your mind'?"

"The story."

A small, wave of relief set in, and I slowed my pace.

"Well, the timing was also weird. The whole thing happened only a couple weeks after you rejected me on text. It's not like I was gonna tell you then." As soon as I uttered the words, I realized we had never talked about the rejection. *Shit*, I thought.

She jumped in. "It wasn't a rejection; it was a 'For now, let's be friends,'" she said.

"It didn't sound like 'Maybe later.' It was more like the total friend zone," I said a bit too sarcastically.

"It was not! You know how important it is for me to develop a friendship before dating someone."

"Well, I took it as a hard no."

"I said 'For now'!"

I again began brisk patio pacing, weighing my regret for not having asked what "for now" actually meant when she sent the text. So much for big-girl pants back then. It was more like leg-halfway-out pants.

"Okay. Fine. Well, here we are," I said.

She didn't offer any consolation or further explanation. Just silence.

I waited a moment before diving into more details about the psychics and the signs. Thankfully, I stayed tight-lipped about the rappelling wedding vision and my marriage mantra. I was sure there was only so much she could take.

"Do you still want to be friends with me?" I asked.

"I'm gonna block you now." She laughed. "Just kidding. Of course we'll still be friends."

After saying our goodbyes, I noticed the huge weight lifted off me was immediately replaced with a big pile of awkwardness. That felt familiar.

The next day came around, and I hadn't heard from Pants, which wasn't unusual as we would sometimes skip a day or two. But I couldn't help but worry about the thoughts going through her head and whether we'd ever talk again.

At the forty-eight-hour mark, I got a text from her right as I was pulling up to Birds's house. I parked the car and opened the message, only to see a photo of a bird-watching event with a note underneath.

> ☺ Lol!!! I didn't know birding was really a sport.

I wasn't sure if this was her way of ribbing me about Birds to remind me we were just friends, a "We're cool. Let's pick up where we left off before you went off the rails" gesture, or simply reflective of an intense bout of amnesia.

And a serious one, too. I learned that people travel like 500 miles to see a bird. I asked, "How do you know what tree it's sitting in, and what if it flies away during the 8-hour drive there?!!!"

I turned the engine off and sat in my car, waiting for a response. She said nothing about the psychics, and instead we messaged about my pet parakeets growing up. It was easy to slip into our usual banter, filled with LOLs and emojis, and ignore the elephant. We were good at that.

Once we wrapped up, I put my phone in my pocket and proceeded with my date with Birds. Everything seemed back to normal, except that Pants knew far too much about my parakeets, and I still hadn't talked to Birds.

I think I found my side job. LOL.

Two days after our parakeet chat, I heard from Pants again. She had forwarded a link to a story about getting paid to watch crime shows. I tapped on it and read the headline.

This could definitely be a get-rich-quick kind of thing for you! Haha!

LOL

You have a few minutes to chat? Just wanted to follow up about the other day.

Yes. Can I call you a little later?

Sure.

I sat outside waiting for the call, knowing I would need to resume patio-pacing once we started talking.

Around six, the phone rang. After a quick exchange of niceties, I got down to business. "I thought about our conversation and realized it probably sounded like I blamed the psychics for my confusion. But in reality, I was already confused about my feelings for you."

"Okay," she said.

Okay?

"Now that you've had a few days to process, do you have any thoughts or questions?" I continued walking in circles.

"Yeah. How are you so sure the psychics were talking about me?"

"The details they *both* shared . . . it had to be you."

"Do you believe them?"

"I did . . . at the time. I don't know what I believe now. Clearly, we passed the three-month window, and we're not together."

I paused, but she didn't say a word.

Big breath. "Had you ever thought about exploring anything more than friendship with me during that time? I mean, you basically rejected me twice. But did you *ever* have feelings?"

"I said 'For now'!"

We both let out uncomfortable laughs. I knew what I was asking wasn't fair. One answer would be disrespectful to Birds, and the other would hurt my feelings.

"There was always a possibility," she said.

I stopped pacing. "What do you mean 'a possibility'?"

"I mean, if you lived here, and we had dinner, like, every Wednesday, something might have happened. I don't know."

Her words hit me to the core. All my confusing emotions swirled back in, full force. This conversation was supposed to quell those, but instead, it was making things worse.

"I'm not telling you this because I'm planning on driving ten hours to your house to profess my love. I just wanted to understand what you were thinking during those three months."

"I know. We're good. I think this whole thing is pretty funny!" Although she laughed, it sounded like an awkward one.

I offered a courtesy chuckle to play along, all while my eyes filled with tears of disappointment for still lacking clarity and the overwhelming guilt for still wanting it.

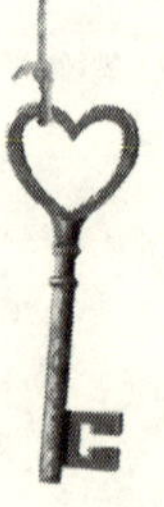

Reality Check

Just days after the confession to Pants, a friend of mine asked if I would be interested in getting a free spiritual reading from some lady she knew. There was one catch—the woman was in training, trying to earn hours for her energy healer certification. Despite the chaos the cosmos had created for me, I couldn't help myself. Maybe I'd get the insight I needed to bypass the journey of discovery and skip to that place of knowing I so craved. Or maybe not—but it was free.

A few days later, the lady and I met online for our session.

"Hi," I said. I was sitting at my desk with a pad of paper and a pen.

"Hello. Thank you for meeting with me. I'm going to share what I feel from your vibrations," she said.

Either she was a get-right-down-to-business person or needed every minute for her certification.

"Okay."

"Spirits are shaking your energy loose because your vibration is off-kilter. Loosening that energy is helping you build up strength."

I started taking notes. I wrote "vibration,""off-kilter,""strength," hoping these words would make sense later on.

"You need to release when you feel agitated. If not, it will be harsh. Misdirection and confusion will take place," she said.

After an hour of this woman droning on and on about what seemed like nonsense, we logged off. I put the pages of my scribbled, incoherent notes in the folder with all my other spiritual resources, including my stick figure worksheets from my intuition coach.

I called Naked and Afraid.

"Well, that was a bust," I said. "She babbled about misdirection and agitation and vibrations. I didn't understand one thing she was saying. Then she made me do these strange breathing exercises while she watched."

"That's kind of creepy."

"I know! I felt like I was getting ready to have a baby, and she just stared at me as I huffed and puffed."

"Weird. Did you learn anything?"

"No. But she got an hour toward her certification. Glad I could help. Just one more experience to put in The Plan and then check off."

We both laughed.

While I wasn't going to abandon the spiritual realm altogether, I started to realize that a healthy dose of skepticism, at least for the shadier advice I got, might serve me well.

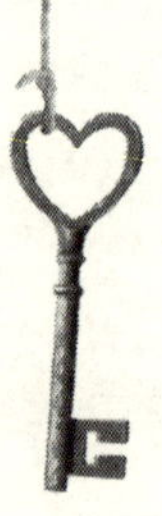

Adventures with Birds

The next day was Birds's birthday, and emboldened by my Yoda cake, I tried my hand at baking once again. This time, no frosting on the counter, shredded bits of cake, or skewers flying about. Instead, I easily crafted a double-decker round cake, covering it with caramel frosting. I then assembled a pretzel nest on top, where I perched a brown ceramic bird I had picked up at the craft store.

On the evening of her birthday, Birds hosted a small gathering with some of her friends. She insisted on cooking for us, to which there were no complaints. We all devoured her mouth-watering veggie burritos—hers doused with hot sauce, of course.

While everyone sat around chatting on the patio, I snuck inside to get the cake stashed in the back of the fridge. I adorned it with candles and tiptoed up behind her as the group burst into song. She looked at me with a huge, glowing smile, and a surge of warmth flowed through my body. It was the first time I had felt such a magnetic connection with her.

Later on, while cleaning up, she rinsed the icing off the little bird and rested it on the windowsill above the sink. She gave me the same smile from earlier, and the warmth rushed back. *Is this* pow, boom, bang*?*

—

The weekend finally came, and Birds and I were only hours from embarking on her birthday adventure to Safford, a small town not far from Tucson. While getting all the snacks organized on the kitchen counter, I shot off a quick message to Pants to check in about her trip with Firefighter.

Getting excited?

Yep! What about you?

Super excited! I can't wait to surprise her with the cool stuff we're gonna do. You nervous?

I bet she's gonna love it! We've talked a lot, so it's almost like we already know each other. But the initial meeting is always awkward.

Butterflies?

Yeah, I'd say so.

When in doubt, eat candy if you get nervous!

I have my snack bag all packed.

Noise machine too? Cached episodes of Dateline on your phone?

I'm taking the fan. And she downloaded shows we both watch.

Oh good!!! You're all set. 😂

Lol! Well, enjoy your weekend and chat next week.
Have fun!!!

Part of me wondered what her trip would be like and if she and Firefighter would fall passionately in love. Thankfully, though, I was preoccupied with my adventure. The General had everything scheduled—down to the minute—and I couldn't wait.

The weekend with Birds began with a short full-moon hike in a remote mountain range just outside of Safford. It was only short because we spent most of our time driving the wrong direction down a precarious dirt road and then struggling to back out. By the time we hit the trail, it was late, and we were hungry. So, we called it quits after a few miles and headed into town for dinner.

"I wonder why they're making us eat out of to-go containers with plastic cutlery. I mean, everyone else has real plates and stuff," I said, after the server brought us our food.

"Maybe because we're on the patio. I don't know. But it's so much waste, especially lids we aren't even gonna use." Birds, being so eco-conscious, always pointed out ways we could save the environment.

Vroom. An amplified muffler let out a deafening sound as a car raced past us down the road.

I shouted over it. "I totally agree."

Vroom. Another flew by.

"Maybe this is why we're the only ones on the patio," I yelled. "And they give us lids so once we've had enough of these mufflers, we can take off and finish dinner somewhere else!"

This was not what I had envisioned for day one.

After a night of snuggling and talking, we headed out for an early morning hike in a beautiful riparian area. She wore one of her many flannels and had her hair tied back in her usual bun. I, on the other hand, sported a zip-up workout top and had on my bright orange baseball hat with the embroidered hiker. It was like outdoorsy lesbian meets sporty lesbian. But we were a cute match.

As we trekked up the trail, it was clear that day two was already off to a better start. The sun was shining, and conversation was flowing. Periodically, we would stop so she could glance through her binoculars to spot a tiny bird nestled on a tree branch high above us. I would wait patiently until she found it. Then, she would make her way over to me and give me a tight embrace. I learned quickly: She sees a bird; I get a hug. I liked that.

Once we got to a shady spot by the river, we pulled out our lunches. I took some photos of her as she nibbled on a sandwich and watched one particular bird fly back and forth between a tree and a rock crevice. Her smile glowed, just like on her birthday, and I lit up just being near her.

We finished lunch and made the short hike back to the car. I had made an appointment for us to spend the rest of the day at a mineral spa.

"I'm ready to just relax this afternoon," I said on the drive over.

"Me too." She squeezed my hand. "And spend time with you."

When we walked into the spa, we were greeted by a wafting smell of essential oils and a lady who, after having us fill out all the liability paperwork, escorted us to a tiny private room with what looked like an oversized bathtub filled with steaming water. Birds and I slowly got in, inch by inch, until we were both fully submerged from the neck down.

"The water is super hot," I said as sweat dripped down my face.

She made a cute joke about how I was super hot.

We both let out an awkward laugh, as flirting wasn't really our thing. We then chatted for a bit about our day, while I tried to convince myself that what I was experiencing in this steam room of torture was actually relaxing.

Finally, I couldn't handle the heat any longer. So, I perched myself on the edge with only my lower legs dangling in the water.

"How long are we supposed to be in here?" she asked.

"Oh, thank God! Can we be done with this?" I wanted to shout. But, in an effort to not ruin the moment, I simply said, "I suppose we can get out whenever we want. You ready?"

I barely finished my question before she hopped out. I followed suit, and we then bundled up in the white, fluffy towels they left for us. I peeked out the door, and a rush of cool air blew in. While taking a few deep breaths, I noticed Paperwork Lady waving from down the hall. Apparently, our timing was perfect. There must be a threshold at which the average human can be in one of those tubs, and Paperwork Lady knew exactly what it was.

Birds and I made our way in her direction, where we were then ushered into a large room with two massage tables about twenty feet apart. I removed my tightly wrapped towel and climbed onto one of the tables. I tried to configure my face in the cushioned hole to ensure I could both breathe *and* not choke myself during this next stage of my relaxation journey. But before I could get comfortable, I noticed a steady stream of cold air blowing directly on me from the vent above. *I wish I was back in the scorching tub.* I yanked the paper-thin sheets up over my shoulders, but it didn't help.

"Would you prefer light, medium, or deep pressure?" my massage therapist whispered, once I got settled in.

"Medium would be good."

He gripped the back of my neck with one of his hands and began repeatedly squeezing. I winced and tightened my muscles even more. He then squeezed harder. Either he was trying to rid me of a nonexistent muscle spasm or strangle me.

While I was contemplating his motives, he moved down to my shoulders. "Ooh, you have a big knot here."

He then dug his thumbs into one of my shoulder blades—not the tight muscles around it, but right on the bone.

"Let me work that out." He put his knee on the table for leverage and jabbed me with the point of his elbow.

The more he exerted pressure using his body weight, the more I had to refrain from screaming. I held my breath while he "worked out the knot" . . . all in the name of being more Zen.

"How was your massage?" I asked Birds when we were getting dressed.

"So relaxing. How about you?"

"Let's just say I'm gonna be very sore tomorrow." I proceeded to share the play-by-play, focusing more on the hilarity of the experience than anything.

She laughed and then said "I wish we could have swapped. I know how much you love massages."

Her kindness drummed up anticipated grief for our imminent breakup, which was sure to happen once I confessed my secret. I just responded with, "You're so sweet."

We savored the aroma of the essential oils one last time and headed to the car to make the short drive to a nearby park for a romantic sunset dinner.

"So, the GPS says to turn here, but it looks all fenced off," I said, slowing the car down. "I swear I researched this, and it looked awesome—big trees, telescopes at night, and people picnicking. This place seems a little sketchy, though."

We drove around for a while longer until we found the official entrance.

"There's a sign." She pointed out the window.

At first, I wondered if maybe the universe had bestowed some mystical symbol upon us. Then I noticed it was an actual sign with the park hours.

"What? I literally looked this up yesterday, and it said they would be open. I'm so sorry!"

"We can find somewhere else to go." She reached over and held my hand, interlocking her fingers with mine. "How about the state park we drove by earlier? It's just up the road."

"Perfect," I said.

By the time we arrived and pulled into the parking lot, it was twilight.

"Everyone's gone," I said. "You still want to eat here?"

"Sure. How about over there on that beach?" She pointed to an area about fifty feet from the car. "We could be right next to the lake."

"Awesome. And we can have the place to ourselves." I smiled at her.

We got out of the car, grabbed everything we needed, and walked toward the water. Once our headlamp beams could reach further, I noticed our "beach" was actually a large gravel boat launch. Neither of us said anything as we laid out the blanket.

While unpacking the spread of food, a chilly wind whipped at our faces and lifted the blanket off the ground. I tossed various packaged items onto the four corners, and then we hunkered down to eat. Nothing says romance like wolfing down pita and hummus while sitting on a pile of rocks on a dark, cold night.

The silence, other than the crunching of carrots and crinkling of the popcorn bag, offered an eerie backdrop. I couldn't eat fast enough and finally jumped up while still chewing my last bite. She followed suit. We threw the food into bags and made a dash for the car.

Although my meticulously crafted romantic weekend was not unfolding as planned, Birds seemed to be in the best spirits. Her ability to embrace Zen reminded me that the whole point of the trip was to enjoy time together . . . and that we were doing.

"You've been everywhere," I said as we hiked up the rocky incline the next morning.

"I have a lot more places on my list," she said.

"Like where?" I asked.

"All of them!"

"Me too!"

We trekked around the bend of a switchback, finally stopping to take in the view of the saguaro-lined canyon below. She took a sip of water from her CamelBak and then put her arms around me. "I'll go with you . . . to all the places."

"I can't wait," I whispered in her ear. And I couldn't.

I was able to send a quick text to Naked and Afraid while Birds was finishing loading her gear into the car.

Despite our misadventures, I've had an amazing time. I'm absolutely sure I'm on the right path. She makes my heart melt.

Good.

I can't believe I almost ruined this relationship with my confusion. But then again, I haven't told her about the psychic stuff. There is definitely still a chance to ruin things.

Enjoy this while you can.

I spent the next few days all-consumed with finding the "perfect" time to tell Birds everything. Although, I was pretty sure there is no "perfect" time to reveal a psychic prophecy in which someone else is your soulmate, I knew if I didn't get it out in the open soon, I would explode from all the angst and guilt.

One evening, while Birds and I were sitting on my patio catching up after work, I just said it. "I need to tell you something."

She turned toward me with a look of concern as if expecting tragic news. "Are you okay?"

I quickly realized my declaration came out far more somber than I had anticipated. *That's what I get for not rehearsing my opening line!* I adjusted myself on the patio cushion and then blurted out, "So, you know how I asked if you wanted to be exclusive back in early March?"

"Yeah?" She furrowed her brow.

"It's a funny story." I had a feeling what I was about to share would likely not get a good laugh from her. "So, back in December, I went to a psychic."

"Okay . . ."

"And she told me my soulmate was Pants." I held my breath and closed my eyes in an ever so slight way, like you do when you are about to get a shot.

She sat there silently, perhaps pondering my confession, all while I was waiting to breathe again.

"Pants?" she finally asked. "Like Utah Pants?"

I let out a small exhale, just enough to mutter, "Um . . . yep."

"Okay." She leaned forward, staring at me in anticipation.

Okay? What do I do with that? Maybe if I just keep talking . . .

"One psychic said Pants was my soulmate—well, actually divine partner, which is basically the same." My voice started speeding up. "Then, a second had a similar message. And both told me something would happen within three months. That three months ended in March on the last day of the Utah trip."

I couldn't tell from the now-stoic look on her face if she was in shock, angry, or hurt. One thing I knew: She did not seem to find humor in this.

I started fidgeting, doing what I could to stop myself from jumping up and pacing. And then I went into a full-blown ramble. "But nothing happened, and there's nothing going on. I was confused. We're just friends, though. The psychics were wrong."

Silence.

"I don't want to be with her. I want to be with you. That's why when I got back from Utah, I asked if we could be exclusive."

After a long pause, she finally spoke. "You saw a psychic?"

"Yes, well, two of them. I went to the first one to find out about my love life. Then I had to double-check everything with the second one."

I then droned on and on about the details of both sessions. She sat still, absent any facial expressions or utterances of even an "uh-huh."

"Okay," I said. "I'll shut up. Say something. Or ask me anything. Whatever. Just something."

More staring and another very long pause. She then said, "Well, we weren't exclusive until after Utah."

Am I really getting off the hook on a technicality?

"I guess my only question is," she started to say, "are you clear *now* that you want to be with me?"

"Crystal clear."

"Then that's all that matters," she said.

"You aren't going to leave me?" It was all I could muster, given that leaving me was something people just did.

"Why would I do that?"

"Because I saw two psychics . . . and was confused about Pants . . . Do you need time to think?"

"There isn't anything to think about. I'm just glad you said something." She snuggled up to me and put her head on my shoulder.

And that was it. After months of anguish, the conversation was finally over. We ate dinner, did our usual routine, and fell asleep cuddling as if nothing had happened. But it definitely had.

Pants texted me first thing the next morning for details.

How did the talk go?

Way better than I expected. Overall, she seemed pretty unfazed. She asked if I was clear I wanted to be with her. I said crystal clear. She told me that was all she needed to hear.

That's awesome.

Naked and Afraid and TikTok, though, had different sentiments about the situation.

"Why she didn't dump your ass, I will never know. I would have kicked you to the curb," Naked and Afraid said. "I mean, here you go waffling between two people, and I was completely devoted to one. How is it I get dumped and you don't?"

TikTok said, "Girl, I don't know how that happened. She has got to be the most forgiving person in the world. I would have been like, 'Uh-uh, we are so done.'"

But we weren't, and I was so relieved. My heart had been aching at the thought of losing her or hurting her.

Part 4

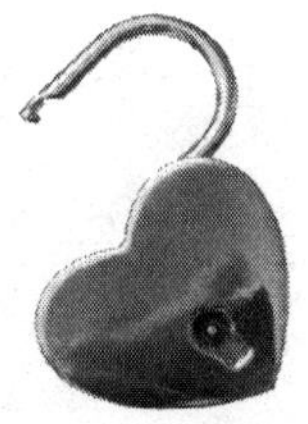

Getting On

Soul Circles

Divulging my secret was supposed to have made all the confusion disappear. But it didn't. I still felt a connection to Pants I just couldn't shake. Only one explanation made sense: Pants and I had unfinished business from a past life. Naked and Afraid had said it. TikTok had said it. Now, Tarot Lady had said it.

As soon as I got into my car after my reading, I texted Naked and Afraid. I'm sure Tarot Lady wondered why I was still parked in front of her house.

> I can't take it anymore. I'm gonna get a past life regression.

> Good. Maybe you can find out more about us.

While I had expected more of a response around my soulmate dilemma, at least she seemed on board.

Another message came in from her.

> I still believe we were Gertrude Stein and Alice Toklas in a past life.

> I know.

Thankfully, she couldn't see me roll my eyes.

Let's not tell too many people yet. They're going to think we're completely out there.

Okay. It stays between you and me.

That would *not* be a hard secret to keep.

Later that evening while eating dinner, I looked online for "past life regression" in Tucson. The headline on one page read, "Quit smoking." Another advertised, "Learn why you are afraid of heights." After scrolling through, I found someone who specialized in uncovering past connections. I left him a voicemail.

After a week with no return call, I decided to restart my search and came across a name I hadn't yet seen. Based on her website, she focused on helping people learn about soul circle intersections across multiple lives. There was no mention of confronting fears of snakes, spiders, or heights. She was exactly who I was looking for. So, I left a message.

The next day, she called while I was out driving. As soon as we started talking, I felt a sense of comfort with her, like being wrapped in a warm blanket. I *knew* she was the one. *Thanks, intuition!* We set an appointment for a couple of weeks out—May 14. While finalizing the details, another call came in, which I let go to voicemail. It ended up being the other regressionist, ten minutes too late.

The Time Capsule

The end of April arrived, and my university's graduation was right around the corner. Typically, I would fly out to Ohio each spring to attend, but with COVID, I hadn't been there in more than two years. Now, I was about to board a plane and revisit my pre-pandemic, pre-breakup life.

The timing felt spot-on. I was finally cruising along with The Plan, had ditched the hundred-pound weight of secrecy I'd been carrying around, and booked my past life regression. I could now put all my energy into coming face-to-face with my old life and get that last bit of closure I was waiting on.

Once I got to Ohio, I drove the rental car to a coworker's house where I would stay during my visits. The room I slept in had furniture, décor, and personal items Runner and I had left there after moving back west years earlier. It looked like a mini version of our old house.

When I arrived, I punched in my entry code and walked inside.

"Hello?" I called out.

"You made it!" I could hear her footsteps coming down the hallway, along with the clickity-click of her dog right behind.

Even though two years had passed, she looked the same—short, stocky, with shoulder-length, sandy blond hair. She was in her late fifties and often wore big-rimmed glasses, reminiscent of a stereotypical professor. We stood in the kitchen for the next hour as she talked my ear off about everything happening at work.

When we finished chatting, I dragged my luggage up the staircase to "my room." I turned the knob, took a deep breath, and opened the door into a flashback of my old life in Ohio. I dropped my bag and gazed around—*our* bed, *our* pillows, *our* lamps, and *our* stuff. A twinge of bittersweet familiarity rushed through me.

Despite my exhaustion from traveling, I began rifling through the closet and dresser, tossing pairs of oversized pants, bulky sweaters, and old T-shirts into a pile in the middle of the floor. "Let go of things that no longer serve me," I said to myself, tossing a horrid jacket I didn't even remember having onto the pile. *Ooh, I have to add that to The Plan.*

Once I had sifted through every item I owned, sheer fatigue kicked in. I stepped over the huge pile of clothing and climbed into bed under my down comforter. I made sure my Sleep Number bed was set to fifty-five. I checked the other side . . . still on her setting. I left it alone.

Hi! Hope you are having a fantastic morning! The Sleep Number bed felt heavenly. It was just missing you to have been a perfect night's sleep. 😊

It seemed both weird and liberating to send that text to Birds, as I imagined her lying on Runner's side of the bed.

Miss you too.

I began the day with a brisk walk around the neighborhood, waving at dog walkers and gazing at all the blooming flowers and trees. Afterward, I had planned to swing by my office to grab any "essential" items to take back to Arizona.

When I arrived, campus seemed quieter than I remembered. No sounds of students bustling in the halls, and no chatter of faculty anywhere to be found. That was what the last day of finals during a pandemic sounded like.

I opened my office door slowly, hearing the creak that had been waiting in the hinges. Things were exactly where I had left them.

"I forgot I had this . . . and this too," I said out loud as I picked up items on my desk. "I knew this book had to be somewhere!" I shouted as I scoured my shelves.

Framed pictures of my adventures with Runner were scattered throughout. I shoved each one into my backpack to deal with later.

While scanning the room for anything I missed, I noticed the handwritten message from Kiddo scribbled on my whiteboard during her spring break visit years earlier. "Runner and I are going to Starbucks. Be back soon." She had squeezed the note in between lots of silly phrases and cat drawings. I grabbed my eraser and lifted it to the board, ready to delete our history. But I stopped short, staring at the words, and then gently placed the eraser back into its holder.

I continued stuffing books into my backpack until it could barely close and then filled two grocery bags with the remaining items. After everything was packed, I looked around, breathing in the near emptiness. *This will never be my life again—living in Ohio, working from this office, or coming home to Runner.* And while I didn't want it to be, sifting through the remnants still felt uncomfortable—like picking through ashes after a fire.

Once my reflective moment passed, I headed over to TikTok's house for a short visit.

"Holy . . . you look good, girl. You are so skinny!" TikTok said, running down her driveway.

"My car is full of clothes to donate," I said.

We started strolling toward the backyard.

"I bet. How was seeing all your stuff? Like a time capsule?"

"Kinda weird. There were photos of her all over my office. And I slept in our bed," I said. "It's as if time stood still, and tomorrow, I'm going back to the future."

"New life, girl!"

After our visit and then graduation festivities that night, I returned to my coworker's house to pack the massive suitcase I bought at a thrift store just to bring home items from a life I didn't miss at all.

Razzing

I hadn't been home from Ohio for even a day before being thrust back into my "situation," this time with a new twist. Pants texted that she wanted to go to the psychic—the divine partner one.

I shot a message back.

What would you ask her?

If I'm gonna be single forever. LOL.

Since her weekend getaway with Firefighter had resulted in another "friendship-only" pact, one she *didn't* initiate, Pants was back out there in the dating world.

She knows things . . . There are no secrets with this lady. So be prepared!

Can't wait! I want to google her.

Here's her website. She has five stars.

I shared the link.

A couple minutes later, another message came in.

She does love spells??? Did you cast one on me?? LOL

Ha ha! Nope . . . Probably why you're single. 😊

A few days later . . .

Did you know today is Bird Day??? LOL. If you didn't already tell Birds Happy Bird Day, you should!! 😂😂

I could never uncover Pants's intentions whenever she would razz me about Birds. Naked and Afraid would just say, "She's teasing you. Remember when a little kid would pull another kid's hair at school? It's what you do when you like someone."

I would then respond, "She has never liked me that way."

Naked and Afraid would come back with, "That's not true. She couldn't put on her big-girl pants and do anything about it."

And I'd snap back, "It's too late now, even if you're right."

We had the same interaction over and over, always ending with Naked and Afraid's assurance of my destiny with Pants. It certainly didn't seem like the recipe to move on with Birds. While I knew that, every time Pants would joke with me, I would lean in anyway and respond with a witty retort. And that's what I did with Bird Day.

Wow! I should get her a card. 😊

😂😂 Did she take the day off in observance?

More razzing. More leaning in on my part.

She didn't. But I will find something special to do to celebrate.

You are going to score some points.

I wasted no time in venturing out to the store to search for a card with a bird on it. After looking through several, either celebrating communion or with the message "Sorry for your loss," I found the perfect one. I snapped a photo and forwarded it to Pants.

Aah, well, that is sweet! She will be so surprised.

A while later, Birds came over for dinner. We sat on the couch afterward, just chatting about our days.

"Here, I got you this." I handed her the card.

She slid her thumb into the groove of the envelope and tore it open. "Thank you oh-so-much," she read out loud. She opened it. "For being oh-so-wonderful." She looked at me and smiled. "What's this for?"

"Do you know what today is?"

"May fourth."

"Yes, but it's also Bird Day! See . . ." I pointed to the card. "I got one with a bird on it."

"I've never heard of Bird Day. Well, that was super sweet of you." She leaned over and gave me a huge hug.

I was happy I could do something thoughtful for her. But the fact that it was inspired by Pants's over-interest in my love life felt incredibly awkward.

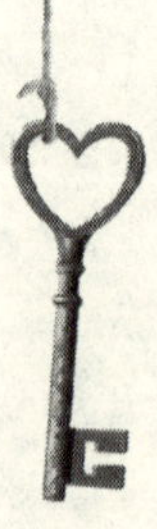

In Another Lifetime

What do you do with the past life lady?

Pants seemed intrigued when I told her about my upcoming regression.

She supposedly hypnotizes me and records the whole session. Then I get to see who is a recurring character from a past life.

You have to tell me if I knew you from before. LOL.

I then joked about her having been a candymaker who fueled my love for jelly beans, making sure to leave out any reference to our supposed unfinished business. She responded with another LOL.

May 14 finally arrived, and I was ready for some answers.

I pulled into the empty parking lot of a nondescript strip mall. I wasn't sure what to expect—maybe a rickety old house teeming with spirits. Instead, her tiny office was tucked in the corner near an accounting firm.

The regressionist was waiting at the door when I walked up. She looked to be about the same age as me, sporting shoulder-length blond hair that encircled her round face. She wore long earrings, and a beaded necklace draped over her black V-neck sweater. *More dangling earrings*, I thought.

"Hi," she said, ushering me in. "You can take a seat on the couch."

She settled into a plush oversized chair across from me and introduced herself. "So, what are you interested in exploring today?"

I told her the backstory of why I was there, filling her in on my supposed past life marriage to Naked and Afraid and divine partnership with Pants. "I want to find out more details about my connections with each of them."

I didn't mention Gertrude or Alice, for obvious reasons. But I also didn't bring up Birds. I wasn't ready to unpack that one yet, especially if I learned she wasn't in my soul circle at all.

The regressionist and I began the session by talking about my upbringing, values, and present life. She took a lot of notes, like a psychotherapist would in dissecting one's childhood. Afterward, she closed her notebook and set it down on a small table beside her chair.

"I'm going to start by helping you relax. You will be in a hypnotic state, but you'll be lucid and remember everything. Go ahead and lie down."

After I nestled into the couch, she had me put on an eye mask and then draped a thin blanket over me.

For the next thirty minutes, her soft voice guided me through a journey where I was taking elevators to the sky and floating on clouds.

"We're now ready to explore one of your past lives. There are three doors. Pick one and go through it." She paused. "What do you see?"

"A meadow with tall grass," I murmured.

"Imagine you are standing in front of a mirror," she said. "What do you look like?"

I focused in on the ornate etchings along the edges of a free-standing silver oval mirror. Then I saw myself. "I'm a woman, wearing a dress, like from *Little House on the Prairie*."

She then asked several questions, until I found myself in what appeared to be a boarding house in the 1800s. I could see the flickering of an old lantern sitting on a worn wooden table and hear the creaking of the floor planks as I walked through a dark bedroom to a hallway.

"There's some lady coming toward me," I said. "She looks like she might be the innkeeper."

I paused. "I'm following her outside to a stable." Another pause. "Now I'm brushing a brown horse. I think it's mine." My conscious mind started bombarding me with reminders that I wasn't really into horses and certainly didn't like grooming them. I didn't mention any of that to Regressionist, though.

"Let's have you leave the stable and go somewhere else."

Her directive came as a relief, since I didn't want to spend the next hour cleaning some animal.

"Okay. I'm walking through the meadow again toward a big tree by a creek. It's so peaceful," I said, smiling.

I saw a journal and a pen under the tree. Before I had a chance to share, Regressionist said, "Someone left you a present beneath the tree. What is it?"

An eerie feeling passed through me.

"A journal and a pen. Maybe I'm a writer." *I like this scene better than the smelly stable.*

I was about to pick up the journal when I saw someone in the distance. "Wait," I shouted. "The innkeeper is coming over! She's with two other women I've never seen before."

"They are going to take you to a different life," Regressionist assured me.

I'm not ready to leave. I want to write in my journal.

Before I knew it, we were all floating on a cloud.

Suddenly, though, everything went dark, as if someone pushed a reset button. Then, I was overcome by the sound of loud traffic.

"Where are you?" Regressionist asked.

"I think I'm in New York City, standing on the sidewalk next to a busy street. It looks like the early 1960s." I glanced down at what I was wearing. "I have on dress shoes, a suit, and a trench coat." I reached up to feel my head. "And a hat. I'm definitely a man, like a company executive."

In a flash, I was at a door. "I'm entering my apartment," I said. "Two little kids are running up to me saying, 'Daddy, Daddy!' I don't know the girl, but the boy seems really familiar."

"Is he a child you know from your current life?" Regressionist asked.

"No . . . I can't place him. But my wife's there too. She's cooking dinner in the kitchen."

"What does she look like?"

"Her back is to me, so I can't tell."

Regressionist then said, "Let's fast-forward and try to learn more about this life."

Before I could say anything, a new scene emerged.

"I'm at a high school graduation. It looks like the same kid from before, but he's older. Everyone else in the scene is blurred out, and I don't see my daughter or my wife, though. Just the boy."

"Hmm. Let's travel to your last day of this life and see if we can't piece this together."

"I don't want to," I said, my voice shaking. "I can't watch myself die. It'll be too scary."

"Trust me. I won't let anything bad happen to you," she said.

"Okay . . ." I took a deep breath. "I'm driving on a country road and about to cross a bridge. But it's only one lane. I'm crossing it. Wait, there's another car coming toward me, and it isn't stopping. I'm swerving off the side of the bridge! Help! My car's in the water, and it's sinking!" I started gasping.

"Listen to me. I want you to come out of your body and watch from above. You are experiencing no suffering," she said in a calm, but direct way.

My breath returned, and I watched, from an aerial view, as the car sank.

"I drowned," I said in a melancholy voice.

Maybe this explains why I've never been a fan of swimming.

Regressionist offered little acknowledgment of my horrific drowning and instead said, "Let's move on to another life."

I guess I'll have to process watching my own death at a later time.

"No. There's one more scene. I'm at my funeral. Everyone is crying. I see my wife, but she has a black veil over her face. She's sobbing. She can't seem to stop."

"Do you know who she is?"

"No. But she seems devastated. It's too much. I don't want to see anymore." I closed my eyes even tighter than they already were. But the scene didn't vanish.

Regressionist was silent for a moment while I took a few deep breaths.

"How about instead of moving on to another life, we meet your spirit council? These guides are with you in each of your lives."

"Okay." I let out an exhale. "Sounds better than watching myself die again."

Just like that, I was somewhere new.

"Now I'm in a castle or something. It's dark and dingy with stone walls all around me. There are five high-back wooden chairs behind a long table, with someone in each of them.

They're all up on a platform or stage, and I'm down below. I feel like I'm at some kind of tribunal." I paused. "Wait! There's Naked and Afraid! Why is she there?"

"She's probably on your spirit council," Regressionist said.

"My spirit council? I thought she was my wife in a past life."

"People can play several different roles *and* be in multiple lives."

If she really was one of my spirit guides, that meant she was one of the stick figures on my intuition handout. I smirked.

"Oh . . . Okay." I paused for a moment. "She just asked if I have any questions."

I shifted my attention to Naked and Afraid and uttered the words out loud, "How do I know Pants?"

A bright light, like a camera flash, went off. Then, the image of my sobbing wife came back into view. I zoomed in through the black veil.

"It's Pants!" I shouted to Regressionist. Then as if the words were channeled through me, I whimpered to Pants, "I'm sorry I left you so soon." Tears started running down my cheeks. "I didn't mean to leave. I should never have driven on that bridge!"

Everything then went dark.

"Where'd she go? She disappeared," I said. "Now I'm back with my spirit council."

"Is there anything else you'd like to ask them?"

Before I had a chance to answer, the boy from the graduation reappeared. "I see my son from New York. But now he looks like my dad from this life. Is my dad my son? How's that even possible?"

"Time is not linear. He could have been both," she said.

"So weird," I mumbled.

"I think we are about done here."

But I felt like we had only just begun.

After making my return float on another cloud, I was up and out of her office in no time.

I called Naked and Afraid as soon as I got in the car. "Hey!"

"How was it?" she asked. "Was I Gertrude, and were you Alice?"

"We didn't talk about that."

Instead, I walked her through every scene, including cloud traveling, my untimely drowning, and the spirit council. "So?"

"First, of course I'm on your spirit council. I could have told you that . . . and saved you tons of money." She laughed. "As for Pants," she continued, "It makes sense. Maybe you're back to apologize for leaving her in a past life, or maybe your job is to not leave again. That's why you won't let go of your connection with her."

While the horse made no sense, Naked and Afraid's explanation sure did.

After the regression, I drove straight to Birds's house. We snuggled on the couch while I shared every detail, even those where Pants was my wife. And I did so all in the name of transparency.

"Do you believe any of this?" I asked her.

"I believe that you believe it's true," she said.

The next day, I messaged Pants about it.

Within one minute, the phone rang.

"What happened? Was Naked and Afraid there? Was I the candymaker?" She laughed.

I described the entire experience in detail. "So?" I asked.

"That's really cool."

I wondered if she meant *cool* like "Neat story" or *cool* like "Glad you are back in this lifetime to finish your business with me."

I just said, "It *was* cool" and left my question unasked, as usual.

Rock That Relationship!

"I wish we recorded our conversations. People would love this," Naked and Afraid said as we cruised up Tumamoc. A week had passed since my regression, and Naked and Afraid and I were still speculating about my supposed unfinished business with Pants. Interspersed in our conversation was contemplating my future with Birds and discussing what we had learned in previous relationships that we were *never* going to do again.

"Well, then, let's stop talking about doing a podcast and really make it happen," I said.

"Yes! We can chat while hiking and record the whole thing." She pulled out her phone as if we were going to start that very moment.

I turned my attention from the path and gave her a serious look. "This needs to be professional. We have to build a website, come up with a tagline, secure social media handles, create an episode list, and find an editing platform. Then, we can record. But not while walking and not on your phone."

"Okay, Commander Corey. You know the business stuff."

The next afternoon, we set up shop at my kitchen table.

"We should start with our webpage." I opened the website builder for www.spinningsisters.com, which we had bought a while back. "What should we put as our tagline?" I asked. "'We spin it around so you don't have to'?"

She gave me a puzzled look. "What does that even mean?"

"I have no idea."

"I don't think we should spin. It makes us sound like we're clueless and just rambling," she said.

"Yeah, but we *own* spinningsisters.com," I said as I searched "spin synonyms" online. "Revolve, rotate, turn, whirl."

Before I could finish reading my list, she jumped in. "Those don't make sense. And Spinning Sisters doesn't make sense. We need to pick something else."

The General gasped and wanted to try to find a way to salvage the domain name we had already invested ninety-nine cents in. "What about 'Spinning around about relationships? Let us help'?" I hated it even more when it came out of my mouth.

"Seriously. We just need a new name."

I leaned back in my chair. "I suppose."

We decided to spend the rest of our time hunkering down on our laptops, surfing the web for inspiration.

After thirty minutes of tossing around several subpar options, Naked and Afraid suddenly hopped out of her chair and started doing push-ups on the rug next to the table. I could barely hear the absurd names she shouted through her heavy breathing.

I was used to her distracted behavior and continued scouring the Internet as she exercised and yelled out ridiculous possibilities. She finally fell to her stomach.

"Let's think about it. Something will come to us." She jumped up and grabbed her laptop. "I gotta go. But we'll figure it out."

I looked at the clock. We had spent over an hour accomplishing nothing other than eliminating our current name.

Heal That Heartache!

That's good, but does it get at the essence of what we're going to do? It's still only about heartbreak.

I had spent the evening bombarding Naked and Afraid with more name ideas, none of which she seemed to like. Suddenly, an idea popped into my head, almost as if the universe had whispered it in my ear.

Rock That Relationship!

Love it!

I waited for the "But . . ." text that was sure to follow. It never came. I then typed "Rock That Relationship" into Google. Nothing. Just punk rock and rock art. *Whew.* And the URL said, "Nothing is parked here yet."

No one is using it. And the domain is available for a penny!

How is that possible?! That is the best. So much better than Spinning Sisters.

I agree!!! Well, anything is better than Spinning Sisters.

I bought the new domain before it was snatched up by some other duo looking to banter about relationships. Back to square one—we had a name, but still no podcast.

Later that week, Naked and Afraid and I reconvened to write a script for the intro. It took thirty or so takes of our ten-second spot to land on one we both could live with. We then drafted an outline of the first episode to record the next day. And no push-ups were done to accomplish any of this.

⟷

"Welcome to Rock That Relationship! episode one," I said in a vibrato radio voice. "So, let me begin by asking, 'What are we doing here? There are so many relationship podcasts. What makes us different?'"

Naked and Afraid leaned in toward her fancy new podcast mic and said, "Well, our listeners can be anyone. Gay . . . straight . . . men . . . women . . . anyone. Even if you are a confused sixteen-year-old boy, we have advice for you."

I started to panic. *What kind of advice would we give a teenage boy in some elusive state of confusion?* I immediately rerouted the conversation to the story of how we met and lessons learned from previous relationships.

Once I stopped recording, Naked and Afraid said, "Let's post it on Facebook now!"

"You don't just put an audio file on social media. We should pilot test the episode with some friends. If it's a go, I'll do some editing and upload it to our feed. Then you can share the link. But we might also decide to re-record it, depending on what people say."

"I think it sounded great! We have to get it out there right away."

Her urgency, while typical, stressed out The Zen Master and even caught The General off guard.

"I want to do it right. Let's wait to get feedback. We only have one chance to make a first impression."

She reluctantly agreed.

Later that day, I sent the recording to some trusted friends. Within hours, feedback started coming in.

"I'm not sure your podcast is for confused boys," Hippie said.

Another friend shared, "You all don't know much about being a teenager these days, or boys, for that matter. I would take that out."

I breathed a sigh of relief.

Our re-recorded version flowed far better and had no references to confused boys.

Afterward, I said, "You know, doing this episode made me realize there's still so much more I need to explore about myself."

"And we get to talk about all of it—in front of the entire world. Maybe the podcast should actually be your plan 2.0!"

It sure felt like it, and we hadn't even recorded the second episode yet.

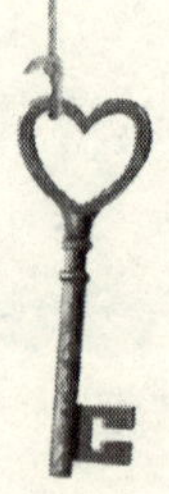

Hotter Than

"So, you sent flirty texts to East Coast?" Birds asked one night while we were lying in bed.

I laughed. "That was like eight months ago."

"What were they about?" Her tone was a blend of playfulness and curiosity.

"I told you all this. I would say something flirty, and she would make little ice cubes fly across the screen."

"What did you say that made her need to cool off so much?"

I hadn't answered *that* question before. "I can't remember. Things like 'I'm about to shower. Wish you were here.'"

As soon as I said it, I felt my stomach turn . . . first, from the thought of showering with East Coast . . . and then from the thought of telling Birds about it.

"Wow! You don't send me that kind of stuff."

I scooted closer to her and held her hand. "Our relationship has always been more sweet and innocent . . . we share photos of cuddly kittens."

"I want a flirty text, though," she said.

I grabbed my phone and started typing.

"What are you doing?"

"Wait . . . Okay, check your messages."

She reached over to the nightstand and picked up her phone. I could see her smiling.

A reply from her popped into my inbox.

"No flirty text back? Just a heart?" I asked.

"I have to think of a good one."

⟷

The next day while at work, Birds messaged me.

You're hotter than Venus. 😊😘

Then came a link to the article "Why is Venus the hottest planet even though Mercury is closer to the sun?"

Love that your flirty text is backed by research. 😊❤

⟷

A few days later . . .

You are hotter than the Earth's core. More cool science for your 🧠.

In came a link to a *Scientific American* article called "Why is the earth's core so hot?"

Wow! You had me at Scientific American. 😃

These exchanges lasted maybe forty-eight hours. Then it was back to clips of penguins holding hands and lightning bugs with the caption "You light up my life." And they were just perfect.

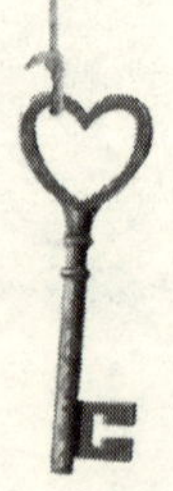

Crack Your Eggs

"You have to see this!" Mom shouted, although I was parked right beside her on the couch. "It's unbelievable!" I looked up from my phone just as a man was about to eat fire.

"That *is* amazing."

After the suspenseful survival of yet another *America's Got Talent* contestant, I gazed back down at the newsfeed on my phone while the judges jabbered on.

"Okay. I won't make you watch all ten episodes I recorded. I'll just fast-forward to some of my favorite parts."

After skipping through several video frames, she blurted out, "This one . . . it's a little girl . . . and she's so talented. Watch!"

I focused back on the show. "Wow, that's pretty cool."

This was how Mom and I spent Saturday night of Mother's Day weekend. Even though I was a bit exasperated watching ventriloquists and glow-in-the-dark dancers, it sure beat our incessant chatter about the absurdity of my love life or having to watch *The Holiday*.

The next morning, after an early walk, I drove to the airport to pick up Birds, who was returning from a trip out east. Once we got back to Mom's condo, I beelined for the kitchen to start cooking brunch for our Mother's Day festivities.

I hadn't even set a pan on the stove before Mom wandered in.

"I'm in charge," I told her. "Go sit down and surf your iPad. I'm sure there's plenty of news about all those politicians screwing up the world."

She laughed. "I could have just picked up a frozen quiche."

"I know, but it's Mother's Day. Why don't you go read about the planet dying and all the horrible laws being passed?"

She went into the den and sat in her usual spot on the love seat. After grabbing one of her many pairs of reading glasses, she started flipping through her iPad.

"What can I do?" Birds asked, standing next to me in the kitchen.

"Wanna make the eggs?" I pulled an egg carton out of the fridge. "You know how I get freaked out about the whole salmonella thing."

She laughed. "I'll always crack eggs for you."

I smiled and handed her the carton. "Thank you. It's one of your many amazing qualities."

Thirty minutes later, we had a full spread ready to go. By that point, my brother and his family had arrived . . . of course, after all the cooking was done.

Once we finished eating, Mom asked us all to sit on the couch. She then disappeared into her bedroom, only to pop right back out holding a couple gift bags. She handed one to my brother.

He looked at me and then back at her. "We're supposed to get you presents, not the other way around."

"It's just something small. Plus, being my kids is the greatest gift you could give me." She smiled.

We all watched as my brother reached into the bag and slowly pulled out a framed photo of his dog.

"This is awesome," he said. "It even has her name on it!"

"I know how much you love that little puppy."

She then handed me a bag. "Nothing sentimental, but I thought these were really cool."

"Okay," I said. I reached in and felt two squishy fabric pads. I pulled them out and then held them up for everyone to see. "What are they?"

"You put one of them under a dish in the microwave. That way, you don't burn your hands when you pull it out."

"That's genius!" I put them back in the bag. "Thanks, Mom!"

"I figured you'd want something practical. And I use mine all the time!"

She then ducked back into her bedroom and emerged with yet another bag. My brother and I exchanged confused glances.

"This is for you, honey." She gave it to Birds. "Mother's Day might be hard without your mom, but you are always welcome in our family."

Birds dug her hand into the bag and slid out something tightly wrapped in tissue paper. She unraveled it, uncovering a little red glass bird.

"I had this in my house. And I thought you might be able to give it a better home," Mom said.

Birds flashed a huge smile, lighting up her entire face. "Thank you."

She then placed the bird gently into the bag and reached over to squeeze my hand. Tears welled up in my eyes. Was this *pow, boom, bang?*

Picking Up the Pieces

Months had passed since Naked and Afraid's breakup, but her heartache wasn't getting any better. After rehashing the same conversation, I finally knew how she felt all the times I had spiraled.

She would start with something like, "Why did she leave? Wasn't I a good partner? Will she come back?"

I would respond, "She probably needs some space to deal with her own stuff right now."

It would devolve from there.

"Doesn't she know how much I love her? Did I make it clear to her?"

"Yes, you were clear."

On one occasion, after being asked dozens of times, I said, "Maybe you should write her a few more love poems just to be sure."

She glared at me.

"Too soon?"

While Naked and Afraid was strong and resilient in many areas of her life, it was evident this was not one of them. She was broken into little pieces . . . pieces I would pick up and try to put back together with her, only to find them scattered about the very next day. This had been the pattern.

All I wanted to do was make her pain go away, like she tried for so long to do with me.

One day while chatting on the phone, I decided to bring up what I thought were the greatest hits from The Plan to see if anything might help.

"How about writing a manifest?" I asked.

"I did that. And she still hasn't come back." She let out a huge exhale of defeat.

"How about Reiki?"

"It was the most expensive nap I ever took," she said.

I tried not to laugh. Finally, I asked, "Is anything working for you?"

"Yes. Processing with people."

"Okay. I'll keep processing with you then."

And I did.

It seemed, though, when I would commiserate with her, she would just get more worked up. So, I came up with different angles I could take to help her stop ruminating. I tried encouragement: "You will get through this;" empathy: "I remember how hard breakups are. They hurt . . . but things do get better;" future thinking: "You will find love again;" cosmic intervention: "See what the psychic has to say;" and distraction: "Did you hear about [fill in the blank with some ridiculous current event]?"

Those didn't work. So, I tried hope: "Maybe she'll realize she made a mistake;" refocusing: "Let's get your website up so you can start your life coaching business;" reverse psychology: "Call her then. Send her more poems;" tough love: "You deserve so much better. It's time to move on;" and Zen: "Just go with the flow. Things will work out like they are supposed to."

One morning while we were speeding up Tumamoc, I said to her, "I've tried every approach I can think of to help you get through this breakup—different things from my plan, some that were your ideas to begin with. And nothing seems to be helping."

"I'm not looking for advice or a pep talk. I just want to process all of this over and over until I'm done talking about it."

"But every time I process with you, it seems like it's making things worse."

"It's helping. It might not look like it, but it is."

All I wanted to do was fix her situation. But as much as I didn't want to admit it, strangleholding my own healing process hadn't exactly worked as planned. Why would I think it would work with hers? But then again, I hadn't yet suggested the five-star-rated sage spray.

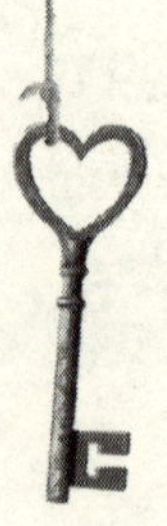

Down and Out

The first weekend in June finally arrived, and Naked and Afraid, Peace Corps, and I were headed to the Grand Canyon for our rim-to-rim-to-rim adventure. Naked and Afraid offered to drive as long as we abided by the rules she texted us the day before.

> So everyone knows, for emotional reasons related to my ongoing feelings for someone I used to date, I can't stop in Phoenix for any reason. So, plan accordingly! 😱

Thankfully, we made it to Tusayan, right outside the park entrance, with no restroom breaks needed.

After an uneventful night in the hotel, we caught the first shuttle to the South Kaibab Trail. This time, we weren't hiking to the bottom and back out the same side. Instead, we would trek twenty-one miles down, across, and out, emerging at the North Rim. We'd then return that same route the very next day.

"Here we go. The Coconino Cowgirls ride again!" Naked and Afraid shouted as she snapped a selfie of us at the trailhead sign.

Not even ten minutes in, she asked, "Are you okay with me going ahead? I can meet you by the bridge like last time."

Peace Corps and I both agreed, and Naked and Afraid took off, scurrying down the dark trail in her Kohl's shorts, but this time with proper trail shoes.

After only a few miles, my left knee started throbbing. I hoisted up my pack, adjusted my gait, and relied more on my hiking poles to provide support. That worked for a while, but then my knee started up again. I tried to ignore it and power on.

When we began descending toward the river, we could see Naked and Afraid below waving to us, like she did during our first trip.

We hadn't reconvened for five minutes before she asked, "Do you mind if I meet you at the lodge? I can get us checked in early."

Peace Corps and I exchanged glances, and then we both nodded.

Naked and Afraid darted off and was out of sight seconds later.

After taking a few pictures of deer gathered under a tree, Peace Corps and I started our more reasonably paced trek across the bottom of the canyon. But before long, my knee pain came soaring back, and I finally decided to fill her in.

"Maybe we should rest," she suggested.

"I'm worried if I stop, I won't be able to get out of this canyon. We still have fourteen miles. I mean, I followed my training schedule to a tee and was super prepared," I said.

"Sometimes things just happen, even with the best-laid plans . . . Well, tell me if you need anything."

"Okay. Let's just keep going for now."

For hours, we wound along the clear creek waters, which alternated from gushing rapids to a trickling stream. I tried to stave off the pain in my leg by at least enjoying the majestic scenery.

"You see these huge rock walls on both sides of us?" I asked.

"Yep," she said from behind me.

"This is The Box I was talking about when we were here in November. I think it's the most beautiful part of the hike, but we need to hurry, or we'll cook."

We sped up, despite my excruciating pain, just until we were clear of the high canyon walls and then returned to our normal pace to begin the ascent on the other side.

Five miles from the North Rim, we decided to take our last long break. I found the perfect spot on a bench and had just propped my foot up when a man in his sixties with a huge, bulging backpack trudged toward me from the riverbed.

"How's the water?" I asked.

"Definitely helpful for cooling off. But my wife is really sick," he said. "She's still down by the river."

"It's pretty hot. Are you all gonna be okay?" Peace Corps asked him. She was spread out on the bench next to me eating a snack.

"I hope so." He took his pack off and dropped it at his feet.

Right then, another older man sat down near us and put his head in his hands. He was a familiar face as we had been leapfrogging with him since the South Rim.

I turned to Peace Corps. "He doesn't look good."

I got up from the bench to fill my water bottle, and lightning-bolt pain shot down my leg.

"I'm hurting," I said.

She sat up. "You wanna rest longer?"

I started a slow walk toward the spigot. "I'm not sure if we stayed here for a month that all the torn ligaments in my knee would heal. And I can't live here." I let out an uncomfortable laugh. "Let's just power through. I am not up for being a part of a ranger rescue mission today."

"Okay. But if we need to slow down or take more breaks—"

"I will definitely let you know!"

After dousing our shirts and hats with water, we headed off to finish our last five miles of switchbacks.

We wound up and around for hours, suddenly cresting the top as the trail came to an abrupt end.

"Welcome to the North Rim!" A man's voice shouted. He was sitting in a lawn chair right at the trailhead. "Grab a cold drink." He pointed to a nearby cooler. "You did it!"

"Thanks! We aren't with your group, though," I said.

"I'm here for everyone. You should be proud of yourselves. Now go get a drink," he said.

We trudged over to the cooler and dipped our hands in the freezing half-ice and half-water mix the drinks were floating in. I found a lemon-lime Gatorade, my favorite, and chugged it so fast that most of it spilled down my face onto my shirt.

"Do you know how we get to the lodge from here?" I asked the man.

"There isn't a shuttle. You have to walk on the path." He pointed to the left. "It's about two miles."

I looked at Peace Corps. "Two more miles . . . Oh my God, I don't think I can take even two more steps." I started massaging my knee.

But I did.

As Peace Corps and I approached the lodge, we heard a familiar voice in the distance. "Over here!"

I could see Naked and Afraid waving at us from just outside the gift shop. We trudged toward her, dropping our packs once we met up. I then let out a huge exhale. *Finally.*

"I got the key and already showered. We're in one of the cabins down the hill," she said, pointing behind me.

"We just came up from there," I shot back. "Sorry . . . It's just my stupid knee. It started hurting right at the beginning and wouldn't let up."

"That sucks. I'll get you some ice in a few," Naked and Afraid said.

"Thanks."

Once we walked in the door of the cabin, Naked and Afraid blurted out, "Did you hear about the lady who died yesterday? Heatstroke, I think." She paused, likely for dramatic effect.

A wave of fear hit me as thoughts of our hike the next day in much hotter temperatures flashed in my head. I pictured myself trapped in The Box in scorching temperatures. I would be rolling on the ground, gripping my throbbing knee, and unable to hike even one more step. Sweat would be pouring from my forehead, my mouth would be so parched I could barely swallow, and my skin would be burning from the beating sun. I would then writhe in pain until my body couldn't take it anymore.

"She was in her early forties and just doing a down and out to the river," Naked and Afraid continued. "It happened on the way up Bright Angel around the two-mile mark." She then looked right at me. "I know your knee hurts, so there's no shame in calling a shuttle and meeting us at the South Rim."

Once she said that, the worry and angst I was feeling about my imminent death disappeared, only to be replaced by a surge of relentlessness and audacity.

"Yes, there is shame. I'm going to do this even if I have to drag my leg behind me!"

"I'm sure you will," she said.

I hauled my gear to the back bunkroom since Naked and Afraid had claimed the queen bed in the front area for herself. Once I got in the shower, she left to find an ice pack for me. I was already dressed when she came barreling back into the cabin.

"I got you ice." She handed me the pack. "Get this. I forgot to tell you earlier. When I checked in, the receptionist told me Twin Flame was a fool for breaking up with me. Then she hit on me."

"Really?" My sarcastic tone was even noticeable to me.

I laid down on my twin bottom bunk and perched the ice pack on top of my knee. A chill ran deep through my skin and into my bones. As I winced, Naked and Afraid went on about how the receptionist thought Twin Flame had made the biggest mistake of her life.

After finishing her scintillating story, she vanished to the front room. I then spent the next hour contorting my body in every which way to get comfortable, all while trying to balance the ice pack on my leg and do a crossword puzzle at the same time. Peace Corps quietly read in the bunk above.

But things in the front of the cabin were far too quiet. I had no idea what Naked and Afraid was doing. I imagined her laying sprawled out on her huge bed, scrolling through Facebook, and replaying the scene with the receptionist telling her she was a true catch.

Once it was dinner time, we all headed over to the lodge. I limped, Peace Corps strolled, and Naked and Afraid ran ahead as usual.

The dining room, perched on the cliff's edge overlooking the canyon, was packed. So, we were lucky to be seated right next to the floor-to-ceiling windows. *We walked across that*, I thought, as I gazed out.

After ordering our food, Naked and Afraid started up about the soulmate stuff. "So, are you Team Pants or Team Birds?" she asked Peace Corps.

I gave Naked and Afraid a stern look.

"Who do you think she's supposed to be with?" Naked and Afraid pressed.

"Why does it matter?" I asked. "I'm with Birds. Just drop it."

"Actually, I'm on Team Corey," Peace Corps said. "She should be with whoever she wants to be with."

The server showed up right then, bringing us another basket of bread, per Naked and Afraid's request.

"Why do you keep ordering so much bread?" I asked.

"Snacks for tomorrow." She picked up the whole loaf, wrapped it in a napkin, and put it in her backpack.

"Good grief," I said.

Not another word was uttered about bread or soulmates.

⟷

A dull ache shot through my leg as I got out of bed that next morning. *I'm not giving up. I'm not calling a shuttle.* While I tried to hide my pain from the others, they knew I was struggling. So, I didn't hesitate in jumping on board when Naked and Afraid suggested she go solo and meet us on the other side of the canyon. Thankfully, Peace Corps wanted to do a more moderate pace with me.

It was still dark out by the time we got to the North Kaibab trailhead. Naked and Afraid immediately took off, and Peace Corps and I started our slower descent into the canyon.

After three miles, we stopped for our first break. I propped my foot up to rest my knee, which was surprisingly not as painful as it had been when I woke up. The day was off to a good start.

I pulled out a bagel and spread gooey peanut butter on it.

"I'm glad we're gonna eat an entire meal every couple miles. A baggie of nuts and my one banana didn't make up for the twelve thousand calories I burned yesterday," I said.

We both laughed.

After our snack break, we hit the trail, powering across the blistering hot canyon with our new "Stay fed; stay wet" strategy. But once we hit the beginning of the switchbacks going up to the South Rim, a familiar throbbing started back up in my leg. I kept quiet and trudged along.

"There's the three-mile rest house!" I shouted to Peace Corps.

"Yay!" Her voice echoed from behind.

As soon as we arrived, we found a place in the shade to sit. I massaged my knee, ate a granola bar, and chugged what was left of a warm Gatorade I had been toting around since our lunch stop hours earlier.

"There's no way I can do it," said a teenage boy lying on a nearby bench.

"I'm exhausted," said another. The sweat had seeped through the neckline of his shirt. "I'm not sure how we're gonna do these last few miles."

Seriously, boys. I'm nearly fifty, have walked to the other side and now back across this canyon with what feels like torn ligaments in my knee, and you all can't get your butts up from a bench?

Guilt washed over me for my horrid thoughts. The canyon is a treacherous place, and each person is on their own journey to conquer it—these boys included.

After my *overly* judgy contemplation, I soaked my clothes and then downed a handful of jelly beans. We then put on our packs and stepped onto the trail while the boys were still heaped over, discussing their exit plan.

"Do you want me to announce every half mile we hike? That might keep us motivated," I said to Peace Corps. "I can track it on my watch."

"Definitely."

"Three miles to the end," I said, still standing at the three-mile rest house.

We both laughed.

For the final stretch, my goal was to keep my head down to avoid looking at the upcoming switchbacks carved into the canyon wall.

After fifteen minutes, I glanced at my watch and called out, "Two-and-a-half miles left!"

"Woo-hoo!"

We continued up the steep and rocky trail, the severe pain of my knee mostly at bay again. Either the ibuprofen I took a few hours earlier had kicked in or, more likely, all the nerves in my leg were dead. At that point, it didn't matter. I was finishing this challenge.

We hiked another thirty minutes before I yelled, "One-and-a-half miles!"

"You skipped the two-mile mark!"

I stopped and turned around, but she continued hiking toward me.

Once she got closer, I said in a softer voice, "That's where the lady died." I paused as a cold rush ran through me. "So, I tried not to look at my watch for a while . . . until I was sure we passed that spot."

Peace Corps came to an abrupt stop and stared right at me. I could sense she had that same cold rush. "Glad you didn't say anything," she said in a somber voice.

"Well, now we're halfway between the top and the rest house," I said, trying to veer from our melancholic moment. "I wonder if those boys are still down there, sprawled out, and moaning about how tired their teen bodies are."

Peace Corps started laughing. "I bet they just end up crashing on those benches tonight."

"Probably!" I turned around, and we both started trudging along.

Once we rounded a few more bends, I shouted, "One mile left!"

Suddenly, we came upon crowds of tourists sauntering down the trail. Most were wearing sandals and carrying lattes. *That can only mean one thing . . .*

"There it is!" I yelled. My eyes filled with tears.

We slogged up the last switchback and then emerged at the top, right among selfie-taking park visitors.

"We did it!" I announced.

"Yes, we did." Peace Corps smiled.

I pulled out my phone and called Naked and Afraid. "We made it!"

"Cool. I've been napping in my back seat. But I'm parked nearby. I'll come to you."

Once she met up with us, we took a picture by the trailhead

and loaded into the car wearing our dirty clothes. She insisted we make the nearly six-hour trip to Tucson that night to save money on a hotel. Thankfully, she drove. But we still weren't allowed to stop in Phoenix to use the restroom.

The next morning, Naked and Afraid posted about the trek on Facebook.

> *Awesome job ladies!* 💪💪🥾🥾 *This trip would not have been possible or even contemplated without Corey's incredible leadership: from her training hikes/walks to her planning all the logistics! And great conversation and positive attitudes kept us going the entire way!* 😊

I smiled when I read it. I loved the post but couldn't help but wonder about the great conversations she had on her nearly solo trek.

Later in the day, Naked and Afraid called. I turned from the hordes of emails I was trying to respond to and grabbed my phone on the first ring.

"Guess who hearted my Grand Canyon post?" she asked.

I knew exactly who she was talking about. My stomach flipped. "Seriously? How did *she* see it? She doesn't even know you."

"I don't know. It's on social media. But what matters is that she saw you accomplished this and how happy you are . . . and how awesome your life is."

I couldn't help but smirk. "True."

"You have a lot to be proud of. Although I still think you should have taken the shuttle back. You probably have permanent knee damage."

"You know me . . . I'm relentless. If I have to hobble for the next two weeks to check this off my plan, it was worth it."

What Comes Around

After returning from the Grand Canyon, Pants and I started planning our next Utah adventure slated for October. We would spend the week hiking, biking, rappelling, and hopefully going to The Wave.

I should ask the psychic if we'll get the permit. Ha ha!!

As soon as I sent the text, I realized we hadn't talked about the psychic stuff since our love spell exchange.

Do it! Let's see if she's right.

Maybe I make another appointment with her. I haven't had some intuitive tell me some weird shit in a few weeks. 😂

You are having withdrawals. LOL.

You should go too.

When I visit, I will!!!

I began typing a response about the possibility of her coming to town and then deleted it. Instead, it felt safer to lean into the silliness of our banter.

What would she have to say for you to believe her???

See what she knows about me.

She would say, "Hmm . . . the crystal ball says you like meat on the bone, endless amounts of Thin Mints, the Celtics, any crime show, mountain biking, and women who shave their legs. In the future, you will be eating a rack of ribs in a small town after hiking."

Then I would know she is legit and whoever she tells me I'm supposed to be with, I'll believe her.

We were starting to go down a dangerous road, one that had the potential of reviving a curiosity I had been trying to keep at bay. But I went there anyway.

Really?? That's what messed me up. She knew tons about me and was pretty specific about who I was "supposed" to be with.

LOL! That's why I need to go. But she said you have multiple soulmates. So how do you know which is the right one??

I have five, supposedly, and she told me I had only met one. So, I can wait to meet the others and then size them all up. Ha ha! Or ignore the cosmos and date whoever I want.

Sounds like a lot to choose from! Ha ha.

Nope. Just five prospects . . . more than the number of women I dated online!! LOL

😂 😂 Did she describe any of the others?

She was pretty adamant about you. I should have asked, though. My head was spinning so much I couldn't muster up any questions.

Adamant how? That I was the one?

She said it probably feels like we have known each other a lot longer than we have, which I've thought from the beginning. I'm not sure if you were "the one" . . . just that you were one of the five. I suppose the other four could be awesome. Who knows?

Hey, you could have met another by now. And it does feel like we've known each other for a while.

This was the conversation I had been wanting to have . . . months ago. All it was doing now was resurrecting my disappointment and jump-starting my confusion. But now, I knew I needed off this road, or I would just slip back into the chaos I had spent so much time reconciling. So, I leaned into humor instead.

I did feel a special bond with the Target lady the other day. She stared right into my eyes when she asked if I was going to use my Target card.

There ya go!!!!

Plus, it's not that horrible to be one of my soulmates. At least I'm not some Forensic Files killer!!!

I'll always be entertained.

So, the only way to confirm this is for you to see the psychic while I hide down the street. If she says your soulmate is some seventy-year-old conservative lady in Alaska, we'll never talk of the subject again. If she says otherwise, you can eat a box of cookies and go into a tailspin.

I guess you have to find a time for me to visit so we can know for sure!

I called Naked and Afraid. Even though it was the middle of the workday, she picked up on the first ring.

"Yo!" she said.

"Pants is talking about seeing the psychic again. Well, I brought it up while we were texting about our Utah trip. So that's on me. But then we got into a *big* discussion about it."

"Again?" she asked, not seemingly bothered by my absence of a "Hello."

"Is she just messing with me?" I leaned back in my chair.

"No. She doesn't know how confusing this has been for you."

"Well, either go to the psychic or don't," I said in a sharp tone, as if I were talking directly to Pants. "Come on, she doesn't even have to go in person."

"I thought she told you she didn't want to give her credit card info over the phone."

"Yeah. I get it. But really? If you want something, you find a way to make it happen." That's one thing I learned from Runner . . . or maybe it was the opposite. If you don't *really* want something, even if you say you do, you find a way to *not* make it happen.

"Maybe she's afraid she'll find out you're her soulmate and then have to figure out what to do," Naked and Afraid said. "Or different theory . . . she finds out you aren't, the whole fantasy implodes, and she's secretly disappointed . . ."

I hardly let her finish before jumping in. "Or she finds out we aren't and breathes a sigh of relief." I then let out a small laugh, more out of my own exasperation than finding humor in our conversation.

"I don't believe that at all," Naked and Afraid snapped back. She then softened her tone and said, "The bigger question is, do *you* want her to go?" I then heard, "No, put it down," which is what she would say when one of her dogs was chewing on something they shouldn't.

While she was wrestling with the dog, I took advantage of the extra millisecond I had to ponder the question. *Do I want her to go?* Truthfully, I had been so focused on whether she wanted to find out about our supposed connection that I hadn't considered if I wanted to open this whole thing back up.

Once the commotion on the other end of the line died down, I said, "If the psychic said we weren't soulmates, I could get some closure and chalk our connection up to only past-life stuff, which I know I still need to resolve."

I could barely finish my sentence before she jumped in.

"Be honest. You'd probably be sad, too."

I paused. "A little." As soon as I said it, I realized *a little* was more like *a lot*. "I've held onto this fantasy for so long. I might not know what to do without it."

"So, what if the psychic told her the same thing, that you *were* divine partners? What would you do?"

I felt a heaviness in my chest. "Nothing, well, except spiral and then probably mess things up with Birds because I couldn't get out of my head."

"Exactly! So, what do *you* want?" she asked again.

"I mean, I want answers. But those answers may make things worse. Really, I just need to close this psychic chapter and move on with my life." I let out a deep breath.

"Then move on."

"I thought you were Team Pants and pro-psychic," I said, with a forced laugh.

"You don't need an outside force to confirm anything," she said. "Plus, you have something great with Birds that you'll screw up if you keep going down this road. Just be done talking about the psychic."

"You're right!"

It hit me—I didn't *have* to stay in what had become an unhealthy situation: my unrelenting quest for the certainty of my soulmate. Nothing about this pursuit was making my life better. Instead, it filled me with self-inflicted confusion, angst, and hurt and got in the way of my relationship with Birds.

I didn't share my epiphany with Naked and Afraid. Instead, I said, "I'm going to put this whole divine partner, soulmate, psychic thing in a box and sit it on a little shelf in my brain. That way, I can't fixate on it every day. I won't initiate or engage in any more discussions about it with her. Even if she brings it up, whatever she says goes into the box. Then I can move forward with my life while simultaneously keeping this box all sealed up."

"Well, that's an interesting approach," she said.

"Yep. Simultaneity. That's what I'm gonna do."

Although I had been back from the Grand Canyon for more than a week, my knee was still aching. I had been propping my ice-strapped leg on the chair next to my desk. Since I had been crowding Phoenix out of her usual spot, she had been spending more time in the garage, going in and out of the cat door in my office. *Clickety-clack.* That was the sound of the flap on the door as it swung back and forth.

While I was hammering away at some emails, the kitty embarked on one of her midday garage excursions.

Clickety-clack. The rubber flaps swung open, and she came barreling in.

"Meee-owww!" she screamed. Her typical meow was a soft and sweet cackle. And this was not soft or sweet.

I turned from my computer to see her standing by my desk, teeth clenched down hard on a lizard at least six inches long.

"Meee-owww!" she screamed again without opening her mouth. The sounds reverberated against the reptilian body.

"Aah!" I screamed back.

Phoenix dropped the lizard, and it scurried across the floor. I hobbled out of the room as fast as I could, slamming the door behind me.

"You two work it out! I'm not coming back until you've resolved your differences!" I yelled through the door.

I was unsure about the nonsense spilling out of my mouth. But it felt empowering to leave it up to them.

I went to the kitchen for a lunch break. I hoped when I was done, Phoenix would have returned the lizard to the garage to live its best life and would be curled up on her chair.

After I finished eating, I tiptoed down the hall, creaked open the door, and peered in. Phoenix was asleep on the chair, and there was no sign of the lizard . . . just as I had hoped.

"Perfect," I said to her. "All is now right in the world."

Once I sat back down and started responding to email, I couldn't help but notice a slight movement in my periphery. I ignored it at first. But when I finally turned my head, I saw a tail sticking out from behind the rubber computer cord organizer along my baseboard. I leaned over to get a closer look. It was alive, and it was stuck. The General wanted me to free it. The Zen Master wanted nature to take its course, even if the lizard met its fate. In the name of Zen, I went back to work . . . with the tail waving in my periphery.

Two days passed, and I could still see the lizard while sitting at my desk. I was sure it would be dead by now. Birds was out of town, and I couldn't do justice in trying to explain this horrific experience to her over the phone. Although I tried.

"I'm just gonna let it be for a while," I told her while staring at my cord organizer.

"It'll rot. Take it outside." Her voice was measured, as usual.

"How about you get it when you come back?"

"Seriously? I can. But that's not for a few more days," she said.

"I don't care. I'm not touching it."

This was one of those situations Runner would have dealt with. In truth, she would have trapped the lizard within moments of its arrival and relocated it outside. But here I was now—a lizard smashed up against my baseboard for three days.

Five minutes after hanging up with Birds, I heard *Clickety-clack*.

"Meee-owww!" Phoenix darted through the cat door with another lizard clenched in her teeth.

I screamed.

She sped down the hallway with her latest catch and ran into the bathroom, where she dropped in onto the cold tile. It laid there on its back, legs thrashing in the air. There were puncture wounds on its torso, and I knew fate was coming for this one, too.

I rushed to the kitchen, grabbed a paper plate, and hurried back. When I returned, the ravaged body was still on the floor, not yet lifeless. I tossed the plate like a Frisbee, and it landed face down, trapping the lizard beneath it. For fear of its brute strength in being able to escape, I put my toilet paper stand on top.

I called Birds in a frenzy.

"There's another one!" I yelled. "I trapped it in my bathroom!"

"It's just a lizard." Her voice was again, quiet and steady.

"It's not just a lizard. It is a bloody, punctured reptile flailing its legs and gasping for breath!" I paused. "I know I can't leave it here. Or maybe I can?"

"Get it outside," Birds said.

"Yuck! Okay." I flipped the plate over with my toe and uncovered the body. "I think it's dead now." I nudged it with my foot. "Definitely dead," I said, kicking it onto the plate.

I then sprinted through the house and out my back door. I had the lizard plate in one hand and phone in the other. At that point, I wasn't thinking about my knee pain.

"I'm gonna chuck it into the yard somewhere," I told Birds in a frenzy.

The lizard bounced up and down on the plate as I ran in circles on my patio, looking for the perfect burial ground.

"Put it in the dumpster so it won't attract other animals."

"But the trash can is in the alley, and I don't want to carry this bloody mess that far!"

"I'll stay on the phone while you do it," she said.

I raced through the gate and jogged toward the dumpster. I opened the lid and flung the lizard and the plate inside.

"That was so gross!" I said to Birds, huffing and puffing.

"You're okay."

"I'm not sure about that. I'll save the other one for you!"

We both laughed and said our goodbyes. I then returned to my office.

"No garage privileges for you anymore," I told Phoenix. "You will have to frolic in the house for a while."

I blocked off the cat door and sat back down to resume my workday. When I glanced over at the cord organizer, I noticed the tail was gone. I looked closer. The whole thing was gone. During the hoopla of lizard number two, something mysterious happened to lizard number one.

The body was discovered a few days later in my daughter's room after a thorough investigation by Birds. She disposed of it with zero fanfare.

I knew I could have eventually handled this situation on my own. But Birds was there for me . . . as she had been, through it all—karate-chop communication, birthday trips that went south, and confession of secrets. It just took a couple dead lizards for it to finally sink in—people I care about don't always leave. Birds hadn't, especially after everything we'd been through. And I didn't need any mystical signs from the universe or some clairvoyant to affirm my path to love. I just had to trust what I already knew.

Be Happy

"Hey," Naked and Afraid said, answering on the first ring.

"Okay, so I'm done with the box," I said. "I want it to go away."

"What box?"

"You know, my simultaneity box, where I put all the psychic stuff . . . signs and symbols . . . the whole Pants divine-partner crap. I tried that for a week, and it didn't work."

"Okay. Where are you?" she asked.

"Driving home from Birds's house . . . Where are you?"

"Walking the dogs. I've already been to the gym and hiked, and it's only seven thirty."

"Figures," I said. "So . . . Birds told me she loves me."

"What? Is that why you're in a tailspin about the box?"

"We were sitting on her couch last night, and she told me she was really glad I was in her life. Then she said, 'I think I love you.' But I effed it up by responding with, 'You think you love me, or you love me?' Then, she said, 'I love you.'"

I took a deep breath.

"You better have said you love her too you fool!" She shouted at me. Then, she turned her attention to the dogs. "Come over here now!"

I waited until the rustling stopped as I wanted her full attention. "Of course I did."

"Do you love her? Be honest."

"Yes," I said, almost interrupting her.

"Good. So, what's up with the box then?"

"I don't want to live with that stupid little simultaneity box in the back of my head anymore." I pressed my foot on the gas a bit more as I hit an open stretch of road. "It doesn't serve me, and I need to let it go."

"Then let it go." She released a breath of what seemed like exasperation.

"Doing all that 'universe' stuff—the psychics, tarot cards, manifests, signs, intuition, even *pow, boom, bang*—was just my way of feeling more in control." I paused. "But trying to solve the mystery of the future has been exhausting and tormenting, not to mention completely unrealistic." As the words came out, I realized ambiguity doesn't actually hurt; it's the quest for certainty that does. The Zen Master smiled.

"Like I've told you before, the entire point of this journey was so you could grow and become a better version of yourself. You did that." She then continued, "I mean, I think you took the most chaotic and roundabout way to do it with that plan. And you tried to force some things. But you did it."

"I know." I laughed. "But my plan *did* help. I learned about the Law of Attraction, made new friends, and exercised more."

"Those are all good. But you also grew from all the unplanned things that came up, especially when you had to deal with some pretty tricky situations, like East Coast's visit, Pants's rejection, and fessing up about all the psychic stuff. All those experiences made you work through your emotions. And you could never have prepared for those."

"Well, that's true. Look at you being all wise." I couldn't help but smile.

"I'm always wise. You just don't listen sometimes."

"Ha ha," I said, sarcastically.

"Just so you know," she said, "as your spirit guide, I won't charge you for all my free advice . . . even the advice you didn't take."

We both laughed.

Deep down, though, I knew she *was* my unwavering spirit guide. And, like Birds, she hadn't left . . . even when I might have been unbearable to take.

"Just enjoy the amazing life you have and be happy." She paused. "I mean, we're all gonna die someday anyway."

We hung up, and I finished the drive home reflecting on her words—the "be happy" ones and not those about my mortality. Underneath all this noise sat the clarity I so craved. It had been there all along. I just hadn't paid attention to it.

Once I got to the house, I ran straight to my office. Phoenix was curled up on her chair as if she were waiting for this moment. I opened The Plan and scrolled through all forty-three items.

I typed "forty-four," took a deep breath, and then added, "Be happy."

I leaned back, turned to the kitty, and read the words aloud: "Be happy." She didn't look up, but I smiled . . . and then checked it off the list.

Reflections

The initial purpose of The Plan was to help me move as quickly as possible through all the awfulness of the breakup and into a happier, healthier place . . . one that would prepare me for and ultimately lead me to my soulmate. Instead of wallowing in sadness forever, I would get up, get out, get through, and get on with my life.

While I had originally believed that doing so would be on my own terms, I came to learn I couldn't control the world around me. And in many cases, I couldn't even control my own life, as old wounds, unrealistic expectations, and emotions bubbled up in ways I wasn't prepared for. In the end, despite my valiant efforts otherwise, I could never have predicted what would happen or who I would become. But it was quite the journey finding out.

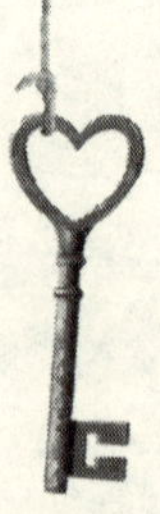

The Plan

During the course of a year, I engaged in forty-four different strategies to move from heartbreak to soulmate. Some worked better than others; some became lifestyle changes; some were one-and-dones; some were added after-the-fact, and even others I came to realize were just ways to try to gain control over a largely uncontrollable situation. Regardless, they all played a role in my journey.

The following are the items in the order I added them to The Plan, along with my reflections on their impact.

1. Distract myself.

While not a cure for heartbreak, I did find value in leaning into distractions, particularly early on. Building Lego art during the witching hours and attending my virtual writing group offered me a sense of purpose, with both resulting in creative outputs. And helping kittens survive and thrive gave me a chance to fixate on something other than my own woes.

2. Talk with anyone who will listen.

Naked and Afraid seemed more prone than me to spill her heart out to the Grand Canyon Lodge receptionist. However, I hardly refrained from sharing my breakup story with old friends, new friends, Mom, and even the kitty on occasion. It's all I talked about for a while. Then, it just wasn't.

3. Get therapy.

Meeting regularly with a trained therapist provided me a great deal of comfort and support. Most of the time, I would spew my feelings, and she would nod, throwing in the occasional question or validation. But having her there each week, ready to listen to the same story again and again, was worth every penny.

4. Feel the feelings.

Even before drafting The Plan, I knew that no matter what happened on this journey, I would need to feel all the feelings. And I did—despair rearing its head as sob fests in my Hyundai, anger leading to the grill giveaway, embarrassment stemming from Pants's rejection, the heaviness of an unmagical Christmas, and the angst of keeping a secret from two people I cared about. While those emotions were awful to experience, once I worked through them, they disappeared, making more room for joy, excitement, enthusiasm, and happiness.

5. Take control.

I had spent much of the year channeling The General with my spreadsheets, rules, timelines, and kick-it-into-action mentality to take control of my life. If it weren't for her, I might not have achieved so many amazing goals I set for myself. So, I am grateful for that.

When on overdrive, though, The General was not helpful. My need for everything to unfold as planned led me to become overly attached to specific outcomes. And when things would veer from what I expected, my propensity to overthink, ruminate, and speculate resulted in unnecessary worry and disappointment.

6. Connect with friends.

Right after the breakup, I reached out to friends to set up hikes, dinners, basketball games, and movie watching nights, and I said yes to every invitation I received. My schedule was full, and I got to spend time with people who cared about me.

7. Show up for others.

Even when I didn't think I could summon the strength, I showed up for others. First Love's cancer treatment and Naked and Afraid's breakup allowed me to be there for two people who had been there for me.

8. Find closure.

I was incredibly grateful to find forgiveness and peace regarding First Love. Releasing the torment I had carried for decades reminded me I never wanted to hold on to old wounds again. And while I desperately felt I needed answers about everything surrounding my breakup with Runner, and Zion for that matter, I came to realize that closure, and ultimately forgiveness, were the gifts I needed to give myself.

9. Figure it out on my own.

While I didn't willingly bring them on, I encountered experiences requiring quick thinking and immediate action, which helped me feel more independent and empowered. Through these crises, I invented the tooth fairy intern and salvaged Baby Yoda. I'm still working on my comfort around lizard disposal, though.

10. Employ the no-contact rule.

One of the most helpful healing activities for me involved employing the no-contact rule with Runner. This meant no communication, looking at her social media, searching online about her new life, or having people feed me information. While it took a while to go *fully* no-contact, once I did, I felt a sense of peace.

11. Walk.

My daily walks were incredibly therapeutic. I could take a mental and physical break, catch up with others, strive toward a fitness goal, and be among beautiful scenery and amazing wildlife. And I always got a kick out of sending pictures of javelina to TikTok.

12. Read books and listen to podcasts about surviving a breakup.

Right after the breakup, I consumed everything I could on surviving heartache. I particularly resonated with people's personal stories, which helped me feel validated and gave me ideas for my own coping. It wasn't long, though, before I wanted to move on from these.

13. Write a "Dear Soulmate" letter.

My "Dear Soulmate" letter, while executed a bit too early, did serve as the foundation for my intricately crafted love manifest, which helped me identify exactly what I was looking for in a partner. However, I realized my search for "the one," whether written in some form or not, was a response to my fear of having yet another failed relationship. I thought if the universe matched me with who I was "meant to be" with, I would be guaranteed success. I learned, though, there is no "meant to be." We get to choose who we want to love. And there are certainly no guarantees. That's the beauty of love.

14. Reclaim my space.

I experienced tremendous relief and liberation in reclaiming my physical space, despite the cleanup I endured after tossing out the gluten-free flour. And I still don't regret the front yard grill giveaway.

15. Let go of things that no longer serve me.

It seemed easy to donate oversized clothing and other items that no longer served me. But through all my coaching and therapy, along with wise exchanges with Naked and Afraid, I discovered I also had a tendency to hold on to *situations* that no longer served me—like fixating on the prophecy of Pants as my divine partner. I was grateful I finally realized that and let it go.

16. Cleanse the house.

Whether saging really did clear negative energy, I will never know. But the spray only cost a few bucks and had excellent online ratings.

17. Get energy healing.

Overall, I found the energy healing sessions incredibly helpful as they infused calmness and light through my body and mind. They also elicited visions, like llamas and bug zappers, which led to foreshadowing of sorts. I wasn't so sure about the energy healing apprentice I met with later in my process. Her messages, riddled with confusing language and extensive breathing exercises, did nothing for me, except remind me that sometimes the cosmos might not know what's best.

18. Make new friends.

Maybe it was serendipity that Naked and Afraid cornered me at the pool party, or perhaps it was common interests that brought all the others into my life. Regardless, both my social circle and my heart filled with amazing people who I came to learn didn't care one bit if I could wall sit.

19. Write a manifest.

Overall, manifesting proved to be a profound activity for me. I enjoyed the thoughtfulness, reflection, optimism, and joy the process sparked. And connecting with my manifesting group helped me feel empowered and supported.

My healing manifest, in particular, gave me agency to decide how long I would be in a state of despair before "feeling better." While I couldn't really control my healing timeline, my manifest offered hope, and that was exactly what I needed then.

On the other hand, the "apple of my eye" manifest was a desperate attempt to feel wanted. Thankfully, it ran its course, and I now know if anyone ever says "Hey, babe" to me, we likely don't have a promising future.

Writing my love manifest, though, turned out to be a beautiful process laid out with great intention. I can't be sure the universe somehow dispatched Birds and sent her right to me. But I do feel confident that articulating exactly what I was looking for made it far easier to find.

20. Have tarot cards read.

Tarot Lady played an important role in my life during this time, despite my initial desire to use the readings as a way to feel more in control. She legitimized my heartbreak with the "burning tower" and gave me hope I would find love again. And she seemed to know, even before I did, what an influence my lawyer-friend, wife-from-another-life would have on me.

21. Journal/write.

My midnight journaling exercise in perspective taking, along with crafting manifests and engaging in personal reflections, all offered opportunities for uninhibited processing. Through writing, I could uncover and make meaning of the hard truths I needed to work through. And, although I relied on verbal processing with others as a way to heal and move on, the solitude of individual reflection, without any insight, judgment, or advice from others, was a critical part of my own meaning-making.

22. Attend self-help seminars and support groups.

I learned a lot about myself through the many online seminars, meetings, and workshops I attended. Understanding my attachment style and relationship patterns was useful, but the women's circle was a once-in-a-lifetime experience for me.

23. Look in places where I could meet the love of my life.

When I was first open to the idea of meeting someone, I flocked to the bookstore, not once, but on several occasions. This fantasy always ended in disappointment, though, because it's hard to control haphazardly running into a random person who would be a perfect love match.

While I was busy lurking at the bookstore and scouring the dating apps, I hadn't thought about making a romantic connection through my Meetup group. I *had* met Runner at an event years earlier. But Meetup had since become my safe haven for friends and nothing else. It turned out, though, to be the perfect place to meet someone—and I didn't have to flip through crusty novels in the process.

24. Find **pow, boom, bang.**

During my quest for love, I became all-consumed with my *pow, boom*, *bang* theory. Although I had heard about people who had experienced this, like Naked and Afraid with Twin Flame, most I knew hadn't. Even Naked and Afraid's relationship ended in heartbreak, leaving me uncertain whether *pow*, *boom*, *bang* served as a proxy for true love or was an idea I had been foolishly holding out for.

Giving up on it, though, didn't mean settling for less or believing I was undeserving of it. I came to see it was just another sign I was using to seek out certainty. I thought if I found it, I would be sure I was with the right person. Ultimately, I learned there is no certainty when it comes to love. Instead, it is one of life's mysteries to be savored and not solved.

25. Meet with a breakup coach.

The four sessions with Breakup Coach changed my life . . . not only in surviving heartache but also uncovering and unpacking old wounds I didn't know I had. Learning about the differences between grief and trauma influenced my healing process in significant ways. It was then I could face my past . . . for the first time ever.

26. Embrace the Law of Attraction.

The Law of Attraction was a game changer for me. With the help of the nice podcast lady, I adopted an abundance mindset, rather than one of scarcity, which resulted in more amazing things coming into my life.

27. Be positive.

After spending much of my adult life as a realist, I began embracing positivity. I shifted my energy to vibrate at a higher level and actually started to see the good in everything. It felt hopeful, exciting, and energizing, which was far less taxing than carrying negativity with me.

28. Walk a labyrinth.

The labyrinth, while beautifully laid out, only served as a distraction, pinned with high hopes and no results. And I did not find my mantra of being "grateful for my healing process" to be truer because I repeated it while strolling through twinkle lights. Instead, it took a year of deep reflection for that gratitude to naturally emerge.

29. Buy crystals.

I'm sure crystals can be powerful, but for me, they did nothing—no clarity, peace, or love. But then again, perhaps my life would have been completely different without them. I'll never know.

30. Eliminate ambiguity.

I originally thought ambiguity was painful, and thus, I needed to know and control how things would play out. I discovered, though, it was the quest for certainty that was actually painful. My need to speed through the healing process and find my soulmate turned out to be a journey about discovering, reclaiming, and loving myself. It just took me a while to figure that out.

31. Date.

While I knew of many others who had success with online dating, for me, it was a bust. The entire charade mostly resulted in a slew of outlandish connections and nothing for my love life. However, it did lead to a friendship with Pontificator, a new adventure buddy in Pants, and a ton of self-reflection. So maybe it was worth it.

On the other hand, in-person dating seemed to work out; just ask Birds.

32. Look for signs and symbols.

For a long while, I saw signs and symbols as indicators of certainty that "the universe knows best," even though the saguaro cactus exercise seemed to prove otherwise. But once I knew my intuitive senses could trump my visionary perception, especially when they were in conflict with each other, I grasped back onto the power of signs and symbols.

But in the end, the signs didn't offer certainty. Instead, many of them drummed up confusion, leading me to believe that maybe sometimes we see what we want to see or notice that which we are looking for in order to feel a sense of comfort or validation. On the other hand, some signs simply have no rational explanation and may leave us wondering if they are a part of a larger divine message. Are signs real then? I'll have to wait for a sign to tell me.

33. See an intuition coach.

The intuitive work was immensely valuable, despite the odd swaying exercise during my coaching session. However, I was unsure if the experience truly enhanced my intuition or simply jump-started that which I already had. Either way, I began to trust my gut more.

34. Put on my big-girl pants.

While I can be courageous in so many other areas of my life, doing so in my personal one seemed to intimidate me. I worried if I said something bold, the situation would backfire, and I'd experience an emotional setback. And, to some extent, I was right. Telling East Coast I didn't want a romantic relationship led to her fleeing the state, and sharing my feelings with Pants resulted in the "for now" text. But just because the outcomes in those cases weren't what I had hoped for doesn't mean taking the initiative to be honest about my feelings was the wrong approach. If anything, doing so just affirmed that I'm worth advocating for my own happiness.

35. Hike the Grand Canyon.

Both Grand Canyon treks were by far the most challenging physical experiences of my life. With the rim-to-rim-to-rim, I hiked further than I ever had, in scorching heat, and with terrible knee pain. I learned I can push my limits and thrive, especially when I have a positive attitude and strong support system. But the relentlessness I summoned to finish the trek with an injury was just a metaphor for what I had been doing in my love life—forcing. I was lucky I made it out safely, both from the canyon and from this quest, with no permanent damage. Maybe I should have listened to Naked and Afraid and taken the shuttle back. Then again, conquering this feat was one of the highlights of my entire journey.

36. Be more Zen.

I also learned that as much as I tried, I couldn't "Be more Zen" just because I wrote it down. However, The Zen Master did show up . . . not when summoned, but when I needed her most. She helped me redirect my approach in asking Birds out, salvage a Yoda cake, and veer from The Plan when new opportunities arose, and others didn't work. She waited patiently as I learned crucial lessons . . . in my own time. And she always knew when to come . . . right when The General would start to freak out. Together, they made for a dynamic duo, balancing the need for control and flow. So, I guess I *was* Zen after all. Check that off the list.

37. Go to a psychic.

After a great deal of reflection, I came to realize that leaning into psychic prophecies was my subconscious attempt at spiritual bypassing. I had been trying my best to "feel the feelings" during my healing process, but when the psychics pointed me to a future filled with soulmate love, I traded my unresolved pain for hope and reassurance. But the unchecked promise of a certain grand future just led me into a state of chaos and angst, torn between two potential love interests. Once I finally let go of the prophecy, I was able to continue moving forward with my healing, both from the breakup and from the prophecy itself. And while I do still trust the universe, I learned the value of embracing my own free will and not overemphasizing the importance of spiritual messaging during vulnerable times in my life.

38. Subscribe to horoscope and other "universe loves you" email lists.

While some of what I received in my inbox was eerie, like references to cupcakes and 555, most messages included universal ideas that could apply to anyone. Regardless, after reading them, I always felt more prepared to deal with the day ahead.

39. Face my fears.

During this process, I engaged in several activities that terrified me. While I was no less frightened by Cujo once she returned to the shelter, scaling cliffs ended up being entirely tear-free and even fun. Tapping into my inner courage with something literally death-defying showed me how strong I really am. And I may have found a new adventure hobby.

40. Get a soulmate sketch.

I don't regret forking out $19.95 for the soulmate sketch. It was humorous on the one hand, while on the other, it may very well prove to be a drawing of one of my four other soulmates I haven't yet met. Only time will tell.

41. Be transparent.

I've never been one to keep a secret. So, holding on to the psychic prophecy not only weighed on my conscience but also put at risk two very important relationships in my life. I will be forever grateful to both of them for accepting my confession and choosing to continue our connections. The whole situation, though, prompted me to add "Be transparent" to The Plan so I would never find myself harboring another secret. However, I think I recalibrated too far in that I felt compelled to tell Birds, in particular, every fleeting thought I had. If I were to do it again, I would have just been open and honest with everyone about the psychic from the get-go, shared my confusion with Birds before becoming exclusive, talked things through earlier with Pants, and let the chips fall.

42. Do a past life regression.

Of every spiritual experience I had, having a past life regression was the most profound, particularly because it didn't entail someone else delivering a prophecy about my supposed future. Instead, it was based on my memories and my experiences.

Understanding my past life connection with Pants helped me make meaning of my confusing feelings, even though I never did uncover what our unfinished business was. I guess that's why it's unfinished. The confirmation of Naked and Afraid as my spirit guide provided clarity about her role during this journey. I was also comforted in knowing I might have been a writer in a previous life and have a soul bond with my father. I'm still not sure about the horse.

43. Do a podcast on relationships.

Co-hosting the podcast during this time served as a major catalyst for my healing. I could ponder difficult questions in a more intentional way, rather than free-range bantering with Naked and Afraid on Tumamoc. I also felt a sense of service in sharing my stories, knowing my bravery in doing so had the potential to transform the lives of others.

44. Be happy.

Even during the twists and turns throughout the year, there were many happy moments. I developed meaningful connections, conquered challenges, experienced personal growth, and even snuggled with kittens. So, although I didn't add it until the very end, it was easy to look back and see that happiness had been there all along.

Acknowledgments

Writing this book provided an unexpected opportunity for reflection, meaning-making, healing, and peace, even well after my journey ended. And I am forever grateful for that process.

I also couldn't be more appreciative of the many people who guided, supported, and loved me through it all. A special thank-you goes out to Naked and Afraid for being my spirit guide; Mom, who I wish I could watch *The Holiday* with just one more time, as we lost her shortly after my year-long journey; Phoenix, my kitty who passed away right before I finished the final draft of the book; TikTok for her wisdom and support throughout; Pants for her friendship during an important period in my life; and most of all, Birds for her relentless patience, understanding, and love while going on much of this chaotic ride with me.

A shout-out goes to the universe as well. Two-and-a-half years after this story ended, I finally made it to The Wave with Pants . . . and Birds.

About the Author

Photo credit: Rachel Marie Castillo

Corey Seemiller is an award-winning professor of leadership and global generational expert. She has authored several books and articles and speaks at events around the world. Her work has been featured in major news publications and media outlets such as NPR, *The New York Times*, *Time Magazine*, and *Newsweek*, and her highly popular *TED Talk* has garnered hundreds of thousands of views. An accredited life coach with specialties in Law of Attraction and intuitive development, Corey also co-hosts the *Rock That Relationship!* podcast, discussing debacles and successes with breakups, healing processes, dating, and relationships. Corey resides in Tucson, Arizona, and is an avid hiker and outdoor enthusiast.

Looking for your next great read?

We can help!

Visit www.shewritespress.com/next-read
or scan the QR code below for a list
of our recommended titles.

She Writes Press is an award-winning
independent publishing company founded to
serve women writers everywhere.